JANE AUSTEN AND FOOD

Dinner, from *Mrs Hurst Dancing* (*c.* 1812–13)
(© *Neville Ollerenshaw 1981; reprinted by permission of*
Neville Ollerenshaw and Victor Gollancz Ltd)

JANE AUSTEN AND FOOD

MAGGIE LANE

THE HAMBLEDON PRESS
LONDON AND RIO GRANDE

Published by The Hambledon Press 1995

102 Gloucester Avenue, London NW1 8HX (U.K.)
P.O. Box 162, Rio Grande, Ohio 45674 (U.S.A.)

ISBN 1 85285 124 4

A description of this book is available from
the British Library and from the Library of Congress

Typeset by York House Typographic Ltd

Printed on acid-free paper and bound in Great
Britain by Cambridge University Press

Contents

Illustrations

TO NIGEL NICOLSON

my collaborator in Bath
friend at Chawton
host and guide in Kent

Acknowledgements

My first thanks are due to the Headmaster and Bursar of Bristol Grammar School and to my colleagues Richard Camp and Carolyn Berkan for devising and enduring the often complicated arrangements which made it possible for me to write this book within one academic year.

I would also like to thank all my good friends in the Jane Austen Society, especially Anne Woodford and Louise Ross who watched the book grow from its beginnings as a paper given in Bath; Jean Bowden and Irene Collins who each made helpful suggestions from their own areas of expertise; Jean Bowden (again) and Penelope Byrde, who helped suggest appropriate illustrations; and Jean Nursten and Robin Vick whose contributions are acknowledged more precisely in the notes.

The Davis family have afforded me many opportunities to see inside 4 Sydney Place, Jane Austen's principal residence in Bath. Their continuing friendship and cooperation are much appreciated.

Martin Sheppard, another member of the Society and also my publisher, has made working on the book a pleasure. His meticulous approach has resulted in many improvements, for which I am duly grateful.

I would like to thank the Jane Austen Memorial Trust for permission to quote from Martha Lloyd's MS collection of recipes preserved at Chawton. Quotations from *Jane Austen's Letters* and *Minor Works* are made by kind permission of the Oxford University Press. I am also grateful to Macdonald & Co. for permission to quote from *Food in England* by Dorothy Hartley and to Penguin Books for permission to quote from *English Food* by Jane Grigson. For permission to reproduce illustrations, I am grateful to the Jane Austen Memorial Trust (pp. 5,

105); the Marquess of Bath (p. 59); and to Neville Ollerenshaw and Victor Gollancz Ltd (pp. ii, 127).

Finally to Rupert Lane, who solved all my computer problems, and Emily Lane, who cheered me ever onward and upward, my thanks and love. Your turn next.

Introduction

One of the characteristics of Jane Austen's style is how sparing it is of physical detail. She never pauses in her narrative to give a lengthy description, whether of faces, clothes, rooms, meals or any other facet of material life. In this she could not be more unlike, say, Dickens, who builds up the solidity of his world through detail. Jane Austen pays us the compliment of letting us imagine for ourselves. In one of her few pronouncements on the craft of fiction she warned her niece Anna, who had begun to write a novel, that she was in danger of giving 'too many particulars of right hand and left'. (*L, 401*)

So we need look for no laden tables, no mouth-watering sights and smells, no big set-piece mealtimes in Jane Austen's work. Yet her characters are forever eating, for the domestic plot inevitably coheres around the give and take of meals. 'It was first necessary to eat' is the comment made by the narrator when the Mansfield party arrive at Sotherton, and it could be said of many a gathering in any of the novels.

But the food itself is rationed, as it were. Jane Austen limits what she tells us to a few particulars which are made to do a great deal of work. For example, out of the dozens of elaborate meals that the characters in *Sense and Sensibility* certainly take together, the only menu that we are told about is Willoughby's snatched lunch at an inn. With an artist of as much mastery over her material as Jane Austen, we can be sure that there is significance in such detail, a significance which would be quite lost if she were habitually loading her text with such description.

My purpose in this book is to examine and understand all the different things which Jane Austen finds to do, artistically, with the humdrum commodity of food. It can safely be said that no reference to food is made which does not contribute something besides verisimilitude to the text. It almost always helps illustrate character – the character in whose speech the detail occurs, and sometimes the character spoken to, or of, as well. For this brings me to another interesting divergence between the practice of Jane Austen and that of most of the great novelists of the eighteenth and nineteenth centuries. It is almost always in dialogue or reported or free indirect speech that a specific food is mentioned. The only exception is the meal at Pemberley:

> The next variation which their visit afforded was produced by the entrance of servants with cold meat, cake, and a variety of all the finest fruits in season; but this did not take place till after many a significant look and smile from Mrs Annesley to Miss Darcy had been given, to remind her of her post. There was now employment for the whole party; for though they could not all talk, they could all eat; and the beautiful pyramids of grapes, nectarines, and peaches, soon collected them round the table. (*P & P, 268*)

This kind of passage, so commonplace in almost any other novelist that it would mean little, is so rare in Jane Austen that it must be given for a purpose beyond mere description of the elegance of the Pemberley scene (which is not to deny that that function has its due importance too). Almost every other mention of a specific foodstuff occurs when one character is talking to another. Thus Mrs Bennet: 'The soup was fifty times better than what we had at the Lucas's last week; and even Mr Darcy acknowledged, that the partridges were remarkably well done'. (*P & P, 342*) Or Mr Woodhouse: 'Miss Bates, let Emma help you to a *little* bit of tart – a *very* little bit. Ours are all apple tarts. You need not be afraid of unwholesome preserves here. I do not advise the custard'. (*E, 24*) Or Mary Crawford: 'Dr Grant is ill . . . He has been ill ever since he did not eat any of the pheasant today. He fancied it tough – sent away his plate – and has been suffering ever since'. (*MP, 171*) These examples, which could be multiplied many times, all bring the speaker, and the speaker's attitude towards other people, into focus.

The economy and vividness with which such utterance can illustrate character, then, is obviously a prime reason why nearly all of the details we learn about food in Jane Austen's novels come in direct or reported speech. But there is another, equally potent, reason: Jane Austen's own distaste, as narrator and on behalf of her most esteemed characters, for discussing food at all. There can be no doubt that vulgarity or triviality or selfishness of some kind attaches to any character who allows the mention of a foodstuff to pass his or her lips. The only exception is Emma, who must respond to a father obsessed with the subject of food, and who even so contrives to mention it only in respect of providing food for other people. Neither Emma, nor any character who enjoys the author's approval, ever describes a meal that has been eaten or a meal anticipated. The same prohibition governs the narrator, whose ladylike persona holds herself aloof from sensual pleasures.

Here is a paradox, for in her letters Jane Austen can write with unselfconscious enjoyment about food. 'Caroline, Anna and I have just been devouring some cold souse, and it would be difficult to say which enjoyed it most.' (L, 6) 'At Devizes we had comfortable rooms and a good dinner, to which we sat down about five; amongst other things we had asparagus and a lobster, which made me wish for you, and some cheesecakes . . . ' (L, 59) 'I always take care to provide such things as please my own appetite, which I consider the chief merit in house-keeping. I have had some ragout veal, and I mean to have some haricot mutton tomorrow.' (L, 28) It is inconceivable that any of her heroines would talk or write like this. In her letters, Jane Austen allows herself licence to particularise on subjects – another is fashion and clothes – which would condemn any character in her books instantaneously as trivial-minded or vulgar.

This is partly owing to Jane Austen's circumstances. She belonged to a family which was sufficiently comfortably off to afford good food, but not so rich that they did not have to practise constant economies – especially after the death of her father, when Jane was twenty-nine. Moreover, though the family always kept a cook, they did not aspire to a housekeeper to plan meals, organise stores and superintend the daily work of the kitchen. This was done first by Jane's mother, later by Jane's sister Cassandra, with Jane herself as subordinate and sometime deputy. Matters of housekeeping were therefore of perennial interest between the sisters, and this is reflected in their correspondence.

A discussion of why the case should have been different when Jane Austen took up her pen to write fiction – or rather, fiction for publication, for her Juvenilia are full of food – forms the concluding part of my first chapter, which looks at her own experiences of housekeeping, and what these tell us about the changes in society, particularly as regards the role of women, during her lifetime.

Drawing on her letters and novels, other Austen family papers, wider eighteenth-century sources and recent scholarly food histories, my next two chapters seek to illuminate the domestic framework to her char-acters' lives: the mealtimes which divided up their days, the etiquette that governed their meals, and the specific foods and dishes (some unfamiliar to us now) which are mentioned in her writings. Attempting to recover such details seems a worthwhile enterprise not because it tells us more about the background to her plots than she wants us to know, but because it helps restore us to the position of her contemporary readers. In reflecting on the economy of her art and the elevated subject-matter of her fictional concerns, it must not be forgotten that part of the reason she is so sparing with information is that she could assume knowledge in her readers – an homogeneous group sharing the same culture and customs – which we no longer automatically possess. For thirty years and many readings of Jane Austen I have confused her characters' habit of 'drinking tea' with the 'afternoon tea' of the Edwardians and ourselves; have puzzled over the oily melted butter in *Northanger Abbey*; and wondered why Mr Woodhouse recommends baking apples three times. These and many other matters, including what exactly *are* rout-cakes and spruce beer, I now understand; and to read Jane Austen with enhanced understanding, even on points of apparent triviality, is to inhabit her world with more enjoyment, and appreciate her artistry with clearer vision.

But it is true that this is merely background; what is really fascinating about food in Jane Austen's novels is how she uses it to define character and illustrate moral worth. My next three chapters examine attitudes towards eating, housekeeping and hospitality among her characters. Not only do these attitudes help us to arrive at a just assessment of individuals; in individual *novels*, they coalesce into themes. *Sense and Sensibility* and *Persuasion*, at the beginning and end of her publishing career, present fictional worlds which ask what true hospitality means, and whether and how it has changed. *Pride and Prejudice* and *Mansfield Park* are both much concerned with good and bad housekeepers – not fortuitously, but because these are the novels in which the heroine may be said to marry above her sphere, at a time when for women class and domestic duties were thoroughly interdependent.

Feminist concerns appear even more specifically in the chapter I have called 'Greed and Gender'. There is no escaping the fact that in the published fiction, all the gluttons are men and all the (near-) anorexics women. Without going so far as to claim Jane Austen as a proto-feminist, the act of focusing on food in the novels supports a feminist reading, if only because female destiny, one way or another, is and always has been intimately connected with food: providing it, avoiding it, being shaped by it body and soul. All these modes bear some relationship to the dominant male desires of a patriarchal system; while male attitudes towards eating inevitably impinge on the lives of the women around them.

The character – theme – morality approach to literary criticism has recently found itself under attack in academic circles, on the grounds that it tells again what the author has already and intentionally told in better words and form. The current interest is in interrogating texts for what the author deliberately or unconsciously *fails* to tell, or tells without realising she has told, about the society from which the work of art sprang. The advantage of selecting a self-limiting topic like food is that it offers *multiple* ways into the texts. As an aspect of Jane Austen's work ignored by the traditional critics (perhaps because they were mostly men and thought it too domestic, too mundane), the study of her treatment of food yields new insights into the skill with which she creates character and establishes her moral values. Equally, it can help us pose the feminist, political and ideological questions which, if not the sole purpose of literary criticism, certainly add something fresh and valuable to the discipline. For example, consideration of Fanny Price's 'niceness' as regards to eating makes some contribution to the political debate between whether the resolution to *Mansfield Park* most supports or subverts the dominant ideology within which it was created. Similarly, the giving and sharing of food which plays such a large part in the life of Highbury is capable of bearing more than one interpretation. I have therefore felt myself at liberty to use any and every approach, providing only that it focuses on food and seems to illuminate something, explicit or implicit, in the text.

Jane Austen's prose is not often held to be poetic, despite the precision of her vocabulary and her exquisite sense of rhythm, two of the poet's essential tools. What is lacking is imagery, figurative use of language, symbol. Thinking deeply about her use of food, however, reveals that this is something she *does* use symbolically: both locally in certain passages, and as an extended metaphor through a complete novel, *Emma*. The last two chapters of this book are an exploration of some of the less obvious, but most resonant, ways in which she makes food work on several levels at once, taking just what she needs for her purposes from the associations that food has acquired through the history of human culture and embedding them into her supremely realist texts.

'much was said and much was ate'

Mansfield Park

Chapter One

Domestic Economy in Jane Austen's Life

'The sweets of housekeeping in a country village!' exclaims Mary Craw-ford archly when her sister, Mrs Grant, is confessing to some difficulties with her plants and poultry. Town-bred Mary knows nothing, and wishes to know nothing, of either the sweets or the difficulties involved in keeping house and providing food for a family in the country; but these were matters which had been familiar to her author since her earliest consciousness.

Born in 1775 at Steventon Rectory in Hampshire, Jane Austen grew up in a household which was virtually self-sufficient in food. Her father, the Reverend George Austen, besides being a parish priest and a teacher of classics to pupils boarding at the Rectory, was a gentleman farmer, working his land with the help of a bailiff. John Bond, who stood very much in relation to Mr Austen as William Larkins to Mr Knightley, was an important personage in the domestic economy of Steventon, and is often mentioned in Jane Austen's early letters.

The glebe lands attached to the benefice of Steventon were only about three acres, but Mr Austen also rented the neighbouring 200-acre Cheesedown farm from his patron Thomas Knight, the principal land-holder of the parish.[1] For the best part of forty years – from 1764 when the Austens were married until 1801 when they retired to Bath – the farm kept the Rectory supplied with pork, mutton, wheat, peas, barley and hops; it also supplied oats and hay for the horses.[2] Surplus produce was sold and could bring in a profit of up to £300 in a year, which made a worthwhile contribution to Mr Austen's income. (*L, 81*)

It was a characteristic of the Austen family that whatever they turned their hands to they did well, taking an honest pride in their efforts. Mr Austen, despite a wholly scholarly background (before his marriage he was Second Master at Tonbridge School and an Oxford Proctor), took to farming with spirit. 'One of his Leicestershire sheep, sold to the butcher last week, weighed 27 lb. and ¼ per quarter', reported Jane in November 1798. (*L, 29*) A fortnight later came news of its consumption: Mr Lyford, apothecary of Basingstoke, 'gratified us very much yesterday by his praises of my father's mutton, which they all think the finest that ever was ate'. (*L, 35*)

The dairy and the poultry-yard were her mother's province. In 1773 Mrs Austen told her sister-in-law, 'I have got a nice dairy fitted up, and am now worth a bull and six cows'. Three years earlier she had written of an Alderney cow which 'makes more butter than we use'; as with the farm, the dairy surplus could be sold.[3]

The Austens eventually had eight children; by the time the youngest, Charles, was born, the eldest, James, was at university. As the youthful population of Steventon Rectory swelled and subsided over the years (and as his own sons grew up, Mr Austen ceased to take in pupils), the number of livestock kept to feed them swelled and subsided too. By the turn of the century only the two daughters remained at home, and Mrs Austen's dairy herd was reduced to three Norman cows and calves. Her collection of poultry at this date comprised ducks, chicken, guinea-fowl and turkeys both black and white. (*L, 73*)

Potatoes, other vegetables, herbs and soft fruit, including strawberries and grapes, were grown in the garden; the Austens also kept bees. The honey was used for mead, which, like beer and home-made wines, was brewed in the brewhouse and stored in barrels in the cellar, which was liable to flood.[4] The 'kitchen, dairy and brewing utensils' at Steventon in 1801 included '13 iron-bound casks'.[5]

Fish and game were brought home on occasion by the sporting sons. In 1785 James, Edward and Henry Austen (the latter only fourteen) all took out a game duty certificate, as the new law required.[6] Henry, particularly, was to be a keen shot all his life.

All this produce was converted into meals or, with certain items, into supplies of preserved food which would last until the next season came round. Vast quantities not only of time but of space indoors and out were devoted to the cultivation, production and storage of food.

The only commodities that had to be purchased from outside were tea, coffee, chocolate, sugar, spices, wine, dried fruit and citrus fruit. These items were valued and guarded accordingly. 'I carry about the keys of the wine and closet', wrote Jane on one occasion, (*L, 23*) and there are many references in her letters to keeping careful watch on the levels of their stocks, particularly of sugar and tea – not so much against pilfering as against running out unawares.

It is not known where the Austens purchased these commodities while they were living at Steventon, but their nearest town was Basingstoke, and the principal grocer there in the 1780s was J. Bickham in the Market Place. The business changed hands in 1791 and again in 1794, the new owner advertising that his stock included 'Old Raisin Wine, Confectionery, Perfumery, Stationery, &c. Oils, fine Westmoreland Hams, Burgess's Essence of Anchovies, Mushroom and India Soy, Sauce Royal, Devonshire Sauce, Lemon Ketchup, Olives, Capers, Vinegar &c'.[7] The purpose of many of these articles would seem to be to disguise tainted meat, a purpose not necessary at Steventon Rectory.

For a household to be virtually self-sufficient in food sounds a happy and healthy state of affairs; and so it was, of course, in terms of economy and wholesomeness. But such a system has its drawbacks, as a moment's reflection will suggest. For if all the food required by ten or a dozen people three times a day, day in, day out, is to be produced on the premises, the burden on the housekeeper is considerable – not just in terms of cooking, but in organisation and planning. Variety and plenty at the table depended on just the right quantities of everything being produced and preserved in season, and then served to the family judiciously throughout the year.

We do not know how Mrs Austen felt about her housekeeper's role. She probably accepted it as a duty, performed it for forty or so years as a skill in which she could take pride, and eventually relinquished it as a burden which she was happy for her elder daughter to take over. Mrs Austen was a religious woman who would have seen the cheerful regulation of her household, the provision of wholesome food for her family and the good management of her husband's income as her share of the marriage partnership. Notwithstanding her aristocratic and intellectual connections and her own highly developed ability to express herself 'both in writing and in conversation, with epigrammatic force and point', she was a practical, down-to-earth woman – whether made so by nature or necessity.[8] Long after her 'retirement', she continued to exhibit a lively curiosity wherever she went, in those little details of domestic economy which are so interesting to someone who has known the satisfactions and struggles of housekeeping on a large scale.

Of course Mrs Austen had servants to help her – there is no suggestion that either she or her daughters were involved in the actual cooking of meals. But the servants were simple country people and required constant direction. Jane Austen wrote in a letter of taking on a new servant who knew nothing of dairy work, but was to be taught. The same maid was to do the cooking 'and says she can work well with her needle', which gives some indication of the unspecialised nature of the servants to be had at Steventon. (*L, 36*) Even when servants were familiar with techniques, however, it was Mrs Austen's responsibility to decide what must be done when; what was the work of that day, what was to be served and what preserved. It was Mrs Austen who had always to be looking ahead and ensuring that stores of food were maintained. In this she would have involved her daughters as they grew up, both as a present help to herself and, more importantly, as part of their training to be wives and housekeepers themselves.

For if Jane and her elder sister Cassandra were to marry men of limited income – and Cassandra, at least, became engaged to exactly such a man, the Reverend Thomas Fowle – such knowledge would be of vital importance to their families' wellbeing.[9] Mrs Austen would have seen it as part of her maternal duty to prepare her daughters to make the full female contribution to any station in life in which they found themselves. The closest Jane herself came to marriage was in 1802 with her acceptance, subsequently withdrawn, of Harris Bigg Wither, heir to nearby Manydown Park. But even had she become mistress of Many-down, with a larger income and more numerous servants than her mother could command, she would still have found her knowledge of housekeeping useful. Certainly Harris's sister Alethea was not above taking an interest in such details, since on one occasion Jane wrote to her for the Manydown recipe for orange wine.

It was this readiness on the part even of well-off ladies to take a practical interest in the provision of food and the running of their households which struck Jane's nephew James Edward Austen-Leigh, in writing his *Memoir of Jane Austen*, as marking a great change in the hundred years between his grandmother's early married life and his own old age. 'I am sure that the ladies there [Steventon] had nothing to do with the mysteries of the stew-pot or the preserving-pan; but it is probable that their way of life differed a little from ours, and would have appeared to us more homely', he wrote in 1870.[10] His Victorian sensibilities prevented him from quite crediting the truth: that although they may not have stirred the pot or the pan themselves, Mrs Austen and her daughters perfectly understood what was going on within them. 'Eliza remembered that Miss Austen had said she did not think it had been boiled enough', reported Jane when one of their preserves was opened and found to be 'neither solid nor entirely sweet'. (*L, 241*) The fact that their friend and one-time house-mate Martha Lloyd made a collection of

Very good white Sauce for boiled Carp

Take half a p.d of Veal, cut it into small pieces, boil it in a pint of Water with an Onion, a blade of Mace, two Cloves, a few whole pepper corns, a little salt & Nutmeg, and a bundle of sweet herbs, till it is as rich as you would have it. Strain it off, & put it into your sauce pan, add to it a piece of butter as big as an egg worked up with flour, a tea cup full of Cream, a tea Cup of white wine, & half a tea cup of Elder Vinegar Mrs Austen

'A very good white sauce for boil'd carp', one of several contributions by Jane Austen's mother to their friend Martha Lloyd's collection of recipes
(*Jane Austen Memorial Trust*)

recipes to which Mrs Austen contributed is proof that the processes of cookery were understood by women of their class.

One of Mrs Austen's contributions to Martha Lloyd's collection was made in rhyme, a demonstration of that blend of unselfconscious interest in practical matters, verbal facility and lively sense of fun which so marked her character – and marked her as a woman of her age. At a later period, how many cooks would have the time, inclination or ability to write verse; how many amateur poetesses would confess to a knowledge of cookery? 'A Receipt for a Pudding' is given in seven stanzas, of which four contain the detailed instruction:

First take 2 lbs of bread
Be the crumb only weigh'd,
For the crust the good housewife refuses.
The proportions you'll guess
May be made more or less
To the size the family chuses.

Then its sweetness to make;
Some currants you take
And sugar, of each half a pound
Be not butter forgot.
And the quantity sought
Must the same with your currants be found.

Cloves and mace you will want,
With rose water I grant,
And more savoury things if well chosen.
Then to bind each ingredient,
You'll find it expedient,
Of eggs to put in half a dozen.

Some milk, don't refuse it,
But boiled ere you use it,
A proper hint for its maker.
And the whole when complete,
In a pan clean and neat
With care recommend to the baker.[11]

With such a mother, there can be no doubt that Jane Austen absorbed from an early age a store of housekeeping knowledge.

In her fiction, however, we find her conforming far more to her nephew's notions of gentility on such subjects. In *Pride and Prejudice* Mrs Bennet boasts several times that, unlike their neighbour Charlotte Lucas, who 'was wanted at home about the mince pies', her girls have been brought up to have nothing to do with cookery. (*P & P, 44*) Mrs Bennet of course is no maternal exemplar and, considering the doubtful financial future of her daughters, she could certainly be considered remiss in neglecting this aspect of their upbringing. Despite her best efforts in another direction, she cannot guarantee wealthy husbands for her girls. Considered realistically, it is more by luck than inevitability that Jane and Elizabeth find themselves, at the end of the novel, each the mistress of a large establishment. (As Jane Austen was to acknowledge elsewhere, 'There certainly are not so many men of large fortune in the world as there are pretty women to deserve them'.) (*MP, 3*)

In *Pride and Prejudice* it is Lydia, and Lydia's children, who are set to be the chief sufferers from Mrs Bennet's mode of education. Lydia will be another Mrs Price, and her home as comfortless. Yet it is Lydia's moral, rather than her practical shortcomings, for which Mrs Bennet is held culpable. Neither Elizabeth nor the narrator ever breathe the slightest reproach on her for bringing up her daughters 'high' (to use Lady Catherine's terminology and meaning). (*P & P, 106*)

An interesting case is that of Catherine Morland. We hear many details of her education, but none of it is in the domestic arts. 'Catherine would make a sad heedless young housekeeper to be sure', is her mother's first remark on hearing that her daughter is to be married. (*NA, 249*) In her brisk, matter-of-fact character and her situation as the wife of a clergyman and mother of a large family, Mrs Morland very much resembles Mrs Austen. Her immediate response to Catherine's news is proof of the practical turn her thoughts habitually take. So why has she neglected this branch of Catherine's training? It is true that the Morlands appear to be somewhat richer than the Austens, but they are far from demanding or expecting great matches for their children. Most probably Mrs Morland has been just too busy with the little ones to 'finish' her eldest daughter's education in this way, thinking there was plenty of time, and being caught unawares by such an early engagement.

Poor Catherine, with all she has yet to learn, will also have to face the ordeal of her father-in-law's scrutiny of her table. Her melted butter is sure to be oiled, or her menu inadequate, on the day General Tilney comes to dinner. But at least, as clergymen go, Henry Tilney has a comfortable income. Elinor Dashwood is the heroine whose married destiny most closely resembles that of Mrs Austen, or of Cassandra had Tom Fowle survived to marry her and take her to his Shropshire rectory. It will certainly be among Elinor's daily concerns to make a small income stretch as far as possible. There is no suggestion that supervising the baking, brewing or churning form part of the Dashwood ladies' 'employ-ments' at Barton Cottage, still less at Norland – but who can doubt that Elinor will be equal to the demands of her new life? Neither Elinor nor Edward has the slightest experience of farming, but they seem to be taking to it with the same enthusiasm as the young Mr and Mrs Austen; our only glimpse of them after marriage shows them mundanely con-cerned about 'rather better pasturage for their cows'. (*S & S, 375*)

As for Emma, she *is* the capable and practised mistress of a household even before her marriage; but it is a wealthy household, well able to afford an experienced cook and a housekeeper. Emma's role is to preside, to give orders and occasionally to consult. (She needs the housekeeper's advice, for example, as to the best invalid food to send Jane Fairfax.) In general Emma probably visits the housekeeper's room once a day, after breakfast, to settle menus. There her involvement ends; certainly it does not appear to occupy a great deal of her time or thought (though she is a little busier just before Christmas, in preparing for the visit of the John Knightleys – a realistic detail passed over in barely a sentence, but evidence of the author's own experience of what a family visit entails). Emma indeed is the model of the gracious Victorian matron, hands unsoiled, so familiar to James Edward Austen-Leigh.

Far more than any of her heroines, therefore, Jane Austen in her girlhood or young womanhood was initiated into the arts of domestic economy. Even had her mother neglected so to train her – which is inconceivable – her own observations of life at Steventon would have impressed upon her consciousness the primacy of food provision in the scale of female duties and occupations.

For it was one of the assumptions on which her society was organised that any woman might at any time be called upon to take responsibility for the smooth running of a household: if not by marrying, then by looking after an aged parent or a single or bereaved male relation. No man could run his own home. The few who did live alone, like Mr Knightley, relied on a paid housekeeper; but this was in general con-sidered a comfortless way to live – especially if the income was smaller than Mr Knightley's, when less good servants could be afforded, or if the man in question was more particular about his creature comforts than the master of Donwell. As a bachelor, Mr Elton is always ready to leave his own lonely hearth for the good dinners and womanly smiles on offer at Hartfield. At the beginning of *Sense and Sensibility* when old Mr Dashwood loses his sister he cannot manage alone; his niece-in-law, with her husband and children, has to leave her own comfortable home to look after him in his. Mr Bingley has his sister Caroline to keep house for him; Mr Rushworth has his mother. Mr Collins, having got himself a house, can't wait to get a wife – any wife will do.

Even the temporary absence of the woman of the house made a difference, if she had no daughter old enough to deputise. In 1770 when Mrs Austen was away from home for about a month looking after her sister in childbirth, Mr Austen wrote forlornly to his own sister-in-law: 'I don't much like this lonely kind of life, you know I have not been much used to it, and yet I must bear with it about three weeks longer, at which time I expect my housekeeper's return.'[12] 'My housekeeper', not 'my wife' – and this from the most affectionate and reasonable of husbands!

The diaries of Parson Woodforde, a contemporary of Parson Austen though unknown to him, are a rich source of information on food and housekeeping in an ordinary country rectory in the last decades of the eighteenth century. Woodforde, who lived in Norfolk and never married, called on his niece Nancy to keep house for him. Receiving just ten pounds a year and board for her services, Nancy found the life dreadfully dull and made frequent complaints. She stuck at it either because she felt a strong familial obligation to her uncle or because she was grateful for any home and occupation – or probably a mixture of the two.

Women were certainly not accustomed to consult only their own preference. When two of James Edward Austen-Leigh's bachelor sons asked their aunt Caroline (Jane Austen's niece) to keep house for them, she accepted out of family feeling and a sense of duty, though as a middle-aged spinster she had been living alone quite contentedly hitherto. Similarly, when Jane's brother Charles lost his first young wife, his sister-in-law gave up her independence to look after him and his three little girls – just as had Elizabeth Branwell, forsaking warm Penzance for bleak Haworth, when Maria Brontë died. It was chance only that Jane Austen herself never had sole responsibility for a household – though she assisted Cassandra and deputised when she was away. Had Cassandra died or married, her responsibilities would have devolved upon Jane. While an uncongenial offer of marriage might in good conscience be refused, the *cri du coeur* of a male relative, which might come at any time, could not.

There is a passage in one of Jane's letters to Cassandra, written on 8 September 1816, which is most revealing of her attitude to housekeeping at this stage of her life, when she was at the height of her literary output and success, but beginning to feel the first symptoms of the illness which was to kill her in less than a year. Cassandra was in Cheltenham with their sister-in-law Mary, while Mary's eighteen-year-old son

Edward (the James Edward Austen-Leigh who was later to write the *Memoir* of his aunt) had been staying with Jane and her mother at Chawton. 'I enjoyed Edward's company very much, as I said before,' wrote Jane,

> and yet I was not sorry when Friday came. It had been a busy week, and I wanted a few days quiet, and exemption from the thought and contrivances which any sort of company gives. I often wonder how *you* can find time for all you do, in addition to the care of the house; and how good Mrs West could have written such books and collected so many hard words, with all her family cares, is still more a matter of astonishment! Composition seems to me impossible, with a head full of joints of mutton and doses of rhubarb. (*L, 466*)

Most women who, at some stage of their lives, have had other things they would rather be thinking about than what to serve for the next meal – and the next – can sympathise with that. The same women have probably, at other times, derived considerable pleasure from cooking and sharing food with family and friends. Jane Austen was no less ambivalent in her attitude. At the other end of her adult life, when it was a novelty for her to take over the housekeeping (her mother indisposed, Cassandra on another visit) she wrote in a different vein: 'My mother desires me to tell you that I am a very good housekeeper, which I have no reluctance in doing, because I really think it is my peculiar excellence, and for this reason – I always take care to provide such things as please my own appetite, which I consider as the chief merit in housekeeping.' (*L, 28*) Later in the same letter she returns to the subject: 'I am very fond of experimental housekeeping, such as having an ox-cheek now and then; I shall have one next week, and I mean to have some little dumplings put into it, that I may fancy myself at Godmersham.' Jane was nearly twenty-three when she wrote this, proving, incidentally, that either of the Miss Austens was quite capable of taking over from their mother when the need arose, long before the post was formally surrendered to Cassandra.

'The sweets of housekeeping in a country village!' As her sister laments the unseasonableness of the weather, Mary Crawford affects to believe that were Mrs Grant to live in London, and have tradesmen to deal with all her wants, no such household cares would plague her. Philosophically Mrs Grant replies that tradesmen can be the cause of just as many vexations as nature, though of a different kind; if Mary sets up house in town, she prophesies, 'their remoteness and unpunctuality, or their exorbitant charges and frauds, will be calling forth bitter lamentations'. (*MP, 213*)

By the time she wrote *Mansfield Park* Jane Austen had experienced both kinds of housekeeping, in country and in town, and she knew the relative drawbacks of each. When Jane was twenty-five her parents made the apparently sudden decision to leave Steventon Rectory to the care of their clerical son James and retire with their two unmarried daughters to Bath. Much has been written about Jane's shock when she heard the news, her initial reluctance, her teaching herself to make the best of it, and the contribution these Bath years were eventually to make to her art, despite the creative failure they seemed to induce in her at the time. Here I simply want to consider the difference – and it was an enormous difference – which living in Bath made to the Austen's household economy.

It was a retirement for Mrs Austen no less than for her husband. Farm, dairy, brewhouse, poultry-yard, hives, all were given up – in Bath they did not have so much as a garden. Georgian terraced houses in Bath had their principal rooms overlooking the street; family and visitors kept their eyes averted from unsightly back yards. Only as the nineteenth century progressed did a private garden come to seem more desirable than public promenading, and architecture to be amended accordingly. Certainly the ground at the rear of the house rented by the Austens, 4 Sydney Place, was little more than a yard, the domain of servants, a utility area for fuel and washing. After Mr Austen's death in 1805 the remaining three were yet worse off, occupying a succession of lodgings formed from just part of a house, with no outdoor space at all.

With the removal to Bath, nearly all Mrs Austen's cares could be shed, together with much that had been used to occupy her time. All their food was now bought in, from the market stalls and specialist shops which served the large number of gentry living or staying in the city. Of course cookery itself continued – possibly even to the extent of baking bread and preserving jams; the details of exactly what was made at home and what bought ready-made are impossible to retrieve, especially as no letters from Jane Austen survive from the Sydney Place period. With a large basement kitchen fitted with dressers and cupboards, other rooms on the same level for scullery and pantry, and a cool wine cellar under part of the back yard, the house afforded space enough for the servants to do their work and for certain stores of food to be kept. But whatever level of cookery went on in Sydney Place, all the raw ingredients certainly had to be purchased.

Shopping itself would have occupied some of the time previously given to the production of food at home. Whether this was found more or less pleasurable than farming and all its related activities was a matter of taste. Presumably Mrs Austen welcomed the change, even if her daughters did not. 'I quite envy you your Farm,' wrote Cassandra wistfully to a cousin ten years later after leaving Steventon, 'there is so much amusement and so many comforts attending a Farm in the country that those who have once felt the advantages cannot easily forget them.'[13] An exhausted Mrs Austen on the other hand might have echoed (or inspired) Mrs Allen's words in *Northanger Abbey*: 'Bath is a charming place, sir; there are so many good shops here. We are sadly off in the country . . . Now here one can step out of doors and get a thing in five minutes.' (*NA, 29*) But whether the change was viewed with relief or regret, there were potentially two serious and unpleasant consequences involved in having to buy all their food.

One was the danger of adulteration, a very common practice before the first Food and Drugs Act of 1875. All kinds of substances were on occasion added to improve the colour or frothiness of beer, which was very much a staple commodity, regularly drunk at home with meals. Chalk (or worse) might be added to flour for bread; Jane Austen once warned Cassandra against the 'very bad Baker's bread' at Streatham. (*L, 367*) There were many other horrors against which the wary shopper had to be on her guard, some of them, of course, impossible to detect until the moment of eating – although one cannot imagine Mrs Austen being fooled by the trick of daubing fresh blood on stale butcher's meat.

Even without fraud, the loss in freshness inevitable with slow transportation and lack of refrigeration was a marked change from the quality of their food at Steventon. Jane Austen had already experienced bad butter in Bath on an earlier holiday there. As for milk, town milk was notorious. Small country towns could be supplied from the surrounding farms, but to provide sufficient milk for a population the size of Bath's required the keeping of cows in the city itself, in cramped, unhygienic barns – and of course without access to fresh grass. The resultant milk was of poor quality to begin with; it was then skimmed of its cream, and very often diluted with water, before being hawked through the streets in open pails into which any dust or debris might be blown. In hot weather, particularly, it must have been virtually undrinkable. Perhaps this, and similar problems with other highly perishable foods, formed part of the reason why the Austens were glad to leave Bath every year in the late summer for a protracted tour to the seaside. Town milk was actually known as 'blue milk' in the eighteenth century, calling to mind the Portsmouth scene in *Mansfield Park* in which, as the warm Spring weather advances, Fanny Price sickeningly observes 'the milk a mixture of motes floating in thin blue'. (*MP, 439*)

The other disadvantage of city life for the Austens was the very material one of having to give ready money for everything they consumed. From the moment of their removal to Bath, Jane Austen became aware of and anxious about money as she had never been before. The family had a much smaller income – not only had several sources of revenue, like the farm and pupils, been given up by Mr Austen, but part even of his clerical stipend had naturally to be left for James to live upon at Steventon – yet their outgoings in cash were greater, both in food and in house-rent. In fact, it would seem that they took a rather better house than they could really afford, as the lease of 4 Sydney Place was not renewed after the initial three years expired. All this added to Jane's feelings of insecurity. Her very first letter to Cassandra on arriving in advance of her in Bath mentions the price of various commodities: meat 8d. per pound, cheese $9\frac{1}{2}$d., butter 1s., cucumber 1s., and salmon 2s. 9d. The cost of the latter was thought to be inflated by the presence in the city of the Duchess of Gloucester. This was another drawback of trying to keep to a budget in a fashionable town – fluctuations in price over which they had no control.

Basic foodstuffs were mostly bought at market. In Bath the sundry groupings of stall-holders of the early and middle eighteenth century had, by the time of the Austen's residence, been gathered tidily and even impressively into the covered Market Place adjoining the Guildhall. Here the Corporation, anxious to attract and keep visitors and residents of the better classes, who were becoming increasingly fastidious in their tastes, did all it could to limit fraud and obnoxious practices through a system of inspectors, bailiffs, licensing and local regulations.[14] Robert Southey thought it a model of its kind for 'order and abundance'.[15]

Notwithstanding that Mrs Thorpe finds 'there was hardly any veal to be got at market this morning' (*NA*, 68), the *Bath Guide* of 1800 (hardly disinterested) boasts:

> The principal markets are kept on Wednesdays and Saturdays and plentifully supplied with every kind of provisions, generally at moderate prices. Fresh butter (equal to any in England) is brought in from the country every morning, and the butchers who live in the city supply the inhabitants with the best of meat every day of the week. The markets for fish are Mondays, Wednesdays and Fridays and are thought to excel those of any inland town in the country.[16]

Certainly Bath was well situated geographically to receive excellent supplies: meat from the Welsh mountains, fruit and vegetables from the Cotswolds and the Vale of Evesham, dairy produce from Somerset and Devon, fish from the River Severn, and imported wines from Bristol.

The city's demanding clientele would have exerted continual pressure in favour of quality and luxury, counteracting the tendency to malpractice to which commercially produced foods at that time were subject everywhere.

Whatever the honesty or otherwise of its shopkeepers, Bath was acknowledged to be second only to the West End of London in the range and luxury of its shops. Some of them dealt in basic commodities – there were the usual bakers, grocers, butchers, poulterers and fishmongers. In Jane Austen's time there was one famous poulterer in Wade's Passage, a fishmonger of high reputation in the High Street and another in Bath Street – the row of shops where the ordeal of Jane's aunt Mrs Leigh Perrot, arrested and imprisoned (and nearly transported) for allegedly stealing a card of lace, began: not a great recommendation of the Bath shops for the Austens. But it was the luxury end of the food market for which the shopkeepers found it most profitable to cater. In 1774 the first ice-cream parlour opened in Bath on Pulteney Bridge. Pastry-cooks also sold ices, together with all kinds of ready-made sweet and savoury dishes to eat in the shop or take away.

Bath had two rival pastry-cooks, to one of which Jane Austen gave immortality by naming it in a scene in *Persuasion*: Molland's, at the foot of Milsom Street. Typically, Jane Austen omits to specify the refreshment taken by Anne Elliot and her companions. Anne's mind is on more important matters: the sudden reappearance of Captain Wentworth. The other famous pastry-cook's, Gill's, in Wade's Passage, is mentioned by Tobias Smollett in *Humphrey Clinker* with more particularity: he names jellies, tarts and basins of soup as among its allurements.

Gill's also featured in a memoir of the 1850s, looking back to a childhood at the turn of the century: 'I particularly remember the pastry-cooks' shops, into one of which we entered, and tasted some delicious tarts, the flavour of which seems to have dwelt on my palette [sic] to the present time . . . The shop I allude to was built against the north wall of the Abbey church, between two buttresses, attached to one of which was the oven chimney.'[17] As a clergyman's daughter, Jane Austen would presumably have deplored such sacrilege; and from what we know of her character there were probably other aspects of the shopping scene in Bath which she viewed with distaste – the commercialism, the ostentation and the deliberate temptation to greed.

The great growth in retailing in towns and cities all over the country was to come after Jane Austen's lifetime, as the population of the country became increasingly urbanised, cut off from the sources of food production, and also increasingly affluent, demanding more and more luxury goods, and less willing to make things for themselves. Living in the fashionable city of Bath, Jane was able to observe the beginning of this trend. It was a trend which would, for the middle and upper classes, lead to material comforts undreamt of in her mother's generation, while reducing the role of women in the home to a combination of decorative plaything and moral guardian. Much misery and frustration for women were to ensue; yet few would have welcomed a return to the drudgery which a life like Mrs Austen's at Steventon must have seemed, by the middle of the nineteenth century, to represent.

Being proficient in all the varied arts of domestic economy had then given pride and meaning to a woman's life; her contribution to the comfort of the home had equal worth with the man's whose means supported it. While holding no brief against wealth and ease, Jane Austen, whose novels always end with the establishment of a true partnership, would not have welcomed any diminution in the domestic importance, and hence the self-respect, of women. To *wish* to live in a town, as do Mary Crawford and Elizabeth Elliot, is to choose a way of life that is empty of useful occupation and the satisfaction of serving others. The life of the urban rich is also detached from the cycle of the year, with its seasons of growth and harvest, which humanity has traditionally linked with religion and held in a proper and healthy awe. Mary Crawford lacks this humility before nature; for her the harp comes before the hay. For Jane Austen, however, the elegancies and fundamentals of life must be kept in balance, an achievement which is almost impossible, or which certainly requires more conscious effort, in the artificial conditions of a town.

Her own next home was also in a town, but a less fashionable one: Southampton. Mrs Austen, Cassandra and Jane, and their friend Martha Lloyd who had recently lost her mother, joined forces with Jane's sailor brother Frank and his new wife Mary. Sharing household expenses would suit them all, and Mary (who was quickly pregnant with the first of her nine children) would have company while Frank was at sea. How household duties were apportioned amongst the five women is not recorded, but there is nothing in Jane's letters from the Southampton period to suggest other than that they lived and worked together in perfect harmony.

As in Bath, most of their provisions still had to be bought in, but their Southampton home had one great advantage: a garden. It was only a walled town garden, abutting the city ramparts, and had been much neglected, but they set to work at once to make it fruitful. 'The Border under the Terrace Wall is clearing away to receive Currants & Goose-berry Bushes, and a spot is found very proper for raspberries', Jane wrote in February 1807. (*L, 178*) By the following summer they were also gathering strawberries.

More letters survive from Southampton than from Bath (though their residence there was of shorter duration), so it is possible to discuss their provision of food with a little more certainty. On the other hand, the house itself, unlike 4 Sydney Place, does not survive, so the space available for cookery and food storage cannot be so easily estimated; but that they were likely to have been greater than in Bath is suggested by the work that was carried out on the premises. We know that Mrs Austen cured six hams for Frank to take to sea; that fruit preserves were made; and that both spruce beer and orange wine were brewed. The inference is that a return to some of their old practices was made possible by a greater amount of space and that, whether from economy, pleasure or healthfulness, these opportunities to produce more of their food and drink at home were eagerly seized.

Another advantage of Southampton was the availability of fresh fish. This was appreciated not only for their own table, but as presents for their inland friends and relations. In February 1808 Jane sent 'four pairs of small soals' to Kintbury Rectory in Berkshire, home of their friends the Fowles, hoping they would arrive while still fresh. The gift was made in return for poultry from Kintbury, the fish being sent back in the basket which had conveyed the birds to Southampton.

The habit of sending foodstuffs among themselves, when any house-hold happened to have a glut or an opportunity to present something they knew would be valued, is one of the charms of the Austen circle's way of life. The Fowles, whose glebe evidently included an orchard, sent hampers of apples to both Henry Austen in London and his mother and sisters at Southampton – in the latter case, sufficient to cover the floor of the garret (the best way to store apples being to lay them out in a cool place without touching one another). At various times in the course of Jane's correspondence we hear of venison being sent from Godmersham to Rowling, and from Chawton Park to the Frank Austens then in lodgings in Alton (neither long journeys); twice of a turkey sent from Steventon to Henry in London, a much greater distance; of '4 brace of birds', 'two pheasants' and 'a pheasant and hare' from the Chawton estates to Southampton (the last consignment being shot by Henry); 'half of an excellent Stilton cheese' from Henry to Chawton Cottage; pork, ham and seakale from Steventon to Chawton Cottage; ham from Chaw-ton Great House to London; a brace of pheasants from Kintbury to

London; a hare and four rabbits from Godmersham to London; and a pot of raspberry jam from Chawton Cottage to London. Poor Henry, cut off from sources of fresh food in London, seems to have been the object of his relations' pity and the most frequent recipient of gifts. On another occasion he accepted his sisters' offer to make him nine gallons of mead. Mrs Austen cured pork at different times for both her sailor sons to take on voyages. She sent biscuits to some grandsons at Winchester College and roots of strawberry plant to a newly-married grand-daughter. All this giving and sending of food – so reminiscent of the world of *Emma* – is only what we hear about when Jane and Cassandra happened to be apart; many more such gifts between the branches of the family must have gone unrecorded, their thank-you letters sadly lost.

Godmersham in Kent and Chawton in Hampshire, referred to above, were two large estates belonging to Jane's third brother, Edward, who inherited property from (and adopted the name of) a distant relation, Thomas Knight. Towards the end of 1808 Edward offered his mother and sisters the use of a house in the village of Chawton rent-free for the remainder of their lives. With great joy they prepared to move into the property now familiarly known as Chawton Cottage, accompanied as before by Martha Lloyd. (Frank's career had taken him and Mary to Yarmouth in the Isle of Wight, where fish could be had, wrote Jane, 'almost for nothing'.) (*L, 212*)

Considerably larger than the average labourer's cottage, and possibly once an inn, the house dated from about 1690. It was accepted sight unseen by Mrs Austen, rather as Mrs Dashwood accepts Barton Cottage, a similarly modest but comfortable establishment for four impoverished women made available by the generosity of a wealthy male relative. At Edward's expense the house was altered and refurbished to suit its new occupants, and in the summer of 1809 they began what was to be one of the happiest periods of their existence, and for Jane certainly the most creative and fulfilling one.

In acknowledgement perhaps of the importance of her writing, she was given a smaller share than Cassandra in the household duties that were now apportioned out. Jane's special responsibility was for the stores of tea, coffee and sugar, precious items which were kept in a locked cupboard in an alcove of the dining-parlour rather than in the kitchen or larder. It was also her job to prepare the breakfast at the dining-parlour fire. That left her free of household cares for the rest of the day – unless Cassandra were away on one of her long visits to Godmersham or Kintbury, when more work of course fell on Jane. Martha appears to have had no specific responsibilities, but as she was another practical, unpretentious woman, who as we have seen collected and wrote down recipes and home remedies in a book which still survives, it is inconceivable that she did not do her share of the work.

At Chawton Mrs Austen confined her activities to sewing and to working in the garden, which she continued to do, for health and pleasure, until almost the end of her very long life. According to one of her great-grand-daughters:

> She dug up her own potatoes, and I have no doubt she planted them, for the kitchen garden was as much her delight as the flower borders, and I have heard my mother say that when at work, she wore a green round frock like a day-labourer's.[18]

Jane was equally interested, if not equally involved, in the progress of the garden and its productiveness. 'What sort of kitchen garden is there?' had been her first eager enquiry about her prospective new home. (*L, 226*) The answer, at least after the family had arranged the plot to suit their own taste and requirements, can best be given in the recollections of a niece, Caroline Austen, who was a frequent visitor there:

> A high wooden fence shut out the road (the Winchester road it was) all the length of the little domain, and trees were planted inside to form a shrubbery walk – which carried round the enclosure, gave a very sufficient space for exercise – you did not feel cramped for room; and there was a pleasant irregular mixture of hedgerow, and grass, and gravel walk and long grass for mowing, and orchard – which I imagine arose from two or three little enclosures having been thrown together, and arranged as best might be, for ladies' occupation. – There was besides a good kitchen garden, large court and many out-buildings, not much occupied – and all this affluence of space was delightful to children, and I have no doubt added considerably to the pleasure of a visit. Everything indoors and out was well kept – the house was well furnished, and it was altogether a comfortable and ladylike establishment, tho' I believe the means which supported it were but small.[19]

'We are likely to have a great crop of Orleans plumbs, but not many greengages – on the standard scarcely any, three or four dozen, perhaps, against the wall', reported Jane in May 1811, when they had been at Chawton just under two years. (*L, 281*) 'The chicken are all alive and fit for the table', she added in the same letter. Later that month she reported that the peas were in a flourishing state, but the mulberry tree less so, and that an apricot had begun to fruit. Strawberries, gooseberries and currants are mentioned a week later.

The style of housekeeping at Chawton thus fell somewhere between what they had known at Steventon and at Bath. Fruit and vegetables were home-grown, poultry home-reared; they were able to keep bees; they had space to bake bread and make wine and brew beer. The bread-oven shared an out-house with the washing copper; if it rained on wash-day the clothes would be hung to dry in the warmth from baking. In an adjoining building a loft was used to store sacks of flour; a small cellar here was used as cool storage for vegetables. Beneath the house itself was a more extensive cellar, the legacy perhaps of its period as an inn, where the Austens could keep their home-produced beer, mead and wine.[20]

Yet there were gaps in their self-sufficiency. 'We have not now so much as a cow', wrote Cassandra, still hankering after a farm two years after the move to Chawton.[21] Meat, flour and dairy produce had to be bought in, whenever possible from the home farm attached to Edward's property. This at least guaranteed freshness and freedom from profiteering. A Chawton villager whose recollections of the 1820s have been preserved recorded that the Austens' manservant would walk up to Chawton House each day accompanied by Cassandra's dog 'Link', who would carry home the pail of milk in his mouth. [22]

Caroline Austen says that her aunts often walked in the afternoon to Alton, just a mile away, for shopping; but whether this included food shopping is unrecorded. The Chawton villager quoted above says that there was only a very small market at Alton, and that 'the principal marketing' was done in Winchester or Farnham. Both a Cheese Fair and a Cherry Fair were held locally, once a year.[23] We do know that the Austens' supplies of sugar and dried fruits came from as far away as Guildford, as Jane Austen mentions paying a Mr Herington there (for goods already received) when passing through on a journey to London. There had been something amiss with the last consignment of currants, and Mr Herington promised to speak to the man who had 'put them up'. Sugar, which could also be variable in quality, came in the form of conical loaves, of which they purchased five or six at a time. They were perhaps especially particular about tea, as this was actually ordered in London, from Mr Twining himself.

That tea and sugar were regarded as expensive commodities is evident from a remark made by Jane in May 1813. She was in London with Henry, while her brother Charles, his wife, their three little girls and nursemaid were staying at Chawton. Anticipating the end of their visit, Jane wrote to Cassandra, 'You will miss them, but the comfort of getting back into your own room will be great!', adding feelingly, '& then the Tea & Sugar!' (*L, 312*) Six extra mouths to feed certainly make a difference to a tightly constructed budget, but we should be unlikely to begrudge our visitors their share of the tea and sugar today.

Though finances were certainly easier for the Austen women at Chawton, and their future more settled, Jane's interest in food prices remained keen. In 1813, replying to a letter from Frank, then stationed in the Baltic, she observed, 'Rostock Market makes one's mouth water, our cheapest Butcher's meat is double the price of theirs; nothing under 9d. all this summer, & I believe upon recollection nothing under 10d. – Bread has sunk & is likely to sink more, which we hope may make Meat sink too.' (*L, 336*) Cassandra also, in 1811, lamented, 'so expensive as everything in England is now, even the necessaries of life'.[24]

Jane Austen was always highly conscious of the difference between households like their own, where economy had to be observed, and others of her acquaintance where expense was no object. It was not that she was snobbish or greedy about food, far from it, but she could not help finding it 'vulgar' to be perpetually preoccupied with prices and small savings. The letter to Frank quoted above was written during a visit to Edward's family at Godmersham Park, and immediately continues: 'But I have no occasion to think of the price of Bread or of Meat where I am now; – let me shake off vulgar cares & conform to the happy Indifference of East Kent wealth.' Godmersham always had this effect on her. On a visit five years earlier she had written to Cassandra: 'The orange Wine will want our Care soon. – But in the meantime for Elegance and Ease and Luxury – the Hattons and Milles dine here today – & I shall eat Ice & drink French wine, & be above vulgar economy.' (*L, 209*) She immediately adds, with perfect sincerity: 'Luckily the pleasures of Friendship, of unreserved Conversation, of similarity of Taste & Opinions, will make good amends for Orange Wine.' Her priorities were impeccable and unassailable; nevertheless she had a value for elegance of mind which was basically incompatible with 'vulgar cares'.

Among the Austens, Knights and Leighs and all their ramifications, the widow and daughters of George Austen had probably the smallest income of all to live upon. Mrs Austen, in accepting an allowance of money from her wealthy brother's widow in 1820, noted that her own income from investments and property came to just £116 p.a., 'my good children having supplied all the rest' which had made an independent home possible since her husband's death.[25] By this date, fifteen years later, only Edward out of all the sons was still in a position to help his mother financially, for James was dead, Henry bankrupt, Frank had also lost heavily in the failure of Henry's bank, and Charles had always been incorrigibly poor. 'Mr Knight is most kind and liberal: he allows me £200 a year, gives me my House Rent, supplies me plentifully with wood and makes me many kind presents', Mrs Austen continued. Aware that 'tho' his income is large, his family is large also', she was reluctant to ask him for more. Edward too had lost money in the 1816 bank crash, he had recently been involved in an expensive law suit which challenged his right to his property and he had eleven children to launch in the world.

If the uprooting from Steventon had left a legacy of insecurity in Jane Austen, to this had since been added a sense of living on her brothers' charity, with all the precariousness and obligation that that involved, even in the most united of families. When she began to earn a little money from her books, she deeply relished the feeling of being able to make a contribution to the expenses of the household. 'Single women have a dreadful propensity for being poor', as she warned a niece who was wondering whether to marry. (*L, 483*)

The Austen women's poverty must not of course be exaggerated: they were comfortable enough to eat delicious things, and to dispense charity to those much worse off than themselves; Jane Austen writes of supplying sugar to a poor old Mrs Williams. (*L, 203*) If she envied richer households it was not so much for the desirable things that money could buy, a French cook or French wine or French bread (all mentioned as bywords for luxury in either her correspondence or her novels), but for their freedom from perpetual contrivance. In this I think she differed a little even from Cassandra, who seems to have relished the challenge of housekeeping, and certainly from her mother. Mrs Austen came from a generation which, as her grandson James Edward Austen-Leigh noticed, was more ready to do things for themselves, and which treated servants as junior partners in the same enterprise, rather than as beings immeasurably beneath them. Mrs Austen had no time for 'idle young people', and, being indisputably well-born and well-connected herself, she had equally no time for silly social pretensions. The labourer's smock she wore for gardening is one example of her unselfconsciousness. If she had a pile of mending to do, she would carry on with it even when company came to call, instead of taking up some fancy work, as most ladies would have done to show they sewed for a pastime, not necessity. This unceremonious habit of her mother's is known to have embarrassed Jane Austen, who belonged to a generation growing more refined.

Yet, to the generation *after* theirs, that of Jane and Cassandra was not refined enough. Not only James Edward in his affectionate reminiscences, but his sharper cousin Fanny (Lady Knatchbull), looking back from her own old age, saw that there had been a great change. 'Yes my love,' she wrote to one of her younger sisters, it is very true that Aunt Jane from various circumstances was not so refined as she ought to have been from her talent, and if she had lived fifty years later she would have been in many respects more suitable to our refined tastes . . . Aunt Jane was too clever not to put aside all possible signs of 'commonness' (if such an expression is allowable) and teach herself to be more refined, at least in intercourse with people in general.[26]

What signs of commonness Fanny had in mind it is impossible to say, but I suspect that preoccupation with the practical aspects of housekeeping and with the need to practise small economies may have had something to do with it, and that Jane Austen herself was very much aware of this. In her fiction, she placed most of her characters above 'vulgar cares' of the sort she herself was never quite free from. Only Miss Bates is in a situation approximating to Cassandra Austen's, 'devoted to the care of a failing mother, and the endeavour to make a small income go as far as possible' (*E, 21*) – and Miss Bates, though treated with respect and pity, is kept at a decided distance by her author. The other hard-pressed housekeeper of the novels, Mrs Price, who has wilfully caused her own degradation, is afforded no sympathy at all. Her home is presented only as a place that any self-respecting heroine would wish to escape from as quickly as possible, never to return.

We have seen how the heroines themselves inhabit a more leisured and affluent world than characterised their author's own immediate experience, though not more than she was familiar with among her relations. James Edward Austen-Leigh put forward the theory that the reason the fragment known as *The Watsons* (written in Bath) was abandoned was that Jane Austen realised she had placed her heroine in too lowly a situation. This has been dismissed as a piece of Victorian snobbery. But there may be some truth in it, particularly as it occurred at a time when, following her father's death, Jane Austen must have felt herself and her sister to be in danger of sliding further down the social and economic scale. There is an unusual preoccupation with humble meals and unfashionable mealtimes in *The Watsons*, a dearth of servants and a consequent demand upon the daughters of the house, 'a great deal of indifferent cooking and anxious suspense', which Jane Austen might have concluded was delicate ground for her. (*MW, 360*)

So there is a sense in which her fiction is more 'refined', in Fanny Knatchbull's use of the term, than her life. The fiction occupies as it were a place a little more advanced along the road towards the Victorian version of gentility than Jane Austen's own lifespan actually reached. Great writers are often endowed with an unusual ability to see the way their society is going. They sometimes combine with this a tenderness for the recent past and an unusually heightened concern lest its better features be lost for ever in the unheeding pursuit of fashion. Jane Austen possessed both these types of vision, both the prospective and the retrospective. The consequence for her novels is a fruitful tension between a value for elegance and elevation of thought, and a desire to preserve the best of the old country ways of living: an attachment to nature, a religious humility about 'the trivial round, the common task' and an equal if separate value for the work of men and women. Food and housekeeping may be mundane topics but in Jane Austen's fiction, sparingly as they are used, they are deeply imbued with significance for the proper regulation of human life.

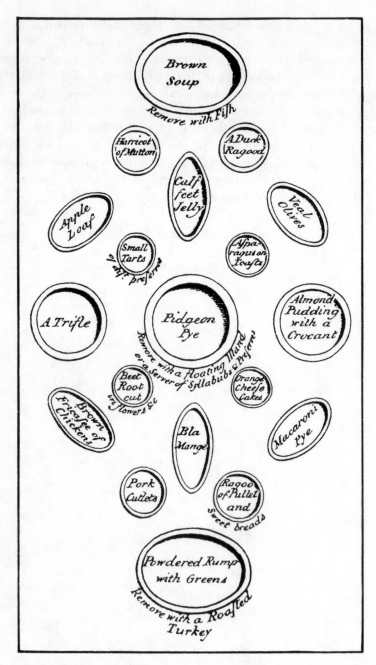

Plan of a typical full course of nineteen dishes, from Mrs Frazer,
The Practice of Cooking (1800)

Chapter Two

Mealtimes, Menus, Manners

The society of which Jane Austen wrote being both more leisured and more formal than our own, the timing and nature of the meals which punctuated daily life, and the conventions and etiquette attaching to them, naturally differed in various ways from those we are familiar with.

At Chawton the breakfast hour was nine o'clock, but this seems to have been unusually early. Possibly it was so arranged that Jane might settle to her writing without delay; more likely, given her self-effacement and accommodating spirit, the entire household of brisk and well-organised women preferred early hours. At Godmersham the clocks striking ten was the signal to go in to breakfast. The planned excursion from Barton Park to Whitwell, in *Sense and Sensibility*, begins with the whole party assembling at Barton Park for breakfast at ten. But it is not only in leisured circumstances that breakfast is taken rather late. Even in the London home of a man of business, Mr Gardiner, the usual breakfast hour is ten.

When Catherine joins the Tilneys for their last breakfast in Bath it must be nine, since 'the clock struck ten while the trunks were carrying down, and the General had fixed to be out of Milsom Street by that hour'. (*NA, 155*) With a longish journey ahead, an early breakfast would be reasonable. But even at Northanger Abbey the breakfast hour would appear to have been nine, since Catherine is woken by the housemaid's opening the shutters at eight, and receives a strong hint from General Tilney about early rising when she eventually makes her appearance in the breakfast-parlour. The General, of course, requires strict punctuality at meals. His combination of greed and dictatorialness overrides his concern to be thought fashionable.

A late breakfast hour, like a late dinner hour, was often a pretension to fashion. The consequent variation between neighbouring houses might lead to awkwardness. Breakfast is over at Longbourn when Elizabeth receives Jane's note informing her of her being unwell. Resolving to visit her sister at Netherfield, Elizabeth debates with her parents, waits for Catherine and Lydia to put on their outdoor clothes, walks the three miles to Netherfield, and finds the ladies there just about to begin breakfast. At Uppercross, 'the morning hours of the Cottage were always later than those of the other house' and Mary and Anne 'were not more than beginning breakfast' when they are interrupted by a party from the Great House, including Captain Wentworth, who has already ridden the three miles from Kellynch before taking breakfast with the Musgroves.

The generally late hour left time for considerable activity before the first meal of the day. At Chawton Jane Austen herself used the interval between rising and making the breakfast to practise the piano in solitude. Caroline Austen found it hard to account for why her aunt kept up her practice in this way. Perhaps the uninterrupted mechanical playing over of simple tunes (Caroline says the music was 'disgracefully easy') was nothing more than a means of inducing her creative juices to flow in readiness for the morning's writing. With nobody else in the room she would 'live with' her characters, decide their development and compose sentences in her mind. Her ideas thus stimulated, her share of the household work dutifully accomplished for the day, her body refreshed by the meal, she would be ready to begin work immediately breakfast was over.

When she was away from home Jane frequently wrote letters before breakfast. In London she even went shopping. 'At nine we are to set off for Grafton House, and get that over before breakfast', she wrote at half past seven in the morning from Henry's house in Henrietta Street. (*L*, *323*) When travelling, a whole stage of the journey could be accomplished before the travellers broke their fast. After making an early start from Chawton in May 1813, 'Three hours and a quarter took us to Guildford, where we stayed barely two hours, and had only just time enough for all we had to do there: that is, eating a long comfortable breakfast, watching the carriages, paying Mr Herington, and taking a little stroll afterwards . . . We left Guildford at twenty minutes before twelve (I hope somebody cares for these minutiae) and were at Esher in about two hours more'. (*L*, *306*) Had a light breakfast already been taken before they left Chawton, I think Jane Austen, with her care for words, would have found it impossible to call a second such meal at Guildford *breakfast*, at least without making some pertinent comment.

Georgiana Darcy, too, travels on an empty stomach, arriving at Pemberley (we know not from where) only to 'a late breakfast'. At variance with both these instances is the scene in *Mansfield Park* in which the travellers Henry Crawford and William Price are served a substantial breakfast, earlier than the rest of the family, to speed them on their way.

An early breakfast might also be provided when the young men of the family were going to hunt. James Edward Austen-Leigh found it worth recording that at Steventon, on hunting mornings, his uncles 'usually took their hasty breakfast in the kitchen'.[1] This struck him as decidedly different from Victorian custom.

'Every generation has its improvements', remarks Mary Crawford. (*MP, 86*) One pre-breakfast activity not so often indulged in during Jane Austen's lifetime was weekday family prayers (as opposed to grace at table). But Jane did experience the tradition in its full solemnity at Stoneleigh Abbey in July 1806. There the old mistress, Mary Leigh, had recently died, and the property had passed to the Reverend Thomas Leigh, Mrs Austen's cousin, with whom the Austens were staying. 'At nine in the morning we meet and say our prayers in a handsome Chapel, the pulpit &c now hung with Black', wrote Mrs Austen. 'Then follows breakfast . . . '[2]

In the country gentlemen often took a brisk walk to work up an appetite for breakfast. This is what John Knightley does when staying in Highbury, taking his two young sons. James Austen frequently walked the mile from his home at Deane to Steventon to visit his parents before breakfast, thus calling forth his wife's reproaches. On the first morning of his visit to Barton Cottage, Edward Ferrars walks to the village to see his horses, returning full of admiration for the surrounding country-side. He does not invite Elinor or Marianne to join him, and they don't appear to expect it. No doubt women were generally assumed to be occupied with the preparations for breakfast. Female walking was usually reserved for a later part of the day, but there might be exceptional circumstances, such as being on holiday, when normal habits were broken. At Lyme, Anne and Henrietta agree to stroll down to the sea before breakfast. They are joined after a while by Captain Wentworth and Louisa, who then remembers she has some shopping to do in the town. It is only 'after attending Louisa through her business, and loitering about a little longer', that they return to the inn for breakfast, doubtless with appetites as well as complexions enhanced by the sea breeze. (*P, 104*)

At an inn, or for travellers leaving home, breakfast might be a substantial meal: Henry Crawford and William Price fortify themselves with boiled eggs and pork chops before setting off from Northampton-shire for London. Parson Woodforde's choice at an inn included 'choc-olate, green and brown tea, hot rolls, dried toast, bread and butter, honey, tongue and ham grated very small'.[3] But it was what Thomas Love Peacock, in his novel *Headlong Hall* (1816), called the 'ordinary comforts of tea and toast' which most people on most occasions found sufficient, and which suited the elegance of the age.

Georgian breakfasts were quite distinct both from the robust meal of bread, ale and cheese enjoyed by former generations, and from the hot dishes of kedgeree, devilled kidneys, scrambled eggs and so forth under which the sideboards of Victorian and Edwardian country houses groaned. Georgian breakfasts were dainty meals of varieties of bread, cake and hot drinks, served (if the house were grand enough to possess one) in the breakfast-parlour rather than the dining-room, and eaten off the new fine china. General Tilney boasts about his breakfast set. 'To his uncritical palate, the tea was as well flavoured from the clay of Stafford-shire, as from that of Dresden or Sêve. But this was quite an old set, purchased two years ago.' (*NA, 175*) Mrs John Dashwood envies her mother-in-law's set of breakfast china as being 'twice as handsome' as her own. (*S & S, 13*)

It was the introduction into this country of tea, coffee and chocolate (from China, Ethiopia and Mexico respectively) which had revolu-tionised breakfast. All had arrived about the middle of the seventeenth century, and had been drunk first in public meeting houses in the middle of the day, before becoming established in the homes of the upper classes at allotted hours. Of the three new drinks, tea became and remained the most popular in England. Between 1693 and 1793 its consumption increased four hundredfold. As a new luxury item which people soon could not live without, it attracted a tax, was very expensive and was kept under lock and key. Jane Austen estimated that the consumption of tea at Godmersham was 12lb. a quarter. Much smug-gling went on, one of those who received contraband supplies being Parson Woodforde.

Tea had not yet been cultivated in India, all supplies coming from China in Jane Austen's day. There was a choice of green tea (which Jane Austen mentions in a letter, and which Arthur Parker, in *Sanditon*, claims acts on him 'like Poison' (*MW, 418*), or brown, the latter being subjected to a lengthier drying process. When tea was first introduced from China, Chinese porcelain bowls or dishes from which to drink it were imported too. Later in the century cups with handles were manufactured in Europe and were soon preferred, but the expression 'a dish of tea'

Taking coffee in morning dress, *La Belle Assemblée* (October, 1810)

lingered on. Jane uses it in a letter of December 1798 when, to celebrate her twenty-third birthday, her three-year-old nephew George was given his first taste of the beverage. Later the expression was heard only in the mouths of the old or the vulgar. 'I could not tell whether you would be for some meat, or only for a dish of tea', says Mrs Price when William and Fanny arrive after a two-day journey (preparations are in hand for neither). (*MP, 379*)

It seems likely that the Austens' habitual breakfast drink was tea, since writing from Bath, where she was holidaying with Edward, Jane warns Cassandra, 'The coffee-mill will be wanted every day while Edward is at Steventon, as he always drinks coffee for breakfast'. (*L, 68*) Jane was perpetually more preoccupied with the state of the tea and sugar stores than with coffee, which she rarely mentions in her letters. Visiting foreigners praised our tea but were very scathing about our coffee. 'The English attach no importance to the perfume and flavour of good coffee . . . . Their coffee is always weak and bitter and has completely lost its aromatic flavour', wrote André Parreaux, while Charles Moritz likened it to 'brown water'.[4]

The third fashionable drink, chocolate, is mentioned only once by Jane Austen, in the Juvenilia, but the gourmet General Tilney, at whose breakfast-table there is more variety than Catherine Morland has ever before seen, drinks cocoa at that meal. Arthur Parker also loves his cocoa, but in the evening, when he 'coddles and cooks' it himself over the fire. 'Cocoa takes a great deal of boiling', he explains. (*MW, 417*) Chocolate, which was bought in cake or roll form and grated originally into hot wine, latterly milk, had been a favourite drink of Dr Johnson – Jane's admiration for whom is not likely to have stretched to his table manners. 'He took his chocolate liberally, pouring in large quantities of cream, or even melted butter', recalled his friend and hostess Mrs Thrale, adding that when he could get them he would eat seven or eight large peaches before breakfast began.[5]

Chocolate, or cocoa, must have been considered by Jane Austen and her family as too luxurious and reprehensibly self-indulgent for everyday consumption. In all the Austen family papers chocolate is mentioned only twice, once at a wedding and once at a rather grand place, Stoneleigh Abbey. Here, Mrs Austen reported to a daughter-in-law in 1806, breakfast consisted of 'Chocolate Coffee and Tea, Plumb Cake, Pound Cake, Hot Rolls, Cold Rolls, Bread and Butter, and dry toast for me'.[6]

Toast was the mainstay of the British breakfast, then as now. It had been invented, foreigners thought, to enable the butter to be spread more easily in our cold rooms. Toast was made in front of the fire by the consumers themselves, rather than by their servants. Toasting the bread and boiling the water for tea in a kettle over the same fire would have comprised Jane Austen's duties in making breakfast at Chawton. Perhaps she also washed, dried and put away the breakfast china too, as many ladies preferred to do for themselves.

On holiday in Bath Jane Austen took rolls for her breakfast; whether she also ate Bath buns for that meal is not known, though she did write mockingly of 'disordering my Stomach with Bath bunns [sic]', that the expense to her Aunt Leigh Perrot of having her to stay might be lessened. (*L, 101*) Giving the recipe for Bath buns in a cookery book of 1782, 'send them in hot for breakfast,' advises Elizabeth Raffald.[7] In the eighteenth century they were decorated not with simple crushed sugar, as today, but with comfits made by dipping caraway seeds into boiling sugar up to a dozen times until they were thickly coated.

The other breakfast dish noticed in the novels is the French bread served at Northanger Abbey. This was not the crusty white baguette we think of today, but more like brioche – a soft yellow loaf or rolls made by enriching yeast dough with butter, milk or eggs. It was the most highly-regarded bread of the eighteenth century. Pure white bread was in any case unknown before the steel-milling process was invented in the mid nineteenth century, taking much of the flavour, goodness and character out of flour.

Two special kinds of breakfast were the public breakfast and the wedding breakfast, the latter a term which has remained in use until recently, although the celebratory meal long ago shifted to much later in the day. Nor were public breakfasts necessarily anchored to an early hour; like many other eighteenth-century rituals, they too got later and later but retained the same name. Outdoor, summer events, with music as well as food and drink, they were profit-making occasions organised by the proprietors of pleasure-gardens. To keep the company select, tickets for them had to be bought in advance. A favourite entertainment of Fanny Burney, they were regularly held at Vauxhall and Ranelegh in London, and at Sydney Gardens in Bath. The Austens' home in Bath actually overlooked Sydney Gardens. Jane Austen joked to Cassandra that if they lived there they need not fear being wholly starved.

As for the wedding breakfast, this was the other Austen occasion when chocolate made an appearance. Caroline Austen's description of her sister Anna's wedding, to Ben Lefroy at Steventon in 1814, gives a good picture of the simple celebrations customary at that level of society. The family began the day with 'a slight early breakfast up stairs', by which

Caroline must mean in their bedrooms or dressing-rooms, since all the sitting- and dining-rooms at Steventon Rectory were on the ground floor. Between nine and ten they set off for the church, the women in a carriage and the men on foot: the distance was half a mile. Apart from the immediate family of bride and groom, says Caroline,

> I am sure there was no one else in the church, nor was anyone else asked to the breakfast, to which we sat down as soon as we got back . . . The breakfast was such as best breakfasts then were: some variety of bread, hot rolls, buttered toast, tongue or ham and eggs. The addition of chocolate at one end of the table, and the wedding cake in the middle, marked the speciality of the day . . . . Soon after breakfast, the bride and groom departed. They had a long day's journey before them, to Hendon; the other Lefroys went home; and in the afternoon my mother and I went to Chawton to stay at the Great House, then occupied by my uncle Captain Austen and his large family. My father stayed behind for a few days, and then joined us. The servants had cake and punch in the evening, and I think I remember that Mr Digweed walked down to keep him company.[8]

In *Pride and Prejudice* Mrs Bennet offers the servants punch to celebrate Lydia's wedding; these are the only references I have been able to find in Austen writings to servants *consuming*, as opposed to serving, food or drink – except for Lady Denham's complaints in *Sanditon* about the cost of provisioning the servants' hall, and Mrs Norris snaffling jellies from Mansfield to take back to her own cottage with the excuse of having a sick maid to nurse. But does the maid actually get to eat the jellies? Mrs Norris *prevents* Dick Jackson from partaking in the servants' dinner at Mansfield Park, and gloats over the fact that the servants at Sotherton are not allowed wine at their table. Mrs Norris herself is the chief beneficiary at her niece Maria's wedding, getting to drink 'a supernumerary glass or two' that evening. (*MP, 203*) Evidently the custom was to drink the young couple's health long after they themselves have departed.

It is notable that the two families from Chawton did not attend the wedding of their niece Anna, despite the distance being but half a day's journey – just as Mr Knightley, oddly, does not attend the wedding of his friends Miss Taylor and Mr Weston. His own wedding to Emma is marked by no 'finery or parade', to the very definite approval of their author. (*E, 484*)

Caroline Austen herself, looking back from the 1870s, was struck by the simplicity of her sister's wedding. She concludes her account with the exclamation, 'Such were the wedding festivities of Steventon in 1814!' Modest though they were, however, they were more than mark the weddings of either Charlotte Lucas or Maria Bertram, both of whom drive directly from the church door to their new homes without any wedding breakfast at all.

After breakfast women who did not have any more pressing household cares to attend to would usually take up some sewing, which they referred to as 'work'. From about twelve or one they might make 'morning calls' on their friends. Emma mentions twelve o'clock as being the earliest time one might expect callers; Mrs Gardiner and Elizabeth leave the inn at Lambton to wait on the ladies of Pemberley after Mr Gardiner's own departure at noon; and Catherine Morland and Isabella Thorpe always arrange to meet at the Pump Room at one.

'Morning' had a different meaning then. The waking hours of the Georgians were divided by dinner, the period before dinner being known as morning, however long that might be, and the period from dinner on as evening. So when the gentlemen of Godmersham had a long meeting at Sittingbourne to attend and the house hours were adjusted accordingly, Jane wrote, 'We breakfasted before 9 & do not dine till ½ past 6 on the occasion, so I hope we three shall have a long Morning enough'. (*L, 89*)

'We three' are of course the ladies left at home. The sexes were very often (though not invariably) apart during the morning, pursuing their duties and their pleasures independently. Morning visits were a chiefly female activity, though Frank Churchill accompanies Mrs Weston on hers, and Bingley even calls on Mr Bennet alone. Evening brought the sexes together again, in a situation of greater formality.

Clothes too were divided into either 'morning dress' or 'evening dress'. Nothing was specified for afternoon, because the concept of 'afternoon' had become detached from its literal meaning. During Jane Austen's lifetime it referred only to that small portion of the early evening between the end of dinner and, an hour or two later, the drinking of tea. 'Morning' then in Jane Austen is virtually synonymous with our 'day'; when she wants to refer specifically to what we call 'morning', she uses the term 'forenoon'.[9]

Dinner had originally been a midday meal, taken very sensibly by a hard-working population midway through the labours of the day. (Plain people have continued to refer to their midday meal as dinner until within living memory, as the term 'school dinners' attests.) As the eighteenth century progressed, and as the idle rich became more numerous and more ostentatious in their idleness, the hour for dinner became later and later, floating through what we should call the middle of the afternoon (which seems the most inconvenient time of all) until it settled at six or seven. The whole point of the movement was that fashionable people were always out of synchrony with the others, for as soon as the others caught up, the fashionable people would set back their dinner hour even later. A great deal of snobbery attached to the subject, the only possible justification for which was that it was cheaper to cook, serve and eat the main meal of the day in natural light, which therefore suited the more impoverished gentry.

I will return to the subject of dinner and its timing, but the point to be made first is that as the meal grew further and further away from breakfast, so some sustenance was required to fill the gap. The name of the snack or meal which came to occupy this slot seems to have a dual provenance. Dr Johnson's *Dictionary* of 1755 defines 'lunch' or 'luncheon' as 'as much food as one's hand can hold': a pie, pasty or hunk of bread would fit this category, and no time is specified for eating it. Henry Brooke uses the word in this sense in *The Fool of Quality*, written in 1760, when he writes 'A large luncheon of brown bread struck my eyes'. Johnson's *Dictionary* has also an entry for 'nunchin' as 'a piece of victual eaten between meals'. The etymology of this derives from 'noonshine', meaning a drink, and by extension a snack, taken at noon. Another variation is 'nooning', used by Susanna Whatman in 1776, both of which tie the word to a time of day more closely than Dr Johnson's definition.[10] Jane Austen uses the word 'noonshine' in a letter written in June 1808 from Godmersham: 'The Moores came yesterday in their Curricle between one & two o'clock, & immediately after the noonshine which succeeded their arrival, a party set off for Buckwell . . .' (*L, 195*)

'Noonshine' was easily corrupted into 'nuncheon', which word Jane Austen uses on just one occasion, in *Sense and Sensibility*, to describe the hasty meal of cold beef and porter which Willoughby swallows at Marlborough on the road from London to Cleveland. From nuncheon to luncheon was an easy next step, and thus noonshine and lunch conjoined – semantically as well as conceptually. The word 'luncheon' is likewise used only once by Jane Austen. In *Pride and Prejudice*, when Elizabeth and Jane travel back from London, Lydia and Kitty meet them with the family carriage at the George Inn in an unnamed town, and order 'the nicest cold luncheon in the world', which consists of 'a sallad and cucumber' and 'such cold meat as an inn larder normally affords'. (*P& P, 222, 219*)

It is interesting, perhaps significant, that both these instances refer to meals taken at an inn. Jane Austen never uses the terms, either in letters or novels, when food is taken in the home at midday. (Caroline Austen refers to 'luncheon' at Chawton Cottage, and the division it made in the way her aunts' activities were arranged: 'working' before luncheon, walking or shopping afterwards – but she is almost certainly imposing her own later terminology.) The verb 'to lunch' did not appear until the 1830s and was at first considered very much a vulgarism.

During Jane Austen's lifetime, in a domestic context, refreshments would be offered without giving them any name, an awkward state of affairs which could not, and evidently did not, long continue. So when Mr Knightley and Mrs Elton discuss the arrangements for the strawberry party to Donwell, they manage to do so without the word 'luncheon' ever passing their lips: 'cold meat' and 'a great set-out' are their respective expressions, while their author merely refers to 'the cold repast'. (*E, 355, 361*) Similarly, when the party of Bertrams and Crawfords set off after breakfast to drive the ten miles to Sotherton, they are taken almost immediately on arrival into the dining-parlour, 'where a collation was prepared with abundance and elegance', before beginning their tour of the house and garden (*MP, 84*). And when Elizabeth and Mrs Gardiner pay a morning call on the ladies of Pemberley, the first awkward attempts at conversation are relieved by 'the entrance of the servants with cold meat, cake, and a variety of all the finest fruits in season'. (*P&P, 268*)

These are very formal occasions. Much more relaxed and friendly is the series of visits Edmund pays to Mansfield Parsonage to hear Mary Crawford play the harp, when sustenance is provided (in the same room) by 'the sandwich tray, and Dr Grant doing the honours of it'. (*MP, 65*) At Godmersham, too, a tray, its burden unspecified, would be brought in to the company in the middle of the day.

The case seems to be that, except on the most formal occasions, such food was eaten not in the dining-room, but in whichever room the family used for sitting in the morning. Even at Pemberley the meal is taken in the saloon, which was the room assigned to receiving morning visitors. As the meal had no name, it is not surprising that it had no fixed hour but was offered whenever guests appeared. There was never a definite invitation to 'come for lunch at one', for example. Indeed, the food might make its appearance more than once, if there was a series of callers. This is certainly the case in the humble Bates household, where on different occasions baked apples and 'sweet-cake from the beaufet' are pressed on their visitors. 'Mrs Cole had just been there, just called in for ten minutes, and had been so good as to sit an hour with them, and *she* had taken a piece of cake and been so kind to say she liked it very much; and therefore she hoped Miss Woodhouse and Miss Smith would do them the favour to eat a piece too.' (*E, 156*)

Even if no visitors called, the family would require some refreshment between dinner and breakfast, but Jane Austen rarely considers it worthy of mention. Two instances are given very much in passing. One is the 'cold meat' eaten at Northanger Abbey between morning and evening service on a Sunday. The other occurs soon after Anne Elliot's arrival at Uppercross Cottage:

> A little farther perseverance in patience, and forced cheerfulness on Anne's side, produced nearly a cure on Mary's. She could soon sit upright on the sofa, and began to hope she might be able to leave it by dinner-time. Then, forgetting to think of it, she was at the other end of the room, beautifying a nosegay; then she ate her cold meat; and then she was well enough to propose a little walk. (*P, 39*)

'Her' cold meat rather than 'some' cold meat gives the impression of a routine; and, as with the other examples, there is no suggestion of adjourning to the dining-room. Nor does her husband join her; when the gentlemen are out shooting or fishing, as Charles Musgrove often is, they do not feel obliged to return to the house in the middle of the day. Whether they take a 'lunch' with them, or repair to an inn, or bear their hunger manfully, Jane Austen gives no hint.

There is little reference to what is drunk with food at midday. Willoughby takes porter, but that is at an inn. Frank Churchill refreshes himself with spruce beer on a hot day at Donwell. Otherwise, we are not told. Emma and Harriet would require something to wash down the cake, but to boil the kettle for tea would involve a lot of bustle in the Bates household that we do not hear about. It is more likely that mead, beer or fruit cordial were customarily served at this time of day, cold drinks that would be ready for visitors at any time they called.

The food itself was invariably cold and, once it had been brought into the room by servants, could be managed by the family themselves. Although there is a waiter in attendance at the George Inn, Lydia takes on the responsibility of dressing the salad; even indolent Dr Grant dispenses sandwiches. Lady Catherine, deigning to take some refreshment at Hunsford Parsonage, 'seemed to do it only for the sake of finding out that Mrs Collins's joints of meat were too large for her family', which suggests they were carved on the spot by the assiduous Mr Collins. (*P&P, 169*) Cold food and little or no waiting relieved the servants of much work, leaving them free to concentrate on the all-important dinner.

Writing from Steventon in 1798 to Cassandra at Godmersham, Jane informs her, 'We dine now at half after Three, and have done dinner I suppose before you begin. – We drink tea at half after six. – I am afraid you will despise us'. (*L, 39*) By 1808, however, she was writing from Southampton, 'We never dine now till five'. (*L, 237*) Presumably, to warrant mention, both occasions marked a shift, perhaps of half an hour. They seem to have taken place almost involuntarily, especially so in view of Cassandra's absence. As the Austens certainly did not increase their pretensions to fashion as they grew older – rather the reverse, they kept much less company at Chawton than they had at Steventon – they could only have been flowing with the tide. Their experience is a striking example of the gradual shift in dinner-time which took place within individual families in the late eighteenth and early nineteenth centuries.

At any one moment in this period, however, the degree of fashion of a family could be decided by its dinner hour. The first quotation above, despite its tone of humour, indicates exactly that. Jane Austen was very much aware of the snobbery attached to the subject as early as 1792, when the juvenile piece 'A Collection of Letters' was written. Though the dinner hour of Maria Williams, the 'young lady in distressed circumstances' who is the heroine of the fragment, is not specified, her rich neighbour Lady Greville, who dines at five herself, frequently and deliberately interrupts Maria and her mother at their dinner by impertinent messages to come out and speak to her at her carriage door. Since her ladyship would have required an hour to dress for dinner, the Williams's dinner probably begins at three.

Eighteenth-century memoirs are replete with references to the significance of the hour at which a person dined. Boswell knew of a London mercer who had settled in Durham and impressed the locals by taking his dinner at two or three o'clock instead of at one. 'How little and how poor he would seem', commented Boswell in 1776, 'to a fashionable man in London who dines between four and five.'[11] But the movement was unremitting. In 1789 Horace Walpole wrote, 'I am so antiquated as still to dine at four when I can, though frequently prevented as many are so good as to call on me at that hour because it is too soon for them to go home and dress so early in the morning'.[12]

Such nonsense was excellent material for Jane Austen's satire. It is at its most pointed in *The Watsons*, a fragment comprising the abandoned beginning of a novel, written some time between 1803 and 1807. Both the earliest and the latest named dining hours of her fiction occur in this piece. The Watson family dine at three; their would-be fashionable bachelor neighbour Tom Musgrave dines (somewhat exaggeratedly) at eight. Like Lady Greville before him, Tom contrives to call at the most inopportune moment, 'as Nanny at five minutes before three, was beginning to bustle into the parlour with the Tray & the Knife-case'. The same servant has to answer a rap at the door and, though charged by her mistress not to let anyone in, is unable to withstand Tom and his friend Lord Osborne. The meal is kept waiting while they converse until

> they were interrupted by Nanny's approach, who half opening the door & putting in her head, said 'Please Ma'am, Master wants to know why he be'nt to have his dinner.' The Gentlemen, who had hitherto disregarded every symptom, however positive, of the nearness of that Meal, now jumped up with apologies, while Elizabeth called briskly after Nanny 'to tell Betty to take up the Fowls.' – 'I am sorry it happens so' – she added, turning good-humouredly towards Musgrave, 'but you know what early hours we keep.' Tom had nothing to say for himself, he knew it very well, & such honest simplicity, such shameless Truth rather bewildered him. (*MW, 346*)

Nevertheless he continues to make himself offensive over the subject of hours. Invited to dinner with the Watsons on another day, ' "With the greatest pleasure," was his first reply. In a moment afterwards – "That is if I can possibly get here in time – but I shoot with Lord Osborne, & therefore must not engage. – You will not think of me unless you see me." And so he departed, delighted with the uncertainty in which he had left it.' (*MW, 360*) Much extra effort is made in the kitchen on his behalf, but he fails to turn up. On another occasion he calls in the evening specifically to boast of being on his way home to an eight o'clock dinner. Invited to share their supper, 'which to a man whose heart had been long fixed on calling his next meal a Dinner, was quite insupportable', he is obliged to leave a pleasant party to go home to his solitary meal. (*MW, 359*)

After the humble Watsons, the next earliest dinner hour in the fiction is the four o'clock of Barton Cottage. Though this is also a modest household, where the price of candles might be considered significant, it is unlikely that the Dashwoods would have changed their hour from what they had been used to at Norland: that would be too degrading. The early hour is more likely attributable to its being the earliest-written of the novels. Emma and her father also dine at four, but in this case it is not difficult to guess that it is Mr Woodhouse's attachment to 'the fashion of his youth', and his general dislike of late hours, which determine the time. It is exceedingly good of Emma, with her regard for elegance and propriety, to humour him in this.

At Mansfield Parsonage they dine at half past four. Five is the hour at Northanger Abbey. The masters of both these establishments relish their dinner and do not want to be kept waiting. For all her unpreten-tiousness, Mrs Jennings is among the later diners at five o'clock, but then, not surprisingly, hours were always later in London than in the country. People who spent most of their time in town would often import their late hours to the country; we can see the effect of this in the difference between the half past six dinner at Netherfield and that at Longbourn two hours earlier.

The first custom associated with dinner was a complete change of costume – at least for ladies. This is what signified the end of the 'morning'. Byron refers sardonically to 'that hour, called "half-hour" given to dress / Though ladies' robes seem scant enough for less'.[13] The fashionable Bingley sisters require as much as an hour and a half's preparation: 'At five o'clock the two ladies retired to dress, and at half past six Elizabeth was summoned to dinner.' (*P&P, 35*) Catherine Morland is more expeditious; when she wants a little time to herself to explore the Abbey, she goes up to dress an hour, rather than half hour, before dinner. Jane Austen does not refer to any change on the part of men except the repowdering of the hair which Mrs Robert Watson thinks essential in her husband. That is not to say that changes were not made. Men who had spent the day in field sports would certainly have required a complete change of dress. Tom Musgrave, who calls one evening on the Watsons dressed for travel (he has just returned from London) apologises for being in a state of 'dishabille'. (*MW, 357*)

Jane Austen's people lived at a time of transition regarding the conventions governing the entrance to the dining-room. Formerly it had been the rule for all the ladies to enter together first, followed by the men. Later etiquette dictated that each gentleman should offer an arm to his chosen – or allotted – lady to take her in; the host always escorting the female guest of highest social standing. At the dinner party given by Emma for the Eltons, we can observe a combination of both customs. 'Dinner was on table. – Mrs Elton, before she could be spoken to, was ready; and before Mr Woodhouse had reached her with his request to be allowed to hand her into the dining-parlour, was saying, "Must I go first? I really am ashamed of always leading the way".' In another moment Emma and Jane Fairfax 'followed the other ladies [there is actually only Mrs Weston unaccounted for] out of the room, arm in arm, with an appearance of good-will highly becoming to the grace and beauty of each.' (*E, 298*) Yet at this party numbers are equal and each lady could have taken a gentleman's arm had it been customary to do so.

In corroboration that this was *not* the custom during Jane Austen's lifetime, in none of her own letters, as far as I am aware, does she mention being taken in to dinner by a particular man. As a humble spinster and a younger sister, she was unlikely ever to have been the principal female guest.

As today on formal occasions, host and hostess sat at the head and foot of the table. If the master of the house was absent, a strict hierarchy obtained as to his substitute. In Sir Thomas Bertram's absence, Tom takes his place, but when Tom too departs for the races, Mary Crawford knows for a certainty that Edmund will be at the head of the table. In this respect, though not in the courtesies attached to the position, Mr Woodhouse has abdicated his place as host; when Emma plans her dinner party she assumes that Mr Knightley will take his seat at the other end of the table from herself. The arrival of Mr John Knightley in the house forces a change, much against Emma's will, for 'she thought it a sad exchange for herself, to have him with his grave looks and reluctant conversation opposed to her instead of his brother'. (*E, 292*) Her wishes in this respect are foreshadowing of their partnership in marriage – another clue to her feelings that she fails to notice. Etiquette dictates the exchange not in this case because John is the elder, for he is not, but because he is the house guest and related to the family by marriage, whereas his brother is merely (at this date) an old neighbour and friend.

The person who gains most in elevation from the lack of a master of the house is Mr Collins at Rosings. 'He took his seat at the bottom of the table, by her ladyship's desire, and looked as if he felt that life could furnish nothing greater.' (*P & P, 163*)

Strict attention to securing an equal number of male and female guests was not observed. The awkwardness of having an uneven number altogether at table is remarked upon in the novels on more than one occasion, however, though no great measures are contemplated in remedy. The unexpected arrival of John Knightley threatens Emma with a table of nine, which, out of defence to her father's dread of noise, she does not seek to make ten (in the event Mr Weston cannot come, restoring the number to the eight originally planned). Mrs Norris, out of humour at Fanny's being invited to dine at Mansfield Parsonage, remarks ill-naturedly, 'I must observe, that five is the very awkwardest of all possible numbers to sit down to table; and I cannot but be surprised that such an *elegant* lady as Mrs Grant should not contrive better!' (*MP, 220*) Again, the hostess is favoured by providence, this time in the arrival of Henry Crawford. Virtually the only reason why Sir Walter Elliot is pleased to welcome his daughter Anne to Bath is that she will make a fourth at the regular family table, though it will be one man to three women.

With the exception of the chief male and female guests, who occupied places next, respectively, to their hostess and host, the company chose their own places at table. At the party given by the Coles, Emma is pleased to find Frank at her side – 'not without some dexterity' on his part. (*E, 214*) At Longbourn, Mrs Bennet refrains from inviting Bingley to occupy the place of principal male guest next to herself, because she is anxious he should sit by Jane. Darcy therefore is given that invitation, much to the distaste and discomfiture of them both. Meanwhile, had it been admissible for Mrs Bennet to direct the seating of all her guests, we can be sure she would have done so with alacrity. As it is, she has to leave it to chance. 'Jane happened to look round, and happened to smile; it was decided. He placed himself by her.' (*P & P, 340*) These two examples, incidentally, imply that the women are already at table when the gentlemen enter.

As the company processed into the dining-room, the table itself presented, in the 1870 words of James Edward Austen-Leigh, 'a far less splendid appearance than it does now. It was appropriated to solid food, rather than to flowers, fruits, and decorations. Nor was there much glitter of plate upon it; for the early dinner hour rendered candlesticks unnecessary, and silver forks had not come into general use: while the broad rounded end of the knives indicated the substitute generally used instead of them'.[14]

He is speaking, of course, of Jane's youth; the tables at Mansfield and Hartfield, twenty years later, are not necessarily deficient in sparkle. Indeed, there are certainly silver forks at Mansfield, together with napkins and finger glasses; these are all new to Susan Price, and occasion her some nervousness. Even at Portsmouth, however, forks are not dispensed with altogether, though they are made of base metal and not properly cleaned. Rosings too bears 'all the articles of plate which Mr Collins had promised' and which are presumably missing from more ordinary establishments. (*P & P, 162*) In 1808 from Southampton Jane wrote humourously, 'My mother has been lately adding to her possessions in plate – a whole tablespoon and a whole dessertspoon, and six whole teaspoons – which makes our sideboard border on the magnificent. They were mostly the produce of old or useless silver . . . a silver tea-ladle is also added'. (*L, 243*)

James Edward Austen-Leigh's remark about table decorations is particularly interesting in its implications for the female role. Notably missing from the occupations of Jane Austen's young ladies is the flower-arranging so common among their Victorian fictional counterparts. The only hint of things to come is in the late work *Persuasion*, with Mary

Musgrove's beautifying a nosegay – appropriate to the modernised, showy but flimsy Uppercross Cottage. This, incidentally, is a fine example of Jane Austen's social prescience: Florence Nightingale, born in 1820, was to rebel against the restriction of female occupations to little more than 'the endless tweedling of nosegays in jugs'.

The *service à la Russe* of James Edward Austen-Leigh's time left the table free for such fripperies because the food would be under the direction of servants, on sideboards and trolleys, carved by them and brought round very much as waiter service today, and served in courses familiar to us, each dish and its proper accompaniments arriving in turn. The *service à la française* of the eighteenth and first half of the nineteenth century was very different. (The change must have occurred between 1850 and 1870, since in *David Copperfield*, written at the earlier date, the old methods still obtain.) One course would comprise a huge variety of dishes and all would be present upon the table together, 'smoking before our eyes and our noses', as Austen-Leigh puts it. Cookery books of the period often carry diagrams suggesting how the dishes might be arranged upon the table to give a pleasing balance. Several large joints of meat and complete boiled or roasted fowl, sometimes garnished with appropriate vegetables (duck with peas, for example) would occupy the central ground. Made dishes and accompaniments (though not many vegetables) would be placed artistically at the sides and corners. There would always be a tureen of soup at one end and very often a whole fish at the other. These would be removed, when the company had finished with them, and more dishes brought in their place. The remains of a fish skeleton were deemed unattractive to be left on the table, whereas a half-carved joint was not.

One of the drawbacks of this style of service was that the meat lost its heat while the soup and fish were consumed. Another was that, despite the huge variety on display, an individual diner might not be served to the dishes he or she liked. Each gentleman carved the meat immediately before him and helped his neighbour and himself to this and other dishes within his reach. Jane Austen mentions one dinner she attended where a lady diner's plate remained empty for some while because her neighbour neglected her, although she asked him twice for some meat. Even for men it was ill-bred to stretch too far or to pass the heavy dishes about and, though there would be servants standing around whose assistance could be sought by catching their eye, it was considered greedy and discourteous to the company to do this too often. It certainly behoved diners, when taking their places, to pay as much attention to the disposition of food as to the identity of their neighbours – unless they happened to be in love.

When everybody had eaten enough of this course, there would be a large-scale disruption and bustle while the servants carried away all the dishes and brought and arranged another complete course. A memorable moment in *Emma* occurs at the Coles' party, when the conversation between Emma and Frank is interrupted at an interesting point. 'They were called on to share in the awkwardness of a rather long interval between the courses . . . but when the table was again safely covered, when every corner dish was placed exactly right', private conversation can be resumed. (*E, 218*)

This second course, which contained as many dishes as the first, just as deliberately arranged, might include some new joints of meat to titillate the jaded palate, but the emphasis this time round was on the lighter savoury concoctions like fricassees and patties, together with a selection of fruit tarts, jellies and cream puddings. Clean plates and utensils were provided by the servants as often as required; the need was signalled by placing the handles of the knife and fork on the plate. While nobody was expected or enabled to try more than a small proportion of the dishes on offer, all that cookery was not wasted. The cold remains served for another day's 'lunch' or supper, and eventually, if the family tired of them or they deteriorated before they were used up, for the servants' table. As a system it was efficient both in terms of labour and fuel; all the cooking for twenty-four hours could be done in one go, while providing the impression – the reality, indeed – of variety and plenty.

Of course it was only in the grandest households, or when company was invited, that two full courses were *de rigueur*. Ordinary family dinners consisted of just one course, though a variety of dishes would be on the table at the same time. A typical family dinner might be this of Parson Woodforde's: 'a couple of rabbits smothered with onions, a neck of mutton boiled and a goose roasted, with a currant pudding and a plain one'.[15] Even this might have been too rich for the Austens; on arriving at Henry's house in London in 1813, Jane, her brother Edward and three of Edward's daughters were served 'a most comfortable dinner of soup, fish, bouillée, partridges, and an apple tart, which we sat down to soon after five'. (*L, 319*)[16]

Mrs Bennet, who is proud of keeping a good table at all times ('I hope *my* dinners are good enough for her', she says of Charlotte Lucas. 'I do not believe she often sees such as home'), (*P & P, 61*) regularly draws attention to the distinction between family dinners and those to which company is invited. When Bingley is first asked to dine at Longbourn,

'Mrs Bennet planned the courses that were to do credit to her house-keeping' – somewhat prematurely, as it turns out, since Bingley is about to go to London. (*P & P, 9*) Almost a year later, when Bingley and Darcy reappear on the scene to revive all Mrs Bennet's hopes, 'she did not think any thing less than two full courses, could be good enough for a man, on whom she had such anxious designs, or satisfy the appetite and pride of one who had ten thousand a-year'. (*P & P, 338*)

Even richer than Darcy was one of Jane Austen's forbears on her mother's side, the first Duke of Chandos, whose second wife, *née* Cassandra Willoughby, brought the unusual Christian name into the family and bestowed her surname on one of Jane's anti-heroes. In 1753 this couple gave a dinner which was attended by, among others, Elizabeth Montagu. 'You may well imagine how well I dined on two and forty dishes, and a dessert of one and twenty, very well ordered and served', she wrote to a friend, adding, rather understandably, 'I came away before supper'.[17]

By contrast the dinner eaten on 4 July 1806 by another of Jane's relations, her uncle James Leigh Perrot, may be taken as typical of the spread provided on a fairly ordinary occasion by a person of comfortable means and middling status in the early nineteenth century. No women were present and the demands of business rather than of fashion probably accounted for the late hour. James Leigh Perrot was in London with his cousin James Leigh to consult his lawyer, Mr Hill. Knowing that the details of his meals while he was away from his wife would be interesting to her, he wrote, 'We dined yesterday at Mr Hill's, not till seven o'clock; Dr Budd came in to Dinner, so that Mr Hill had no opportunity of talking with me upon Business. Our Dinner was Mackerell at Top, Soup at Bottom removed for a Neck of Venison, one Chicken on one Side, and Beans and Bacon on the other; Pease and Cherry Tart succeeded'. He added, 'Not choosing to fast so long, I made a good Luncheon here upon some exceeding good giblet Soup'.[18] He was referring to his hotel, Hatchetts: another instance of the term 'luncheon' being associated with an inn at this date.

In order to pace themselves it was necessary for the diners, viewing the first course spread before them, to know whether there was more to come. 'You see your dinner' had been the phrase used by the plain-spoken mid-Georgians to indicate that there was just one course. In *The Watsons*, when an extra effort is made by Elizabeth to entertain guests, her sister-in-law, Mrs Robert Watson, instead of being gracious and appreciative, protests 'against the appearance of the roast Turkey, which formed the only exception to "You see your dinner".' Evidently Elizabeth has announced that, contrary to their normal custom, there is more food to come – perhaps when the soup is removed. Mrs Robert seizes the opportunity to appear self-denying while effectively drawing attention to her hostess's poverty:

'I do beg and entreat that no Turkey may be seen today. I am really frightened out of my wits with the number of dishes we have already. Let us have no Turkey I beseech you.' 'My dear,' replied Elizabeth, 'the Turkey is roasted, & it may just as well come in, as stay in the Kitchen. Besides if it is cut, I am in hopes my Father may be tempted to eat a bit, for it is rather a favourite dish.'

'You may have it in my dear, but I assure you I shan't touch it', replies her sister-in-law, an example of the worst kind of guest. (*MW, 354*)

When enough had been eaten of the second course the dishes were taken away, the tablecloth was removed, and what was known as 'the dessert' was set out. The word was taken from the French *desservir*, to clear the table, and bore a meaning quite different from its common modern usage. Most of the table utensils having been removed with the cloth, and the waiting servants dismissed, dessert was a way of prolonging the meal with titbits which could be eaten using the fingers. Traditionally it comprised a variety of dried fruits, nuts and sweet and spicy confections, made with the most expensive imported ingredients. When Mrs Jennings seeks to cure Marianne's broken heart with offers of sweetmeats, olives and dried cherries she is describing a typical dessert.

By the early nineteenth century cheese, the reputation of which had formerly suffered from being thought labourers' food, was establishing the place at that stage in the meal which it has retained ever since. Only with the improved transport of the period could a variety of cheeses from different parts of the country be brought in their prime to the rich man's table, and begin to acquire their individual names after their places of origin. Thus when Emma unwillingly catches up with Mr Elton and Harriet in Vicarage Lane, she is disappointed to find that 'he was only giving his fair companion an account of the yesterday's party at his friend Cole's, and that she was herself come in for the Stilton cheese, the north Wiltshire, the butter, the cellery, the beet-root and all the dessert'. (*E, 89*) A fine cream cheese is served after dinner at Sotherton in high summer when the milk is at its richest.

Wine seems not to have appeared until the dessert – it was certainly very much associated with it. At Barton Cottage, when this stage of the meal is reached, 'Thomas [the servant] and the table-cloth, now alike needless, were soon afterwards dismissed . . . the dessert and the wine were arranged', though this is only Mrs Dashwood dining with her eldest daughter. (*S & S, 355*)

'Who can now record the degrees by which the custom prevalent in my youth of asking each other to take wine together at dinner became obsolete?' James Edward Austen-Leigh enquires.[19] The custom he refers to is that whereby a gentleman diner would fill the glasses of his female neighbour and himself and they would drink with each other to a toast of his proposal. Dr Chapman thinks this is what is meant by Edmund Bertram's being glad to put an end to Mr Rushworth's speech 'by a proposal of wine', presumably to his neighbour Mary Crawford;[20] though as host on the occasion he might equally, if manners were already changing, be concerned to see everybody's glasses filled. (*MP, 55*) The old custom, however, certainly still prevailed at the time *Sense and Sensibility* was written, accounting for this little vignette between Sir John and Elinor: 'Since Edward's visit, they had never dined together, without his drinking to her best affections with so much significancy and so many nods and winks, as to excite general attention.' (*S & S, 125*)

After taking one or at most two glasses of wine, the ladies would gracefully withdraw from the dining-room. The hostess had to ascertain by a glance that her female guests were ready for the move; her rising to her feet was the signal for all the ladies present to do likewise. A dozy woman like Lady Bertram might not be very alert to this duty; she never willingly rises to her feet in her life. When Fanny Price is longing to escape Henry Crawford's presence at Mansfield Park, 'she thought Lady Bertram sat longer than ever, and began to be in despair of ever getting away'. (*MP, 304*) A gentleman would politely step forward to open and close the door for the departing ladies. After another dinner at Mansfield, that preceding the ball, Edmund, holding open the door as Fanny follows her aunts out of the room, asks her to keep a dance for him.

Strict precedence was observed in the order in which the ladies processed out. At the opening of *Persuasion*, Elizabeth Elliot has for thirteen years been 'walking immediately after Lady Russell out of all the drawing-rooms and dining-rooms in the country'. (*P, 7*) It could be awkward when seniority of age clashed with seniority of rank. The Miss Musgroves complain that their sister-in-law, the daughter of a baronet, makes too great a point of taking her due precedence over their mother. Women in their own home gave way to guests. 'Remember,' Mrs Norris tells Fanny, when she has been invited to the Parsonage to dine, 'wherever you are, you are the lowest and the last; and though Miss Crawford is in a manner at home, at the Parsonage, you are not to be taking place of her.' (*MP, 221*) The daughters of the house filed in and out according to age, until one of them married, when she went to the top of the queue. On the day of Lydia's return to Longbourn as Mrs Wickham, Elizabeth, sickened by her sister's folly, withdraws from the family

till she heard them passing through the hall to the dining-parlour. She then joined them soon enough to see Lydia, with anxious parade, walk up to her mother's right hand, and hear her say to her eldest sister, 'Ah! Jane, I take your place now, and you must go lower, because I am a married woman.' (*P & P, 317*)

This passage is interesting because it shows the formality observed even within a family party. It also shows the women trooping in together; Lydia does not claim her husband's or her father's arm.

The withdrawal of the women from the dining-room left the men free to enjoy an hour or so of uninhibited conversation and drink, though there is nothing of this in Jane Austen, who famously never gives a scene at which no woman is present. Excessive after-dinner drinking is hinted at only in Emma's suspicion, during Mr Elton's unwelcome proposal, that he has over-indulged himself with Mr Weston's good wine; and even this suspicion is unfounded, for Mr Elton has drunk just enough 'to elevate his spirits, not at all to confuse his intellects'. (*E, 130*) We need not suspect Mr Collins and Sir William Lucas of over-indulging in order to appreciate how much they must have enjoyed having the freedom of Lady Catherine's dining-room when she leaves them to its possession – for the separation of the sexes still takes place, albeit with some awkwardness, when there is no host to preside over this part of the evening.

If this was the hour most looked forward to by many of the men, it could be the most tedious hour for the women, thrown on their own resources in the drawing-room, with neither alcohol nor male company to inspirit the scene. At the Dashwoods' dinner-party in town, there is poverty of conversation enough at table, but 'when the ladies withdrew to the drawing-room after dinner, this poverty was particularly evident, for the gentlemen *had* supplied the discourse with some variety – the variety of politics, inclosing land, and breaking horses – but then it was all over; and one subject only engaged the ladies', which is the comparative heights of two of their little boys. (*S & S, 233*) Even Elizabeth Bennet can sometimes flag at this hour. 'Anxious and uneasy, the period which passed in the drawing-room, before the gentlemen came, was wearisome and dull to a degree, that almost made her uncivil.' (*P & P, 341*) On the other hand, with no gentlemen to draw their attention off, some ladies improved in pleasantness, Bingley's sisters for example: 'Elizabeth had never seen them so agreeable as they were during the hour which passed before the gentlemen appeared'. (*P & P, 54*)

In the early novels, the gentlemen return to the ladies *en masse*. At Mrs Philips's, 'The interval of waiting appeared very long. It was over at last however. The gentlemen did approach . . . . Mr Wickham was as far beyond them all in person, countenance, air and walk, as *they* were superior to the broad-faced stuffy uncle Philips, breathing port wine, who followed them into the room'. (*P & P, 76*) In the case of the ladies, it was the hostess who led the way, but with men the host brought up the rear. John Dashwood also follows the body of gentlemen guests into the drawing-room of his London home.

Later the habit established itself of each gentleman leaving the dining-room when he wished. At the Randalls dinner-party there are five men and three women. Mr Woodhouse soon follows the latter into the drawing-room. 'To be sitting long after dinner, was a confinement that he could not endure. Neither wine nor conversation was anything to him; and gladly did he move to those with whom he was always comfortable.' (*E, 122*) Later in the novel, Mrs Elton takes his habit as a compliment to herself: 'Here comes this dear old beau of mine, I protest! – Only think of his gallantry in coming away before the other men!' (*E, 302*) Not only feeble old men but smart young men in love might wish to get back to the ladies. At the Coles' dinner-party, 'They were soon joined by some of the gentlemen; and the very first of the early was Frank Churchill. In he walked, the first and the handsomest . . . .' (*E, 220*)

If there was no company in the house, the family were free to spend this interval between dinner and drinking tea in a more informal way than in sexually-segregated conversation. This was the period denominated 'afternoon', and in the summer (when there were fewer social engagements anyway) it could be pleasantly spent out of doors. Lydia Bennet proposes a walk to Meryton in the afternoon of a very busy day in May; Elizabeth and Jane have already travelled from London, had lunch at the George with Lydia and Kitty, and dinner at Longbourn with the entire Lucas family as guests. The people of Highbury frequently take walks at this time of the early evening (to use, for a moment, our own terms). When Emma has no companion, she walks only in the grounds of Hartfield, as in the July 'afternoon' when Mr Knightley proposes marriage to her. The weather has just cleared, and 'on Mr Perry's coming in soon after dinner, with a disengaged hour to give her father, she lost no time in hurrying into the shrubbery'. (*E, 424*)

Afternoon walks of relaxation were more often undertaken by men, or by men and women together, than the predominantly female morning walks and visits – doubtless because the men had, with the advent of dinner, given up their pursuits of the day, be they sport or business. Mr Woodhouse expresses the wish that Mr and Mrs Cole, instead of giving dinners, 'would come in one afternoon next summer, and take their tea with us – take us in their afternoon walk'. (*E, 209*) On another occasion Emma and Harriet are just setting off for a stroll when Mr Knightley, walking up from the Abbey after dinner, agrees to join them; on returning they fall in with 'Mr and Mrs Weston and their son, Miss Bates and her niece, who had accidentally met. They all united; and on reaching Hartfield gates, Emma, who knew it was exactly the sort of visiting that would be welcome to her father, pressed them all to go in and drink tea with him.' (*E, 344*)

Even in the winter, and in situations of some ceremony, however, the period between dinner and tea was known as the afternoon. On arriving for dinner at Mansfield Park, Henry Crawford gives Fanny a note from his sister (why has *she* not been invited?) urging her to 'smile upon him with your sweetest smiles this afternoon'. (*MP, 303*) In *The Watsons*, Emma dines with Mr and Mrs Edwardes and their daughter Mary prior to going to a ball for which they are to set out at eight o'clock. She is a stranger to their house and, 'with nothing to do but to expect the hour of setting off, the afternoon was long to the two young ladies . . . The entrance of the Tea things at 7 o'clock was some relief.' (*MW, 326*)

Both beginning and ending later than present-day afternoons, those of Jane Austen's time, whether spent formally or informally, always closed with this drinking of tea. The time for tea seems to have been set at about three hours after the commencement of dinner (when the Austens dined at half past three, they drank tea at half past six), which would give on formal occasions two hours to eat, and one for the after-dinner separation of the sexes; and on simple family days, perhaps an hour to eat and two hours for walking or any other activity.

At Hartfield tea is taken on 'the large modern circular table which Emma had introduced at Hartfield and which none but Emma could have had power to place there and persuade her father to use, instead of the small-sized Pembroke, on which two of his daily meals had, for forty years, been crowded'. (*E, 347*) In other establishments the tea things would be brought in by the servants to the family or assembled company in the drawing-room, as in the Edwardes' house in the passage quoted above. When Henry Crawford is trying to force Fanny to engage in conversation with him, while Lady Bertram dozes and Edmund hides behind a newspaper, Fanny is relieved to hear 'the very sound which she had been long watching for, and long thinking strangely delayed. The solemn procession, headed by Baddeley [the butler], of tea-board, urn, and cake-bearers, made its appearance and delivered her from a grievous imprisonment of body and mind.' (*MP, 344*)

Part of her deliverance is that she now has something to do: 'she was busy'. It is not surprising that, of Lady Bertram and Fanny, it should be Fanny who makes the tea. In fact Lady Bertram feels herself incapable of it: on the occasion when Fanny has been invited to dine at the Parsonage, Lady Bertram tells her husband plaintively, 'She always makes tea, you know, when my sister is not here.' (*MP, 219*) But there are other examples which show that this was often the duty of the young ladies of the house. No doubt it set off their charms. At Longbourn, Jane makes the tea and Elizabeth pours the coffee. Elinor Dashwood 'presides' at the tea-table in Mrs Jenning's London drawing-room. However, at Mansfield Parsonage, it is Mrs Grant, not Mary, who is 'occupied at the tea-table' after dinner. (*MP, 224*)

Although the ceremony was invariably known as 'tea', coffee was often also available. Coffee is drunk very frequently in *Pride and Prejudice*: at the Philips's, Netherfield and Rosings as well as Longbourn. It is also mentioned at Sotherton, Mansfield Park, Woodston Parsonage and the Dashwoods' London lodgings. Arthur Parker, a molly-coddled invalid, is unique in taking cocoa at this hour; his sisters are equally unique in each having a different kind of herb tea – an early instance, this, of health foods for fanatics. Jane Austen also mentions dandelion tea in a letter – but this was an economy measure, perhaps. Following so shortly on a large dinner, little sustenance was required or provided with the beverages, but there is cake at Mansfield Park, toast at Sanditon and muffin both at Hartfield and at the Philips's. This may have been particularly welcome to those guests who had not been invited to dinner with the family, but just 'to drink tea' and spend the rest of the evening.

After tea something more than conversation was usually required to vary the scene. Mr Bennet habitually retires to his library after tea but he is the exception, for most people took it for granted that they must amuse one another during these last hours of the day. In Jane Austen's own family there was often reading aloud. Emma is doomed to evening after evening playing backgammon with her father. Her only respite is when she can assemble the old dames of the village to 'win or lose a few sixpences by his fireside', but even then she must sit and listen to their 'prosings'. (*E, 22*) Whenever much company was assembled, it was usually cards or music, or a combination of both, which whiled away the hours. The young ladies present would be begged to play and sing; or card tables would be organised by the hostess for the pleasure (usually) of the gentlemen. 'A whist table was formed after tea – formed really for the amusement of Dr Grant, by his attentive wife, though it was not to be supposed so.' (*MP, 227*) During Elizabeth's visit to Netherfield, Mr Hurst, who lives only to eat, drink and play cards, is indulged the first two evenings, with loo and piquet respectively, but on the third evening he is not so lucky: 'When tea was over, Mr Hurst reminded his sister-in-law of the card table – but in vain. She had obtained private intelligence that Mr Darcy did not wish for cards'. (*P & P, 54*) On one of the Netherfield evenings Miss Bingley and her sister sing; the game of whist at Mansfield Parsonage is accompanied by Mary Crawford playing the harp. Marianne plays the piano at Barton Park; Mary Bennet at Netherfield; Elizabeth at Rosings. Emma plays at the Coles' and later Jane and Frank sing together. At Mansfield Park, all the young people except Fanny gather round the pianoforte for a glee.

Impromptu dancing often closed the evening. In her youth Jane Austen herself danced this way at Goodnestone Park, with Lady Bridges accompanying on the piano. Anne Elliot plays country dances for the hour together that the young people at Uppercross may have the pleasure of dancing; Mrs Weston performs the like service at the Coles's. But Fanny's first experience of dancing at Mansfield Park is consequent upon 'the late acquisition of a violin player in the servants' hall'. (*MP, 117*)

The last meal of the day was supper. When dinner had been eaten early in the day, supper had necessarily been a substantial repast; but as dinner itself became an evening meal, all that was normally required last thing at night was a tray of elegant light refreshments. Consequently it is the more old-fashioned characters who are attached to the idea of supper. This is made most explicit in the notions of Mr Woodhouse, who 'loved to have the cloth laid, because it had been the fashion of his youth'. (*E, 24*) This is not because he is greedy, for indeed he takes nothing but gruel himself and recommends his guests to take the same. It is simply habit.

The schoolmistress Mrs Goddard is another such elderly, homely body who has not moved with the times. When she receives, from the mother of a former pupil, the gift of a fine goose, she consumes it not at dinner but at supper. 'Mrs Goddard had dressed it on a Sunday, and asked all the three teachers, Miss Nash, and Miss Prince, and Miss Richardson, to sup with her.' (*E, 29*) Dinner for these hard-working women is probably still the middle of the day, when the pupils eat theirs.

By her early supper-time, however, Mrs Goddard can relax and enjoy her food. She – or rather Harriet, but surely in echo of her words – is the only person in any of the novels to use the verb 'to sup', though Jane Austen frequently used it herself in her letters.

When Mrs Philips promises her nieces, if they will come in the evening, 'a nice comfortable noisy game of lottery tickets, and a little bit of hot supper afterwards', we know she is betraying vulgarity as much in the second component of her invitation as the first. (*P & P, 74*) Mrs Bennet, her sister, also offers supper, and is disappointed when the party from Netherfield will not stay for it. Between the writing of *Pride and Prejudice* and its publication, mealtimes and manners changed and Jane Austen herself realised that she had slipped up a little. 'There might as well have been no suppers at Longbourn,' she wrote to Cassandra when the book came out and she read it for the first time in print, 'but I suppose it was the remains of Mrs Bennet's old Meryton habits.' (*L, 300*)

'Duets after supper' are mentioned at Netherfield but not similarly commented upon in Jane's letter. (*P & P, 40*) It could be that while families continued to take some light refreshment at the end of the day, this would be done in what Jane elsewhere calls 'unpretending privacy', and that to offer supper to dinner guests (who had probably, anyway, eaten a more substantial dinner than usual) was the *faux pas* of Mrs Bennet. Certainly no supper closes the evening at Rosings or Randalls – or at Mansfield Parsonage, despite the famous appetite of the master of that house. However, returning to Mansfield Park between ten and eleven o'clock from taking dinner at the Parsonage, and finding the family assembled in the drawing-room and Fanny with a headache, Edmund goes to a table 'on which the supper-tray yet remained' and pours a glass of madeira for his cousin. (*MP, 74*)

The diminution of supper to a few oddments which could be served on a tray led to the manufacture of an elegant new possession for the home. Mrs Philip Lybbe Powys, a friend and contemporary of Mrs Austen, but rather richer, wrote in her diary for 31 August 1798:

> In the morning we went to London a-shopping, and at Wedgwood's, as usual, were highly entertain'd, as I think no shop affords so great a variety. I there, among other things, purchas'd one of the new invented *petit soupée* trays, which I think equally clever, elegant and convenient when alone or a small party, as so much less trouble to ourselves and servants.[21]

Even at Hartfield the cloth is not laid on the dining-table, but on some smaller table which, at the appointed time, is set out and moved towards the fire in the drawing-room, where the guests are playing piquet or quadrille. At Northanger Abbey, however, where there seems to be a separate room for every purpose, many of them dedicated to the production or consumption of food, one room is nominated the supper-room, which is where Eleanor and Catherine are sitting at eleven o'clock on the last evening of Catherine's visit. To heat a room especially for this purpose seems the height of pretension and of conspicuous consumption of resources, and thus highly consistent with the General's domestic law.

When Jane Austen stayed in 1808 with the family's benefactress Mrs Knight, an elderly woman of refined manners, supper for the two of them was taken in the dressing-room, and consisted of tart and jelly. In the same year the Austens themselves provided a tray of widgeon, preserved ginger and black butter to some elderly ladies who had come for the evening. If this does not sound particularly digestible for old ladies late at night, neither does the toasted cheese which Jane Austen elsewhere mentions as being her own favourite supper dish. With greater discretion, Emma orders the Hartfield suppers so that they are warm and comforting for her father's guests, who dine early, yet delicate enough to do credit to her housekeeping: on different occasions we hear of minced chicken, scalloped oysters, fricassee of sweetbread, asparagus, boiled eggs, biscuits, baked apples, apple tart and custard. Probably many of these were uncommon fare in the Goddard and Bates establishments, thus all the more a treat.

Wine, or wine and water, is drunk with supper at Hartfield and Mansfield. Such drinks, with the addition of hot soup, were often provided late at night to people who have been out at the theatre or a public assembly of any kind. Jane Austen and a party of brothers and nieces, returning to Henry's house from a visit to the Lyceum in 1813 (on the same day as the dinner already mentioned), took soup and wine and water before retiring to bed. In *The Watsons*, after the monthly public ball, it is the Edwardes' habit to come home to some 'welcome soup': taken on this occasion, rather unusually for a meal which is not dinner, at their dining-table. (*MW, 336*) Catherine Morland takes 'warm wine and water' after one evening out in Bath, and on another appeases her hunger (we are not told with what) as soon as she gets back to the Allens' Pulteney Street lodgings. (*NA, 29, 60*)

It is at a private ball, however, that suppers really come into their own, regaining for one dazzling evening the glory that has otherwise long departed. The late hours of a ball and the energy expended in dancing made suppers essential. In 1800 Jane Austen attended one such private ball of fifty people. 'We began at 10, supped at 1, & were at Deane [where she was staying] before 5'. (*L, 91*) In a mocking passage in *Sense and Sensibility*, when Robert Ferrars is spouting drivel about the comforts of cottages, he assures Elinor that even balls can be held in them: 'The library may be open for tea and other refreshments, and let the supper be set out in the saloon.' (*S & S, 252*)

More seriously, when Mrs Weston is planning the ball at the Crown – which is to be a private ball, despite its being held in an inn – she at first, because of the awkward access to the only room large enough to accommodate a sit-down supper, 'proposed having no regular supper; merely sandwiches, etc, set out in the little room; but that was scouted as a wretched suggestion. A private dance, without sitting down to supper, was pronounced an infamous fraud upon the rights of men and women.' (*E, 254*)

The odd thing about the arrangements at the Crown is that 'at the time of the ball-room's being built, suppers had not been in question'. This is a mystery. The ball-room had been added to the Crown 'many years ago . . . while the neighbourhood had been in a particularly populous, dancing state'. (*E, 197*) Had the young Henry Woodhouse, and Hetty and Jane Bates, once danced there? Or even Mrs Bates before she was married; and Mr Knightley's parents? Surely these good people would have wanted supper? It was, after all, the fashion of their youth, and there was *no* previous period when supper was not eaten.

In the event the supper provided at the Crown is a plentiful one. 'Dear Jane,' cries Miss Bates as she sees the spread, 'how shall we ever recollect half the dishes for grandmama?' We do not learn what the dishes were, with the exception of 'Soup too!' (again in Miss Bates's words). (*E, 330*) Soup was certainly *the* essential component of supper at a ball. There is soup at the private ball at Mansfield Park; and one of Mr Bingley's two conditions for fixing the date of the ball at Netherfield is that his housekeeper should have time to make 'white soup enough' for the assembled party. (*P & P, 55*)

Chapter Three

From White Soup to Whipt Syllabub

Some of the specific foodstuffs and dishes mentioned by Jane Austen in her letters and novels are unfamiliar to us today; with others the social cachet or particular significance attaching to them then have since been lost and need to be retrieved for a full understanding of the novels. Soup is a good beginning. In *Pride and Prejudice*, Mr Bingley promises to hold his ball 'as soon as Nicholls has made white soup enough'. (*P & P*, 55). We have seen how balls always included supper, and how supper at a ball invariably included soup. The kind of soup taken at balls is not specified elsewhere in Jane Austen, either in her letters or novels. The joke here – and Mr Bingley is speaking humorously, of course – is that only the most elegant concoctions would suit the notions of his house-guests Mr Hurst (who favours French cookery) and Mr Darcy (who can afford to keep a French cook). Plain homely Nicholls must therefore put forth her best, and the best soup of all was 'white'.

Jane Grigson, in her fascinating book *English Food*, reveals that white soup goes back to the courtly cookery of medieval England and France, when its name was *soupe à la reine*.[1] Obviously, over such a long period of time and place, there were variations in recipe, but the soup was based on veal stock, cream and – the essential ingredient – almonds. Sometimes rice or white breadcrumbs were added as a thickener, sometimes the soup was enriched with egg yolk or given texture by the white part of leeks. One eighteenth-century version, from a private collection, is yet more substantial:

To Make a White Supe: Take a Nuckell of Veale and boyle ye broth to jelly and straine it and when cold take of all ye fatt and then put in two Chickings just to boyle, and when they are enough beate ½ a pound of almonds with a little Creame (to keep it from oyling) and thickening your broath up with it put a blade of mace. In boyling the jelly broath, cut some Chickings or Partridges in pieces into ye broath with a little salt.[2]

The only other soup named by Jane Austen in any of her writings is pease-soup, which formed part of the dinner at Steventon on 30 November 1798, when, in consequence of her mother's indisposition and her sister's absence in Kent, Jane herself was in charge of the housekeeping. Her efforts survived that greatest of all trials, an unexpected visitor who arrives just as the family is sitting down to eat, making addition or disguise impossible. The visitor was Mr Lyford, the apothecary from Basingstoke, who called (probably well aware that it was dinner-time) to see Mrs Austen. 'He came while we were at dinner,' wrote Jane, 'and partook of our elegant entertainment. I was not ashamed at asking him to sit down to table, for we had some pease-soup, a spare-rib, and a pudding.' (*L, 34*)

Pease-soup had evolved from the pease-pottage or pease-porridge of early English cooking and nursery-rhyme fame. If white soup was French and courtly in origin, pease-pottage was thoroughly English and everyday. For centuries, the main meal of the ordinary working people was pottage, a thick but liquid mixture of whatever happened to be available – roots, greens, grains, a little bacon, perhaps – simmered together over the open fire in the pot and eaten with a spoon. 'Older than Europe itself', says Fernand Braudel of this method of preparing daily sustenance.[3] As the gentry and middle classes came to scorn such labourers' food, however, soup as we think of it parted company from more solid fare, and was relegated merely to the start of dinner or to the minor repast of supper. As part of this evolution, pease-pottage became pease-soup, but it was still a homely dish, made in the winter with dried peas, which would be simmered in stock or water with celery, onion and seasoning. The capability of peas to be dried made them a very useful foodstuff when there were so few methods of food preservation available; they were grown in large quantities and eaten throughout the winter by all classes of people, besides forming one of the staple supplies of sea voyages.

Peas, celery and onion were all Roman introductions to the British Isles, so this soup, or pottage, went back to time immemorial. In a somewhat desperate effort to give the soup as modern and elegant a finish as possible Hannah Glasse, in *The Art of Cookery Made Plain and Easy* (1747), recommended 'Let a fried French roll swim in it'. One imagines this refinement was dispensed with at Steventon Rectory, at least for ordinary family dinners.

The pudding served at Steventon that day might have been either savoury or sweet; an accompaniment to the spare-rib or a dish to follow it. I am inclined to think it an accompaniment, for if a sweet pudding Jane would probably have specified what kind; moreover, there are no potatoes mentioned to give starch and bulk to the meal.

James Edward Austen-Leigh, writing in 1870 of the Steventon household a hundred years or so before, observed, 'Potatoes were used, but not so abundantly as now; and there was an idea that they were to be eaten only with roast meat. They were novelties to a tenant's wife who was entertained at Steventon Parsonage . . . and when Mrs Austen advised her to plant them in her own garden, she replied, "No, no; they are very well for you gentry, but they must be terribly costly to rear".'[4]

In giving this advice, was Mrs Austen acting on government orders? In March 1795, when the effects of the previous year's poor harvest were being severely felt, the Board of Agriculture circulated a paper entitled *Hints Respecting the Culture and Use of Potatoes*, to which this note was added:

> The Board takes the liberty of desiring the Clergy, in their several parishes, to have the goodness to communicate the above to their neighbours; and at the same time to encourage, as much as they can, the farmers and cottagers to plant Potatoes this spring, in order that the kingdom may experience no scarcity, if the next harvest should prove either very late, or not sufficiently productive in bread corn.[5]

Potatoes were certainly under cultivation at Steventon for a good twenty years before this; writing in 1773 to her sister-in-law Mrs Walter, Mrs Austen thanks her 'for the receipt for potato cakes', adding, 'I have not yet found time to try it, but dare say they must be very nice and light'.[6]

It is interesting to find the reluctance among the Steventon villagers to try the crop corroborated by the testimony of Gilbert White, writing from the Hampshire village of Selborne in 1778: 'Potatoes have prevailed in this little district . . . within these 20 years only and are much esteemed by the poor, who would scarce have ventured to taste them in the last reign' (the last reign having ended with the death of George II in 1760).[7]

There was a great deal of prejudice to be got over, not only among the poor themselves, but sometimes on their behalf. As late as 1821 William Cobbett, who cared deeply about the well-being of the labouring classes, greatly deplored the increase in the cultivation of potatoes. Comparing potatoes with bread, he wrote in *Cottage Economy*:

Suppose a bushel of potatoes to be cooked every day in order to supply the place of . . . bread, then we have nine hundred boilings of the pot, unless cold potatoes be eaten at some of the meals; and in that case the diet must be cheering indeed! Think of the labour, think of the time, think of all the peelings and scrapings and washings and messings attending these nine hundred boilings of the pot! For it must be a considerable time before English people can be brought to eat potatoes in the Irish style; that is to say, scratch them out of the earth with their paws, toss them into the pot without washing, and when boiled turn them out upon a dirty board, and then sit round that board, peel the skin and dirt from one at the same time and eat the inside.[8]

Mrs Austen was evidently more enlightened (or more obedient?) in recommending to the village people a foodstuff which would vary, not dominate their diet, and which turned out to provide a valuable source of vitamin C throughout the year. Her daughter Jane, perhaps, was less enthusiastic about them. The only reference to eating potatoes in either her letters or her novels is, I believe, during dinner at Mansfield Park, in a somewhat scathing remark by Dr Grant: 'These potatoes have as much the flavour of a moor park apricot, as the fruit from that tree.' (*MP, 54*)

Potatoes were eventually to replace not bread but *pudding* in the English diet – savoury pudding, that is. Pudding has always been the starchy filler, the traditionally English accompaniment to meat. The basic idea was a combination of wheat flour or oatmeal and fat (suet, lard or butter) boiled in a pudding cloth, or baked in the oven. To this of course could be added any number of fillings or flavourings, either savoury or sweet, and it could be served with a corresponding sauce. Foreign visitors were frequently struck by the variety of English puddings. 'They bake them in the oven, they boil them with meat, they make them fifty several ways: BLESSED IS HE THAT INVENTED PUDDING', wrote François Mission.[9]

Beef pudding was mentioned by Jane Austen in 1814, when she expressed the hope that Cassandra and her mother, whom she had just left at Chawton, had been able to finish it up. We don't talk of beef pudding today, but we do still have steak and kidney pudding, one of the last of the savoury puddings to survive. In her letters Jane Austen mentions one other beef dish (besides the 'sandwiches all over mustard' that she ate at Oakley Hall, and which may or may not have been of beef; after all, mustard was eaten with cold pork at breakfast at Mansfield Park). In 1798, travelling back from Kent, Jane and her parents were served beefsteaks at the Bull and George, Dartford, together with a boiled fowl, 'but no oyster sauce'. (*L, 21*)

A picnic at Longleat (1816), by Humphry Repton
*(Reproduced by permission of the Marquess of Bath,
Longleat House, Warminster)*

I think this was probably a joke (rather than an expression of disappointment), oysters being all too common fare at inns, for they were very cheap. At the King's Head, Norwich, Parson Woodforde's dinner in January 1783 consisted of fresh salmon with oyster sauce, boiled turkey with oyster sauce, lamb and mince pies.[10] The only other mention made of oysters by Jane Austen is also connected with an inn: Tom Musgrave in *The Watsons* talks of ordering a barrel of oysters for himself while staying at the White Hart.

Mutton almost seems to have become the generic word for meat – or for dinner itself. Inviting someone to take their mutton with you was a common formula used even by *bon-vivants* who certainly hoped for something more elaborate for their dinner. Dr Grant invites Edmund Bertram 'to eat his mutton with him the next day' without supposing, for a moment, that 'the bill of fare' as he calls it is actually mutton (in fact it's turkey). (*MP, 215*) When Henry Tilney is about to spend a few days in his own home, Woodston Parsonage, his father proposes that the rest of the family should 'take him by surprise there some day or other, and eat their mutton with him', thus obliging Henry to hurry off earlier than planned in order to organise a suitably sumptuous repast. (*NA, 209*)

Lower-bred characters also use the phrase. At Portsmouth, Mr Price asks Henry Crawford 'to do them the honour of taking his mutton with them'. (*MP, 406*) It seems to be a masculine expression, suitably rough and ready, boasting an ignorance of domestic detail.

Miss Bates may be using the word mutton in a generic sense when she forces people to hear how small a slice of mutton Jane eats. A real saddle of mutton features at the Randalls dinner-party on Christmas Eve, while earlier the same day, nursery dinner for the little Knightleys at Hartfield is the plain wholesome fare of mutton and rice pudding.

As excellent mutton was reared on Mr Austen's farm, it is not surprising to find it regularly on the menu at Steventon. Another dinner provided for the household by Jane Austen during her mother's indisposition of November 1798 was haricot mutton. A recipe for this is given by Elizabeth Raffald in *The Experienced English Housekeeper* (1782):

> Cut the best end of a neck of mutton into chops, in single ribs, flatten them, and fry them a light brown, then put them into a large saucepan with two quarts of water, a large carrot cut in slices, cut at the edge like wheels; when they have stewed a quarter of an hour, put in two turnips cut in square slices, the white part of a head of celery, a few heads of asparagus, two cabbage lettuces fried, and Cayenne to your taste, boil them all together till they are tender, the gravy is not to be thickened.

Pork was also plentiful at Steventon. In 1801, when the farm livestock came to be sold, twenty-two pigs and three sows were mentioned in the advertisement.[11] 'We are to kill a pig soon', Jane had written to Cassandra in the same letter in which she mentioned haricot mutton. She does not go into further particulars of the cookery of this pig, but less than two months later another pig from their Cheesedown farm was killed, cut up and cured to be sent to sea with Second Lieutenant Charles Austen. Mrs Austen, Jane wrote humorously, meant to 'pay herself' for the salt and the trouble involved by keeping back the spare-ribs, the souse and the lard. Souse was a pickled version of brawn, the face-meats of the pig boiled, chopped and set in jelly from the trotters. The sousing-drink, as it was called, might be a strong brine, wine, ale or verjuice – this latter a common eighteenth-century ingredient consisting of the sour pressings of unripe English grapes. Pigs were traditionally killed in November, as was the one at Steventon in 1798; and, because the brawn or souse kept well in its jelly, it lasted well into Christmastide. As early as 1542, Andrew Boorde, in his *Compendyous Regyment, or a Dyetary of Helth*, says that brawn is 'an usual meate in wynter amonges Englysshe men'.[12] Indeed, brawn was in many households regarded as the traditional Twelfth Night dish. In the boisterous Christmas scene at Uppercross House, little boys are holding high revel at tables laden with 'cold pies and brawn'. (*P, 134*) On 14 January 1796 Jane wrote from Steventon, 'Caroline, Anna and I have just been devouring some cold souse, and it would be difficult to say which enjoyed it most'. (*L, 6*)

Bacon kept even longer. Among the Austens' household effects advertised for sale in April 1801 was a 'side of bacon' – the only item of preserved food which they had not either eaten themselves, given to James, or decided to take with them to Bath.[13] The value of such an item must have made it worth including in the auction. The previous autumn, when that particular pig had been killed and cured, the Austens had not made their plans to leave Steventon.

At a different time of year a different kind of pig would meet its doom. 'Porkers', that is pigs to be eaten as pork, differ in many ways from those destined to be bacon and hams. The type of animal is different and its feeding is altered to suit the purpose for which the pig is required. As Dorothy Hartley writes in *Food in England*: 'Bacon and ham pigs used to be wanted large, and in country places, 40 or 50lb. hams, and sides of bacon to match, glistening with salt, sparkled aloft between the top of the grandfather clock and the dresser; but for pig-keepers in a small way, pigs are usually killed when just "full-grown" and used partly as fresh pork and partly for salting.'[14]

It is very evidently this latter kind of pig which has been killed (in the Spring) at Hartfield, and which Emma and Mr Woodhouse discuss with reference to the Bateses:

'Now we have killed a porker, and Emma thinks of sending them a loin or a leg; it is very small and delicate – Hartfield pork is not like any other pork – but still it is pork – and, my dear Emma, unless one could be sure of their making it into steaks, nicely fried, as ours are fried, without the smallest grease, and not roast it, for no stomach can bear roast pork – I think we had better send the leg – do not you think so my dear?'

'My dear papa, I sent the whole hind-quarter. I knew you would wish it. There will be the leg to be salted, you know, which is so very nice, and the loin to be dressed directly in any manner they like.'

'That's right, my dear, very right. I had not thought of it before, but that was the best way. They must not over-salt the leg; and then, if it is not over-salted, and if it is very thoroughly boiled, just as Serle boils ours, and eaten very moderately of, with a boiled turnip, and a little carrot or parsnip, I do not consider it unwholesome. ' (*E, 172*)

Alas, his advice is unattended to. 'If there is one thing my mother loves better than another it is pork – a roast loin of pork', says Miss Bates, happily unaware of his prohibition (for deference might have made her observe it). So much for the loin. There is no such controversy over the leg, which prudence dictates must be salted for later consumption. There is some doubt about whether the Bates household possesses a salting-pan large enough to hold the joint; Mrs Bates, taking the interest of a long-retired housekeeper in the details of cookery, fancies not. So Patty, the maid-of-all-work goes 'down' to look. Evidently the kitchen is downstairs, presumably at the back of the shop over which the Bateses rent a few rooms on 'the drawing room floor'.

The salted leg will eventually be boiled, and then Mrs Goddard will be invited to partake of their bounty, for 'I really do not think she cares for anything but boiled pork', muses Miss Bates, quashing her generous impulse to invite her immediately to share the roast; 'when we dress the leg it will be another matter'. This verb 'to dress', meaning to prepare food, used only in a few contexts today (salad, crab), has a more widespread application in Jane Austen.

The food which gives the most desirable social message in Jane Austen's world is undoubtedly venison. Reared on some of the larger country estates, such as Godmersham, its presence on the table indicated either that one had extensive grounds oneself, or at least that one was connected with those that had. Prior to the eighteenth century the keeping of deer implied that the owner had been granted the right to 'empark' land for that purpose by his sovereign.[15] There was no park without deer, and 'Park' in an ancient place name – as in Godmersham Park or Mansfield Park – carried that significance. Jane ate venison in 1796 at Rowling, when it is specified as having come from Godmersham, and in 1816 at the Alton home of her brother Francis, when it was almost certainly a gift from the Chawton estate. General Tilney boasts of sending half a buck every year to his neighbours who are less well-endowed with land than himself. Venison is eaten at Mansfield Park and is common fare among Tom Bertram's circle of friends; and Mrs Bennet serves it to impress Bingley and Darcy on their return into Hertford-shire, highly gratified with the praise she extracts that nobody had seen so fat a haunch. (Fat as opposed to meagre, or fat as opposed to lean? Venison is an exceptionally lean meat, but until very recently people prized fatty joints, which tend to have more flavour.) It is worth noting by the way that on all these occasions when venison is eaten – in life and in fiction – it is September.

Turkey makes a very frequent appearance in Jane Austen – the most frequent of any of the meats. This is rather surprising, since during her lifetime there was quite a lot of prejudice against it as a recent import (from South America) and it was often held to be tasteless and tough. No doubt this was the truth for those whose only experience of turkey was of the birds who had been forced to walk on their own two feet from East Anglia to London before being killed. They actually set off in August for consumption at Christmas. But the Austens had always reared their own turkeys at Steventon, which made all the difference. Henry in London received the gift of a turkey sent by carrier from Hampshire from time to time, ideal for his French cook to exercise his ingenuity upon. 'Pray note down how many full courses of exquisite dishes M. Halavant converts it into', wrote Jane to Cassandra, who was staying with Henry at the time of one such gift. (*L, 118*)

Turkey was certainly associated with Christmas by the Austens, while many other families (Parson Woodforde, for example) maintained the older tradition of beef for Christmas Day. At the end of November 1812 Jane wrote to her friend Martha Lloyd, away on a visit, for the address of a Mr Morton to whom they were to send a Christmas turkey. She continued, 'We are just beginning to be engaged in another Christmas Duty, & next to eating Turkies [sic], a very pleasant one, laying out Edward's money for the Poor'. (*L, 501*) Back in 1796, brother James had 'cut up the turkey with great perseverence' at the supper during a ball on 8 January. (*L, 3*)

In 1807 Robert Southey published a book which Jane Austen is known to have read. Entitled *Letters from England*, it purported to be the impressions of a Spaniard named Espriella travelling through England; but being actually the work of an Englishman and a contemporary of Jane Austen, it provides us with some useful insights into the customs of her times. 'On the feast of St Michael the Archangel, everybody must eat goose for dinner; and on the Nativity turkey, with what they call Christmas pies,' Southey wrote.[16] Goose was traditional at Michaelmas because it could be fattened up on the stubble and gleanings left by the reapers. An old proverb went, 'Who eats goose on Michael's day / Shan't money lack his debts to pay'. Jane Austen, having eaten goose at Godmersham on Michaelmas day 1813, remembered this saying and wrote to Cassandra: 'I dined upon Goose yesterday, which I hope will secure a good Sale of my 2nd Edition.' The goose which Mrs Martin sends as a present to Mrs Goddard at the end of Harriet's visit to Abbey Mill Farm is a Michaelmas goose.

The other kind of goose was green goose, killed at three or four months old. On 10 June 1784 Parson Woodforde was at what he called 'a very genteel dinner' where 'a green goose and peas' made its appearance as part of the second course. It is a disappointing green goose which puts Dr Grant out of humour one evening in mid August and makes his young visitors, the Crawfords, seek an escape from his black mood in an impromptu walk to Mansfield Park; poor Mrs Grant has to stay and bear it.

If foreigners admired our puddings and marvelled at the amount of meat on British tables, they also scoffed at the way we had only one sauce in which all our vegetables were smothered. A young German, Moritz, residing in England in 1782, wrote: 'An English dinner for such lodgers as I am, generally consists of a piece of half-boiled or half-roasted meat; and a few cabbage leaves boiled in plain water; on which they pour a sauce made of flour and butter, the usual method of dressing vegetables in England.'[17] It is said that Voltaire was the first to observe that the English had a hundred religions and only one sauce.

When General Tilney dines at his son's house, he is in a good enough humour to overlook 'the melted butter's being oiled'. (*NA, 215*) This used to puzzle me. Surely melted butter *is* oily? To Jane Grigson, again, I am indebted for elucidation. Under the heading 'Melted Butter' she writes,

In early recipes you will often notice that fish or a vegetable are to be sent to table with 'good melted butter'. This does not mean literally what it says – a piece of butter melted and perhaps flavoured with lemon juice – but a sauce composed of butter, thickened with flour rather than the egg yolks of *sauce Hollandaise*. This is the 'one sauce' of bad English cookery of the past; by adding shellfish or herbs or mustard or anchovy, its flavour and name became different. But only slightly so, as the general texture and weight of the sauce remained identical. The problem of this sauce is not of course curdling, but oiling; overheating is the cause.[18]

It is interesting that the word vegetable was not used to denote something edible before the middle of the eighteenth century, the first instance of such usage in print being in 1767, by the agriculturalist Arthur Young; and he was speaking in the context of cultivation rather than of cookery. Before that, the word was applied to anything in the vegetable kingdom. The traditional term for the edible varieties was potherbs – because they went in the pot – or, in more refined circles, garden stuff. Hannah Glasse, writing in 1747, instructed: 'In your first course, always observe to send up all kinds of Garden Stuff suitable to your Meat etc. in different Dishes, on a Water dish filled with hot water on the Side Table.' It is garden stuff with which the kind Sir John Middleton is said to supply his newly-arrived tenants, the Dashwoods. (*S & S, 30*) Jane Austen does not use the word vegetable until *Sanditon* of 1817, and then in the mouth of the modern and modernising Mr Parker, while his wife remains faithful to the old term:

> 'It was always a very comfortable House – said Mrs Parker – looking at it through the back window with something like the fondness of regret. – And such a nice Garden – such an excellent Garden.' 'Yes, my Love, but *that* we may be said to carry with us. – *It* supplies us, as before, with all the fruit and vegetables we want; and we have in fact all the comfort of an excellent Kitchen Garden, without the constant Eyesore of its formalities; or the yearly nuisance of its decaying vegetation. – Who can endure a Cabbage Bed in October?' 'Oh! dear – yes. – We are quite as well off for Gardenstuff as ever we were.' (*MW, 380*)

Jane Austen uses the word sallad [sic] in the French manner, meaning just lettuce, or at any rate leaves; Lydia Bennet talks of dressing 'a sallad and cucumber'. (*P & P, 219*) Although tomatoes had been introduced to Britain a century before, there was a great deal of prejudice against them because of the unpleasant smell of the plant, and at this date tomatoes were still rarely eaten, especially raw. The Austens and Knights must have been among the first to do so, as in October 1813 Jane refers to herself and her niece Fanny Knight 'regaling' on them every day. (*L, 346*) They were evidently grown at Chawton too, since she enquires whether Cassandra has any.

One unusual home-grown vegetable enjoyed by Jane Austen was sea-kale. From Chawton, in March 1817, Jane sends thanks for a gift of seacale (as she spells it) from Mrs James Austen at Steventon. 'Sea-kale is delicious; and very English', Jane Grigson tells us:

> It is the one vegetable we have developed from a wild species. Along the beaches of Kent, Sussex and Hampshire sand was piled round the young shoots to blanch away their bitterness. 'Very delicate', John Evelyn wrote in 1699 of this *Crambe maritima*, this wild sea-cabbage which tastes of anything but cabbage. It was soon found to do well in gardens, blanched under old crocks. Two of the master gardeners of the eighteenth century, Philip Miller and William Curtis, worked out the ways of cultivating sea-kale. Antonin Carême, the great French chef, who worked for the Prince Regent for a while, commented on the 'sikel' of the London markets which he found 'very appetising'.[19]

Asparagus is another vegetable mentioned by Jane Austen. It was one of the supper dishes at Hartfield which Mr Woodhouse would not let his guests eat, as he fancied it not boiled enough, much to Mrs Bates's disappointment. Jane Austen herself ate it in May 1799 at an inn in Devizes *en route* for Bath. Also on the menu on that occasion was lobster, one of the relatively rare mentions in either letters or novels of seafood or fish; there is cod and salmon in *Sense and Sensibility* – but again they are on the menu at an inn. Salmon was available (but at a high price) at the Bath market in May 1801. Improved methods of transport were bringing fish of all kinds to inland markets (but not, as Mrs Bennet laments, on Mondays). As a consequence the fish from stewponds, on which many communities had formerly depended, began to fall out of favour because of their muddier taste. Carp was one such fish, and a recipe for a sauce for carp (perhaps masking the flavour) was one of Mrs Austen's contributions to Martha Lloyd's recipe collection.

Another was for shortcrust pastry. Jane writes of one servant, 'Her Cookery is at least tolerable – her pastry is the only deficiency'. (*L, 287*) Venison pasty and cold pigeon pie are two pastry dishes which make more than one appearance in Jane Austen and in eighteenth-century writers generally. It is amusing to find Mrs Elton, who believes herself the last word in modernity, planning to take 'pigeon-pies and cold lamb' on the exploring party to Box Hill (*E, 353*), and then to turn to George Turbeville's *The Noble Art of Venerie* of 1575, with its description in verse of an Elizabethan picnic beginning with the servants spreading the cloth 'upon the grassy bank', containing the line, 'With pigeon pies, and mutton cold, are set on hunger loose'.[20]

Sweet puddings using a pastry case mentioned in Jane Austen's writings are apricot and apple tarts, mince pies, apple dumplings and even rice pudding, though this could also be made without pastry. Sometimes however there were lighter concoctions on the table: jellies and stewed pears are mentioned by Jane Austen. Though the Bates's maidservant Patty makes excellent apple-dumplings, delicate Jane Fairfax prefers the less stodgy baked apples, as Miss Bates informs us:

'Then the baked apples came home, Mrs Wallis sent them by her boy; they are always extremely civil and obliging to us, the Wallises, always – I have heard some people say that Mrs Wallis can be uncivil and give a very rude answer, but we have never known anything but the greatest attention from them. And it cannot be for the value of our custom, now, for what is our consumption of bread, you know? Only three of us [endearingly, she counts Patty] – besides dear Jane at present – and she really eats nothing – makes such a shocking breakfast, you would be quite frightened if you saw it. I dare not let my mother know how little she eats – so I say one thing and then I say another, and it passes off. But about the middle of the day she gets hungry, and there is nothing she likes so well as these baked apples, and they are extremely wholesome, for I took the opportunity the other day of asking Mr Perry; I happened to meet him in the street. Not that I had any doubt before – I have so often heard Mr Woodhouse recommend a baked apple. I believe it is the only way that Mr Woodhouse thinks the fruit thoroughly wholesome. We have apple dumplings, however, very often. Patty makes an excellent apple dumpling.' (*E, 237*)

Lacking an oven of their own or unable to afford the fuel to light one, poorer people, such as the Bateses, often sent their pies to be baked by the local baker (marking them with initials for later identification: 'pat it and prick it and mark it with B'). Interestingly, in view of the early-morning delivery of the Bateses baked apples by Mrs Wallis's boy, *Good Things in England*, a collection of old recipes made by Townswomen Guild members all over the country in 1954, says of baked apples that they were 'baked all night in the still warm oven of a stove that has been heated all day by a coal fire. In the morning the oven would be cold.' Bakers like Mrs Wallis would thus gain a few extra pence from the residual heat of their ovens. The minimal amount of heat remaining in the oven perhaps explains why Miss Bates has her apples baked twice, and Mr Woodhouse even recommends three times; to reduce them to the pulpy state no doubt preferred by him would take three nights' worth of diminishing heat. There was a great deal of prejudice against eating fruit in its raw state throughout the eighteenth century, which Mr Woodhouse retains. Raw fruit was believed to cause not merely indigestion, but all manner of ills, including the plague. We think of baked apples as retaining their peel, and being cored and stuffed; but the same old recipe says they should be peeled and halved, a little water, sugar and flavouring such as lemon, cloves or cinnamon added, and covered with their own peelings to prevent drying out before being sent to the oven.

Another apple concoction was the black butter which was not a complete success when made at the Austens' Southampton home – 'neither solid nor entirely sweet'; its more common name was apple butter. It was a good way of using up windfalls. Complete apples were roughly chopped and cooked to a mush, strained, then sugar was dissolved in the pulp, which was boiled for several hours until stiff and then potted, when it would keep for up to a year. In the case of the Southampton experiment, it was decided that it had not been boiled long enough. The result was fit to be eaten 'in unpretending privacy', but not to be offered to guests.

One person who would certainly not have allowed his guests to touch it, however well it had turned out, was Mr Woodhouse; he boasts of having 'no unwholesome preserves' at Hartfield. (Neither fresh fruit nor preserves!) However, apricot 'conserve' is made at Mansfield Parsonage, and apricot 'marmalade' at Barton Park; while at Chawton the Austens made raspberry jam.

When Jane Austen, in a rare reference to bought food, wrote 'You know how interesting the purchase of a sponge-cake is to me' (*L, 191*), she referred, of course, not to the Victoria sandwich we often call sponge but to the true fatless sponge-cake, made with just flour, eggs and sugar. Raising powder was not available before the 1850s, so the lightness of a sponge had to come from the amount of air that could be beaten into the mixture. Fortunately labour was cheap and uncomplaining. Hannah Glasse, writing in 1747, advises that the mixture should be beaten for an hour.

Also requiring a great deal of labour was the eighteenth-century 'bride-cake' recipe recorded in the Townswomen Guilds collection mentioned above. Ingredients are 4lb. fine flour, well dried; 4lb. fresh butter; 2lb. loaf sugar, pounded and sifted fine; ¼oz. mace; ¼oz. nutmeg; 32 eggs; 4lb. currants, picked over and dried well; 1lb. sweet almonds, blanched and cut lengthwise very thin; 1lb. each shredded orange and lemon peel; and half a pint of brandy. Part of the method was to beat the whites and yolks of the eggs separately, the latter for half an hour.[21]

The recipe includes a marzipan, or 'almond icing', and a white or 'sugar icing'. 'It appears that in the eighteenth century wedding cakes were not decorated, but were left plain white', observes the editor. This would accord with the simplicity of weddings before the Victorian era. Jane once had reason to enquire whether a family of her acquaintance sent out their wedding cake; so the custom was not yet universal, though the dispersal of the Westons' wedding-cake makes so humorous – and apt – an opening to *Emma*.

The other famous cake in *Emma* is rout-cakes: the poor attempt at rout cakes made by the good dames of Highbury, as seen through Mrs Elton's eyes. This is the recipe for 'Rout Drop Cakes' given by Maria Rundell in her *Domestic Cookery for Private Families* (1806):

> Mix two pounds of flour, one ditto butter, one ditto sugar, one ditto currants, clean and dry; then wet into a stiff paste with two eggs, a large spoonful of orange-flower water, ditto rose-water, ditto sweet wine, ditto brandy; drop on a tin-plate floured, a very short time bakes them.

Midway between a pudding and a drink, and frequently served at late-night suppers, was the old eighteenth-century favourite, syllabub. This had begun life as very definitely liquid: warm milk from the udder being squeezed directly into glasses of cider or ale. 'We have had a syllabub under the cow', wrote Horace Walpole from Strawberry Hill in 1752.[22] The next refinement was to replace the milk by cream and the ale by white wine, giving a separated concoction of creamy froth on a liquid base. Hannah Glasse's version has cider or wine sweetened and flavoured with nutmeg, milk and then cream. Sensibly recognising than an elegant evening party did not often take place in dairy or field, she writes, 'You may make this Syllabub at Home, only have new Milk; make it as hot as Milk from the Cow, and out of a Tea-pot or any such Thing, pour it in, holding your Hand very high.' Later, whipped syllabub became the fashion: by 1806 Maria Rundell was giving a version in which thick cream, wine, sugar and lemon are beaten together for half an hour. Made this way it did not separate and would keep in a cool dairy or larder for days; it was solid enough to be eaten with a spoon. This solidification gave rise to one of the very few similes to be found in Jane Austen. In the juvenile fragment *Lesley Castle*, Charlotte Luttrell (to whom cooking is everything) describes her sister 'with her face as White as a Whipt Syllabub', running in with the news that her lover has cracked his scull and is in danger of losing his life. (*MW, 113*)

Mr Woodhouse's famous gruel is a far cry from syllabub (one would like to hear his strictures on that) but it is of a similar consistency, neither liquid nor solid, and it is consumed at the same time of day, or rather evening. Gruel is simply a large spoonful of oatmeal boiled in a pint of water, with a little butter stirred in at the last minute if wished; in these proportions, 'it will be fine and smooth, and very good', promises Hannah Glasse. But will it be 'thin but not too thin' as Mr Woodhouse and Isabella like it, but as the cook at Southend never could achieve? 'Some love a little pepper in it', adds Hannah Glasse; not Mr Woodhouse, one imagines.

Not infrequently wine was put into gruel, which made it into even more of a nightcap. Another such was caudle, mentioned in some of the Austen family writings, a mixture of hot ale or beer with sugar, nutmeg and egg yolk. There was certainly a penchant in eighteenth- and nineteenth-century society for these hot, fortified, semi-alcoholic mixtures that fall somewhere between food and drink. The coldness of homes heated only by open fires made them particularly welcome last thing at night, before braving the chilly stairs and passages on the way to bed, or even worse the cold night air out of doors. Negus was another late-night drink that was nourishing and warming, and mildly alcoholic; a mixture of lemon, spices, calves-foot jelly, wine and boiling water, it was mixed twenty minutes or so in advance of drinking so that the jelly melted and the flavours blended together in the heat. Traditionally served on winter evenings before the company departed, to warm them on their way, it was especially popular after balls. As she makes her weary way upstairs after as much dancing as she has strength for at the Mansfield ball, Fanny Price is 'feverish with hopes and fears, soup and negus'. (*MP*, 281) In *The Watsons*, when Lord Osborne's party has departed in great show from the ball at the inn, Tom Musgrave is left with a choice between shutting himself up in a corner with a barrel of oysters, or helping the landlady to make fresh negus for the dancers still remaining. (This being a public assembly, not a private ball, the only refreshments on offer are tea and negus; for the 'comfortable soup' with which to wind up the evening, Emma Watson and the Edwardes have to wait until they are back home, and gathered round their own fireside.) Negus is not mentioned as being provided at the ball at the Crown in *Emma*, probably because it took place in early summer; Mrs Weston and Mrs Stokes between them would not have failed to provide everything proper to the occasion and expected by their guests.

'Henry desires Edward may know that he has just bought 3 dozen of Claret for him (Cheap) & ordered it to be sent down to Chawton', wrote Jane in May, 1813; being at war with France evidently did not prevent the import of French wine. (*L*, *313*) However, madeira was becoming the most fashionable and patriotic wine. There was madeira and port in Henry's house in October 1813, and madeira on the supper tray in *Mansfield Park*, which was being written at about the same time, while in Maria Edgeworth's *The Absentee* of 1812 a picnic is washed down by madeira and champagne.

While the well-off brothers like Edward and Henry drank French and Portuguese wine, the Austen ladies produced home-made wines of various kinds. But it was not only in modest households that home-made wine eked out imported supplies. Manydown, home of Jane's friends the Bigg family, was a grand enough establishment, but not ashamed to practise this branch of domestic economy. Writing to her friend Alethea Bigg in January 1817, Jane added a postscript: 'The real object of this letter is to ask you for a receipt, but I thought it genteel not to let it appear too early. We remember some excellent orange wine at Manydown, made from Seville oranges, entirely or chiefly & should be very much obliged to you for the receipt, if you can command it within a few weeks.' (*L, 477*)

The Manydown recipe appears to be the one copied into her household book by Martha Lloyd, using as it does both Seville and sweet oranges:

> Take ten gallons of water, 30lbs of fine Lisbon sugar and the whites of 6 eggs well beaten. Boil together – of an hour, skimming it well. Then add the chop't pieces of 33 Seville oranges (reserving the peel of 24 of them to be thrown into the barrel); the juice of 36 sweet oranges and of fifteen lemons. Mix all well together and boil it up again.
> When cold for working take a large toast, cover it with good yeast and let it stand for 2 days and 2 nights. Then turn it. Cask it off at the end of four months and add to the liquor a bottle of brandy and three lbs of lump sugar – you may bottle towards the end of the year.[23]

Seville oranges are of course available only in the first months of the year, which is why the Austens needed the recipe within a few weeks; wine made in February would be ready to put into casks in June or July, hence Jane's remembering at Godmersham in June 1808 that 'the Orange wine will want our care soon'. (*L, 209*)

The fruit or flowers for many home-made wines would be grown or gathered at home, whereas oranges, Seville or otherwise, had to be bought. In 1811 the Austens had to buy in currants for their currant wine, as their garden did not yield enough that year – so that, even when the main ingredient was not free, it was thought worth purchasing supplies in order to keep up the stock of wine.

A similar difficulty arose one year as to the honey for mead, which the Austens made regularly. 'There is to be NO HONEY this year. Bad news for us', Jane wrote in 1816. (*L, 466*) There are very many references to mead in Jane Austen's letters in the Chawton years, despite the fact that it was going out of fashion in the country generally (probably because it was becoming so much easier to obtain sugar than honey). In medieval times mead had been made with honey and water alone, no yeast; fermentation came from the fact of the ingredients and utensils being less than sterile. With increased cleanliness came the need to add brewer's yeast or barm, which is the froth on top of fermenting beer. The recipe noted down by Martha Lloyd has nutmeg, mace, cloves and ginger 'sewed up in a linen bag', sweet-briar and lemons. Another eighteenth-century recipe also uses sweet-briar, together with rosemary, but no spices; another, of an earlier date, includes marjoram and thyme. Parson Woodforde put elderflowers in his. Indeed, no fewer than fifty-six different recipes for mead had been collected by Sir Kenelm Digby from his acquaintance for one of the earliest cookery books to be published, *The Closet Opened* of 1669.

Another, more up-to-date, home brew made at Chawton was spruce beer. The spruce fir is not native to our shores, so this cannot be one of our oldest beers. It appears to have been a novelty at Highbury in 1816. Mr Knightley and Emma like it, and Mr Elton resolves to like it too; he notes down the recipe in his pocket-book, and Harriet snatches up the remains of his pencil. What did Mr Elton write? Dorothy Hartley quotes a nineteenth-century recipe for spruce beer which certainly has the 'elegant terseness' which Emma mocks in *Mrs* Elton: 'One pint good spruce extract, 12lb treacle, 3 gallons of water. Boil all and let stand 1 hour. Add 3 or 4 gallons of water, 1 pint of yeast (the water should be hand warm). Pour into a 10-gallon cask. Fill her up, – let her work. Bung her up. Bottle her off.'[24]

This text is attributed to a New England housewife, and it is interesting that Robert Southey, writing in 1807 in his guise as a Spanish traveller in England, says, 'They have a beverage made from the buds of the fir-tree and treacle; necessity taught the American settlers to brew this detestable mixture, which is introduced here as a luxury'.[25]

More expansively, Dorothy Hartley explains:

The gummy tassels of the spruce are brought gradually to the boil to release the essential oil and flavour. As soon as the oily scum shows on the surface, pass a large plate across the surface drawing the scum aside and slip out the spruce, put in another bough, and continue doing this until you have a thick scum of spruce oil, and the water is well impregnated with the essence. Strain, and to 16 gallons of warm spruce liquor, add 16lb of treacle, stir till dissolved, and put in about ½ pint of fresh yeast. Let it work, covered, for three days, and then strain off into a cask. Do not bung up until fermentation has practically ceased. It can be drunk within a week or so, but it is better kept some months.[26]

Spruce beer was at this date held to be an anti-scorbutic – Captain Parry took a consignment of essence of spruce on his voyage of discovery to the North-West Passage in 1819 – though how much vitamin C remained in the extract must be doubtful. Although the efficacy of fresh fruit and vegetables in preventing or curing scurvy on long sea voyages had been observed for the last two hundred years, the reason was not properly understood. So reluctant, on economic grounds, had the British Navy been, despite empirical evidence, to accept that other changes in the diet were ineffectual, that lemon or lime juice were not issued to sailors until 1795. Captain Parry's faith in spruce beer, therefore, was a late remnant of the prejudices of the authorities on this subject.

The elder of Jane Austen's two sailor brothers, Frank, first went to sea in December 1788 (at the age of fourteen), his first voyage lasting three years, though his ship the *Perseverance* was able to take on fresh supplies in India. Nevertheless, there was certainly a risk to him in the early part of his career of suffering from scurvy or from a pre-scorbutic condition. Not that this risk was confined to seafarers. A dearth of fresh fruits and vegetables through the long British winter rendered the general population liable to sufferings caused by vitamin C deficiency. This must surely account for the loss of Mrs Austen's front teeth before she was fifty; with consumption of sugar as low as it was in the eighteenth century, no other explanation seems so likely as pre-scorbutic softening of the gums.[27] The increased frequency of potatoes in the diet of succeeding generations afforded them greater protection against this scourge, which, in its limited seasonal form, presented an unrecognised jeopardy to health.

In a rare reference to anything medicinal, in 1805 Jane wrote to Cassandra: 'You continue, I suppose, taking hartshorn, and I hope with good effect.' (*L, 170*) Hartshorn actually was the antlers of deer and, shaved fine, boiled and strained, was the chief source of ammonia. What good effect was expected from it I would not like to surmise; no particular ailment of Cassandra's is referred to in the correspondence of the time, though Cassandra was not above destroying a letter that mentioned anything embarrassing.

It was available in three forms: spirit of hartshorn, an aqueous solution of ammonia; hartshorn jelly, a nutritive jelly made by boiling half a pound of hartshorn shavings in four pints of water for three hours; and salt of hartshorn, or carbonate of ammonia, the 'smelling salts' familiar from much Georgian and Victorian literature. Used to revive fainting young ladies, it was so often needed that many women carried a supply about with them. When Louisa Musgrove is 'taken up lifeless' after her fall on the Cobb, Anne Elliot can immediately produce salts; so can Mrs Jennings (probably not much to the purpose) at the John Dashwoods' dinner party when Marianne bursts into tears. On an earlier occasion in *Sense and Sensibility*, however, Marianne has to wait until her return home before hartshorn can be procured to 'restore her a little to herself'. This is the party at which Willoughby rebuffs her and, as it takes place in a particularly hot, crowded room, it is hardly surprising that Marianne is in danger of fainting away. Mrs Jennings is not present, however and Elinor uses lavender water to revive her sister. As Marianne goes to bed immediately after taking the hartshorn and, Elinor must hope, to sleep, it is a little perplexing that a stimulant should be applied.

Lady Bertram carries her salts to the wedding of Maria and Mr Rushworth in case she should feel any perturbation (she does not). She also keeps a supply of aromatic vinegar, which Fanny is given (to sniff?) when she has a headache.

With no synthetic drugs available, medicine and foodstuffs were of course closely related in Jane Austen's lifetime. One thinks of the arrowroot from the Hartfield housekeeper's stores with which Emma tries to tempt the appetite of the ailing Jane Fairfax. Arrowroot was a recent introduction to these shores – indeed, one authority gives the 1820s as the date of its introduction from the West Indies, which postdates *Emma*; Jane Austen herself seems a little unfamiliar with it as she spelled it 'arraroot' in her MS, which was queried by the compositor. It is not clear in the novel whether the 'finest arrowroot' which the Hartfield housekeeper suggests be despatched from her stores is the raw ingredient, or the made-up dish. This was a forerunner of our corn-flour-thickened blancmange. The arrowroot was first dissolved in a small quantity of cold milk; then boiling milk, sweetened and flavoured with cinnamon and lemon peel was poured on whilst stirring briskly, since it thickened instantly. It was put in a mould and turned out the next day. Just the food for a temporary invalid such as Jane Fairfax – or a perpetual one like Mr Woodhouse. No wonder it formed part of the stores at Hartfield.

Another and more traditional invalid food was asses' milk. It was particularly recommended for the nourishment of tubercular patients (which Jane Fairfax is sometimes feared to be, 'the standing apprehension of the family', her mother having died of consumption), and often advised to be drunk warm from the animal. Lady Denham has two milch asses and, always keen to turn a profit, is in hopes that some of those attracted to Sanditon 'may be consumptive & want Asses milk'. (*MW*, 393) Containing a very small proportion of protein and fat, asses' milk is less nutritious but more easily digestible than that of cows or any other milk apart from human. Although the reason was not understood, the truth of this was recognised even in the sixteenth century:

> In great consumptions learn'd Physicians thinke,
> 'Tis good a Goats or Camels milke to drinke
> Cowes-milke and Sheepes doe well, but yet an Asses
> Is best of all, and all the other passes.[28]

Lady Denham is a shrewd businesswoman, and could certainly have charged a premium for the produce of her milch asses: in 1796 it was selling at 3s. 6d. a pint, a remarkable price when one considers that meat cost less than 1s. a pound. When she finds that one of the new arrivals in Sanditon is an heiress, and, being half Mulatto, 'chilly and tender', she is overjoyed, on her nephew's account and her own.

> In Miss Lambe, here was the very young Lady, sickly and rich, whom she had been asking for; & she made the acquaintance for Sir Edward's sake, & the sake of her Milch asses. How it might answer with regard to the Baronet, remained to be proved, but as to the Animals, she soon found that all her calculations of Profit wd be vain. Mrs G. would not allow Miss L. to have the smallest symptom of a Decline, or any complaint which Asses milk could possibly relieve. 'Miss L. was under the constant care of an experienced Physician; – and his Prescriptions must be their rule' – and except in favour of some Tonic Pills, which a Cousin of her own had a Property in, Mrs G. did never deviate from the strict Medicinal page. (*MW*, 422)

Sanditon was written at a time when Jane Austen's own health was failing her, but is full of jokes about hypochondria and quack remedies. All her life she had had little patience with these, and her letters contain remarkably few references to the substances and home concoctions with which eighteenth-century sufferers attempted to cure their complaints. Not for her Parson Woodforde's faith in healing a sore eyelid by rubbing it with the tail of a black cat.

In September 1816 Jane Austen expressed relief that the house was again empty of visitors. 'Composition seems to me impossible with a head full of joints of mutton and doses of rhubarb.' (*L, 466*) And in 1813 she wrote to Cassandra of Henry, who was to visit at Chawton, 'His stomach is rather deranged. You must keep him in Rhubarb and give him plenty of Port and Water.' (*L, 326*) The rhubarb referred to in both these letters is not the plant we think of, the stalks of which are eaten as fruit; though it had been commonly grown in English gardens from the early eighteenth century, Jane Austen, I believe, makes no reference to it. She is referring rather to the medicinal rootstock of the species of rheum grown in China and Tibet and for a long period imported into Europe through Russia and the Levant, and used as a purgative by the overfed part of the population. In *Northanger Abbey*, Catherine, awakening from her delusions, admits to herself that poisons and sleeping potions were not to be procured, 'like rhubarb', from every druggist. Its exotic provenance, and its availability only through druggists and apothecaries, rendered powdered rhubarb an expensive commodity. Parson Woodforde gave on different occasions sums ranging from 2s. 6d. to 3s. an ounce.

Such were the eating and drinking habits of Parson Woodforde's household that they were frequently in need of this remedy for over-indulgence. It is not unreasonable to assume that – with a few notable exceptions – Jane Austen's people, both real and imaginary, did not so often over-eat themselves, despite all the rich and delicious food on their tables.

Chapter Four

Greed and Gender

Jane Austen was not quite twelve years old when the Reverend John Trusler's book *The Honours of the Table for the Use of Young People* was published. In this work Trusler declares, with perfect seriousness, that to eat very much 'is now deemed indelicate in a lady, for her character should be rather divine than sensual'.[1] One can imagine Mrs Austen's snort of impatience with that. Whether the Austens owned a copy of the book is not known, nor whether Jane ever read this particular contribution to the cult of female sensibility. What *is* certain is that, from a very early age, she was atune to the mental currents of her times and alive to any absurdity inherent in them. Her earliest literary efforts were written to amuse her family by mocking the attitudes and excesses found in books. Just two years after the appearance of Trusler's work, when she was only fourteen, she included this passage in her burlesque of the sentimental novel, *Love and Freindship*:

> 'But still I am not without apprehensions of your being shortly obliged to degrade yourself in your own eyes by seeking a Support for your Wife in the Generosity of Sir Edward.'
> 'Never, never Augusta will I so demean myself (said Edward). Support! What support will Laura want which she can receive from him?'
> 'Only those very insignificant ones of Victuals and Drink' (answered she).
> 'Victuals and drink! (replied my Husband in a most nobly contemptuous Manner) and dost thou then imagine that there is no other support for an exalted Mind (such as my Laura's) than the mean and indelicate employment of Eating and Drinking?'
> 'None that I know of, so efficacious,' (returned Augusta). (*MW, 83*)

Noble contempt for the necessities of food and drink is here made fun of, shown to be a ludicrous affectation. There can be no elevated thoughts, no rectitude, no love, without a well-fed body to sustain them.

The youthful author's sympathy is evidently with the clear-headed Augusta, as her sympathy was to continue to be, throughout the development of her fiction, with all that was rational and unaffected.

While this is undeniably true, it is, however, very far from being the whole truth. Jane Austen's emphasis on the moral life lifts her imaginary world above materiality to an unusual degree. Of all writers she is the one who seems most ready to eschew physical detail in order to concentrate on a higher plane of existence altogether. Her most esteemed characters are rarely if ever preoccupied with 'the mean and indelicate employment of eating and drinking'. They eat to live, but certainly do not live to eat. To take an interest in food in a Jane Austen novel is to be almost certainly condemned as frivolous, selfish or gross.

Here then is a second approach, one which is much more in line with Trusler's dictum. In her narrative persona, Jane Austen apparently comes close to the young lady who deems it indelicate to require food. Wouldn't we be inclined to say, if we had to choose between the two terms, that her heroines are more divine than sensual? Anne Elliot, for example – can anybody remember that slender form of hers ever consuming anything? Does it experience so much as a pang of hunger through the whole course of the novel – or is it merely the medium of those 'musings of high-wrought love and eternal constancy' which seem to spread purification and perfume through the streets of Bath?

Of course a close reading of the complete Jane Austen corpus reveals, what we might have expected, that she refuses to fall into either an excess of refinement on the one hand, or preoccupation with bodily satisfactions on the other. The two are always kept in play together. In matters of eating, as in other aspects of life, she is concerned with achieving balance. Nevertheless, it is true that what she presents as a reasonable balance seems to err on the side of spirituality in comparison with either the uninhibited Georgian novelists or the lavishly material Victorians. Then again, in saying that, one may be comparing her with men – with Fielding and Smollett, with Dickens and Trollope. Fanny Burney and Charlotte Brontë are as concerned as Jane Austen – indeed, perhaps more so, being less committed to realism – to present their heroines as free from earthy appetites.

There is more food in the Juvenilia than in any other of Jane Austen's fiction before *Emma*. This could be because the young Jane Austen was not mentally editing out the mundane as in work intended for publication (the same applies to her letters). It could equally be because the clash between the wholesome enjoyment of food at Steventon Rectory and the treatment of female incorporality in literature struck her as a fruitful source of ridicule.

The gulf between the divine and the sensual is certainly one with which the Juvenilia are much concerned. At this stage in her writing there is no attempt at balance, unless it be in showing the ludicrousness of both extremes. The young women in these early pieces are divided into those who won't eat at all, and those who eat and think about eating too much.

'The two ladies', we read in the very first mention of food in Jane Austen's preserved writings, 'sat down to supper on a young Leveret, a brace of Partridges, a leash of Pheasants and a Dozen of Pigeons.' (*MW*, 9) One of these ladies has just accepted proposals of marriage from two different men. To be so ready to eat at such a time reveals a sad want of sensibility, which the cataloguing of all those poor creatures underlines. Had we been told that Charlotte and her aunt simply sat down to 'a large supper' it would not be anywhere near so telling; already Jane Austen is learning to insert the precise detail exactly where it will be effective, in literary terms.

The fun arising from the incongruity between greed and heroineism continues in 'The Beautifull Cassandra' in which the eponymous heroine 'proceeded to a Pastry-cooks where she devoured six ices, refused to pay for them, knocked down the Pastry Cook and walked away'. (*MW*, 45) Men too, though less often, can be subject to the demands of sensibility. In 'Amelia Webster', George Harvey offers it as a proof of love at first sight that he has 'not tasted human food' between seeing the object of his affections (through a telescope!) on Monday and Saturday, the date of his letter.

In another epistolary fragment, entitled 'A Beautiful Description of the Different Effects of Sensibility on Different Minds' the food mentioned is amusingly indigestible, just right for the ailing young lady who 'lies wrapped in a book muslin bedgown, a chambray gauze shift, and a french net nightcap', and whose appetite is 'Bad, very bad'. As all her friends gather round her bedside, unable to sleep except 'for five minutes every fortnight', the writer of the letter is 'usually at the fire cooking some little delicacy for the unhappy invalid, – Perhaps hashing up the remains of an Old Duck, toasting some cheese or making a Curry which are the favourite dishes of our poor friend'. (*MW*, 72)

Jane Austen's Juvenilia include several fragments of drama. In one, the heroine, having been shown the bill of fare at an inn (two ducks, a leg of beef, a stinking partridge, and a tart) breaks into song:

I am going to have my dinner,
After which I shan't be thinner,
I wish I had here Strephon
For he would carve the partridge if it should be a tough one. (*MW, 174*)

Of the two scenes in 'The Visit', one is set in a dining parlour, where the company talk of nothing but food and drink, and where all (except Sir Arthur, who neither speaks nor eats) betray, in every sense of the words, a coarse taste:

The Dining Parlour

MISS FITZGERALD *at top.* LORD FITZGERALD *at bottom. Company ranged on each side. Servants waiting.*

CLOE.	I shall trouble Mr Stanly for a Little of the fried Cowheel & Onion.
STANLY.	Oh Madam, there is a secret pleasure in helping so amiable a Lady.
LADY H.	I assure you my Lord, Sir Arthur never touches wine; but Sophy will toss off a bumper I am sure to oblige your Lordship.
LORD F.	Elder wine or Mead, Miss Hampton?
SOPHY.	If it is equal to you, Sir, I should prefer some warm ale with a toast and nutmeg.
LORD F.	Two glasses of warmed ale with a toast and nutmeg.
MISS F.	I am afraid Mr Willoughby you take no care of yourself. I fear you don't meet with anything to your liking.
WILLOUGHBY.	Oh! Madam, I can want for nothing while there are red herrings on table.
LORD F.	Sir Arthur taste that Tripe. I think you will not find it amiss.
LADY H.	Sir Arthur never eats Tripe; 'tis too savoury for him you know my Lord.
MISS F.	Take away the Liver & Crow & bring in the suet pudding. (*a short pause*) Sir Arthur shan't I send you a bit of pudding?
LADY H.	Sir Arthur never eats suet pudding Ma'am. It is too high a dish for him. (*MW, 53*)

From this point in her youthful writings we can feel Jane Austen gradually losing her taste for downright burlesque and coming to care, almost despite herself, about her characters. A more sustained treatment of the relationship between young women and food comes in the epistolary *Lesley Castle*. One of the correspondents, Charlotte Luttrell, is a comically heightened forerunner of the unromantic and capable housekeeper Charlotte Lucas in *Pride and Prejudice*. Some of the themes which were to engage Jane Austen's serious attention well into the Steventon novels were now emerging, though still subject to a playful approach. In another kind of foreshadowing, Charlotte Luttrell is one of a pair of sisters, the one all high-mindedness, the other all pragmatism. The contrast is more humorous and exaggerated than in *Sense and Sensibility*. As Charlotte says herself, 'Never to be sure were there two more different Dispositions in the World. We both loved reading. *She* preferred Histories, and *I* Receipts. She loved drawing Pictures, and I drawing Pullets. No one could sing a better Song than she, and no one make a better Pye than I.' (*MW, 129*)

While Eloisa falls in love, Charlotte cooks. She writes to her friend:

Imagine how great the Disappointment must be to me, when you consider that after having laboured both by Night and by Day, in order to get the Wedding dinner ready by the time appointed, after having roasted Beef, Broiled Mutton and Stewed Soup enough to last the new-married couple through the Honeymoon, I had the mortification of finding that I had been Roasting, Broiling and Stewing both the Meat and Myself to no purpose. Indeed my dear Friend, I never remember suffering any vexation equal to what I experienced on last Monday when my sister came running to me in the store-room with her face as White as a Whipt syllabub, and told me that Hervey had been thrown from his Horse, had fractured his Scull and was pronounced by his surgeon to be in the most eminent [sic] danger. 'Good God! (said I) you dont say so? Why what in the name of Heaven will become of all the Victuals! We shall never be able to eat it while it is good. However, we'll call in the Surgeon to help us. I shall be able to manage the Sir-loin myself, my Mother will eat the soup, and You and the Doctor must finish the rest.' (*MW, 113*)

As Eloisa lies upon her bed in convulsions, Charlotte and her mother lament the waste of the provisions. 'We agreed that the best thing we could do was to begin eating them immediately, and accordingly we ordered up the cold Ham and Fowls, and instantly began our Devouring Plan on them with great Alacrity. We would have persuaded Eloisa to have taken a Wing of Chicken, but she would not be persuaded.' Indeed, she has given way to 'almost perfect Insensibility'. Charlotte tries to rouse her by arguing that she is herself the greater sufferer: 'For I shall not only be obliged to eat up all the Victuals I have dressed already, but must if Henry should recover (which however is not very likely) dress as much for you again; or should he die (as I suppose he will) I shall have to prepare a Dinner for you whenever you marry anyone else. So you see that tho' perhaps for the present it may afflict you to think of Henry's sufferings, Yet I dare say he'll die soon, and then his pain will be over and you will be easy, whereas my Trouble will last much longer for work as hard as I may, I am certain that the pantry cannot be cleared in less than a fortnight.' (*MW, 115*)

The family travel to Bristol for Eloisa's health, whence Charlotte reports:

> I have the satisfaction of informing you that we have every reason to imagine our pantry is by this time nearly cleared, as we left particular orders with the servants to eat as hard as they possibly could, and to call in a couple of Chairwomen to assist them. We brought a cold Pigeon pye, a cold turkey, a cold tongue, and half a dozen Jellies with us, which we were lucky enough with the help of our Landlady, her husband and their three children, to get rid of, in less than two days after our arrival. Poor Eloisa is still so very indifferent both in Health and Spirits, that I very much fear, the air of the Bristol downs, healthy as it is, has not been able to drive poor Henry from her remembrance. (*MW, 120*)

Charlotte's thoughts perpetually run on food. When dining out with another family in Bristol, 'We spent a very pleasant Day, and had a very good Dinner, tho' to be sure the Veal was terribly underdone, and the Curry had no seasoning. I could not help wishing all dinner-time that I had been at the dressing of it.' (*MW, 121*) Her reason for wishing to go to London and particularly Vauxhall is 'to see whether the cold Beef there is cut so thin as it is reported, for I have a sly suspicion that few people understand the art of cutting a slice of cold Beef so well as I do'. (*MW, 129*)

Charlotte is unique in Jane Austen, not only in actually cooking rather than superintending the cooking of the food, but in thinking and speaking figuratively. She describes her sister's face as 'white as a whipt syllabub'; she herself, when provoked, remains 'as cool as a cream-cheese'. (*MW, 130*) Jane Austen very rarely indulges in similes: the other famous example, remembered for its rarity, is the sudden accession of self-knowledge in Emma when 'it darted through her with the speed of an arrow, that Mr Knightley must marry nobody but herself'. (*E, 408*) It is amusing that the most practical character Jane Austen created should employ some of the devices of poetry; but after all it is very apt that her language should be the least abstract of any character's.

After the Juvenilia, Jane Austen imposed on herself a greater delicacy in her handling of food. Her art became more subtle, her characterisation less crude, her satire more oblique. But while there are no further greedy, food-obsessed anti-heroines to laugh at, the subject still engaged her interest sufficiently for her to give us one more portrait of the self-starving heroine of sensibility, treated now to the full weight of her mature judgement (which implies censure *and* sympathy). That heroine is Marianne Dashwood.

Refusal of food is one of the several ways in which Marianne endeavours to 'feed' and 'nourish' her grief at Willoughby's loss. (The verbs are Jane Austen's and contribute to the irony for the attentive reader.) It is perhaps not unreasonable that at dinner on the very day of Willoughby's sudden departure from Devonshire, Marianne 'could neither eat nor speak'. (*S & S, 82*) But at the next morning's breakfast she is equally 'unwilling to take any nourishment'. 'Her sensibility was potent enough!' remarks the narrator, underlining her point. (*S & S, 83*) On their first night in London, in a fever of hope for the arrival of Willoughby, Marianne 'could scarcely eat any dinner'. (*S & S, 161*) On the morning after being rebuffed by Willoughby, 'At breakfast she neither ate, nor attempted to eat anything'. (*S & S, 181*) When his letter is delivered later that morning, Elinor reaches her 'just in time to prevent her from falling on the floor, faint and giddy from a long want of proper rest and food; for it was many days since she had any appetite, and many nights since she had really slept; and now, when her mind was no longer supported by the fever of suspense, the consequence of all this was felt in an aching head, a weakened stomach, and a general nervous faintness'. (*S & S, 185*)

She does make an effort later that day to eat more at dinner than her sister expected; but at dessert Mrs Jennings' offer of sweetmeats, olives and dried cherries as a consolation for disappointed love is too much for her sensibility and drives her from the room. Thus, and for many further weeks, she persists in that negligence of her health of which she subsequently accuses herself and to which she attributes her serious illness later in the novel.

But though her self-reproaches on this subject are sincere, and sincerely endorsed by her author, the theme receives an ironic flourish at the end. The chastened Dashwood women being reunited at Barton Cottage, they hear from their servant Thomas, waiting at table, that he has seen Lucy and Mr Ferrars, newly married, in Exeter. Marianne has hysterics and retires to her room; Mrs Dashwood asks questions on Elinor's behalf; and then:

> Mrs Dashwood could think of no other question, and Thomas and the table-cloth, now alike needless, were soon afterwards dismissed. Marianne had already sent to say that she should eat nothing more. Mrs Dashwood's and Elinor's appetites were equally lost, and Margaret might think herself very well

off, that with so much uneasiness as both her sisters had lately experienced, so much reason as they had often had to be careless of their meals, she had never been obliged to go without her dinner before. (*S & S*, 355)

This is to be Jane Austen's final joke bounced off a literary convention which had amused her since youth, the incompatibility of fine feelings and a normal intake of food. Henceforward she was to look less satirically and more profoundly at the subject of eating disorders in young women. Even in Marianne's psyche there are other forces at work besides a misguided addiction to the cult of sensibility. Unlike the heroines of the Juvenilia, she is a complex person inhabiting a fully realised society. Her negligence of her health, therefore, is a response not only to the imaginary demands of sensibility (for which she is found culpable), but to the very real difficulties encountered by a young woman in a world organised largely by men for their own benefit (for which she is held to deserve a measure of sympathy). It is a world in which women, especially shielded young women of the respectable classes, are disabled by ignorance, immobility and impotence, while the decisions that affect their lives are made – deliberately or casually – by men. The difference between the freedom of action of a Willoughby and a Marianne is enormous. It is as a psychological and physiological truth, and not a matter of gender politics (though we may choose to see it that way), that Jane Austen presents Marianne and other disempowered women as seeking refuge in one aspect of their lives they *can* control, the consumption of food.

In the novels composed in her maturity at Chawton, Jane Austen shows both Fanny Price and Jane Fairfax suffering extended loss of appetite as they struggle to defend their personal integrity against male strategems. Fanny and Jane have much in common. Most notably, they are poor. They have no money of their own, and Jane Austen is always a realist in equating money with independence of action. They are also alike in owing large debts of gratitude for such educational and material advantages as they enjoy to people who are not their parents. Nothing is theirs of right; their social status is precarious. To all these disadvantages they add the usual handicaps associated with their youth and sex. Though the circumstances surrounding their struggles are very different, each is concerned with preserving her moral rectitude: Fanny in rejecting Mr Crawford against Sir Thomas's advice and his own sustained assault; Jane in first making allowances for Frank Churchill and then giving up her engagement to him when she thinks he is weary of it, accepting instead the post of governess. In clinging to what they think is morally right, both young women risk condemning themselves to a lifetime of real poverty (were Sir Thomas to cast Fanny off).

The trials of both Fanny and Jane are sustained and intensified over a period of weeks, and both have also to contend with the misery of being misunderstood even by those who seem to love them. They are at the mercy of male initiative; experience comes to them in a series of stabs or shocks. Isolated, immobilised, unable to express their anguish in any other way, Fanny and Jane reject food.

It is true that the food which Fanny rejects at Portsmouth is disgusting, while Jane, like Marianne, is tempted and coaxed to eat by all the delicacies her friends can procure. In the words of Miss Bates, 'Jane would hardly eat anything; Mr Perry recommended nourishing food; but everything they could command (and never had anybody such good neighbours) was distasteful' (*E, 391*), and of course she particularly refuses to touch the arrow-root sent by Emma. But the effect on the two young women is the same. During her residence in Portsmouth Fanny 'had lost ground as to health', 'starved [in] both mind and body', (*MP, 409, 413*) while Jane, whose appetite has been diminished for the whole duration of her secret engagement, loses even what little she had in the crisis: 'her health seemed for the moment completely deranged – appetite quite gone'. (*E, 389*)

Even Emma herself can see, when the truth about Jane's engagement is revealed, that Jane rejected Emma's food because Emma seemed her enemy. 'Emma could now imagine why her own attentions had been slighted . . . No doubt it had been from jealousy. – In Jane's eyes she had been a rival; and well might anything she could offer of assistance or regard be repulsed. An airing in the Hartfield cariage would have been the rack, and arrow-root from the Hartfield store-room must have been poison. She understood it all.' (*E, 403*) With this authority, readers too can understand that similar semi-conscious impulses might motivate Fanny and Marianne. It is not implausible to suggest that *in part* at least Fanny rejects her mother's food because her mother has rejected *her*; and that Marianne rejects Mrs Jennings' food to punish the woman for whom Mrs Jennings is an inadequate substitute, Marianne's own mother, who has ordered her to stay away from home when what Marianne desperately craves is the solace of Mrs Dashwood's 'personal sympathy'. Here are two very different mothers, Mrs Price and Mrs Dashwood, who fail their daughters in their most basic needs of love and/or food at a crisis point in their lives.

Such readings focus on a wholly female interplay of inadequacy, rejection, punishment and self-deprivation. But these dramas, so feeble and insignificant perhaps compared with the great male dramas going on in the world, are enacted within the context of a firmly established patriarchal system. They spring from that system and are a comment upon it.

The eating disorders of Marianne, Fanny and Jane may thus be said to mirror a degree of social disorder. The patriarchy, justifiable on the grounds that it provides a relatively stable framework for personal and social life (and it would be wrong to suggest that Jane Austen saw it only as oppressive), is, like any power system, in need of constant surveillance. To use a term with a modern ring, it should be self-regulatory. Those whom it makes strong must have due regard for those whom it renders weak. Especially vulnerable to any abuse are young women with scrupulous consciences, those who like Fanny Price strive to be of 'sound intellect and honest heart' despite having few weapons of defence or attack at their disposal. Jane Austen is quite clear that both sexes must be allowed the full play of their moral autonomy and that a healthy society values equally the contributions each can make. Danger arises when the sex which has the monopoly of money and mobility assumes that the pick of the world's pleasures must be therefore theirs to plunder. Marianne, Fanny and Jane are unfortunate in being desired and trifled with by men who have been used all their lives to having their own way. That these women, of no feeble character any of them, should be crushed to the point where their only resource seems to be self-destruction, must be a reflection on their society and on those in whom its power resides.

The attitude towards food of the remainder of Jane Austen's heroines can be expressed in just one word: indifference. By this I don't mean just that Jane Austen does not trouble to give them feelings on the subject, but that their positive indifference is at some point in the text clearly demonstrated and approved. Despite the author's preference for imperfect heroines who learn by their experiences to correct their faults, there are certain imperfections, and interest in food is one of them, which are for her intrinsically anti-heroic.

Jane Austen's heroines eat to keep themselves healthy, to be sociable, to conform. But not one of them ever anticipates or expresses pleasure in a meal, or admits to liking a particular food. Elinor is quite Marianne's equal in this respect. On the three-day journey from Devonshire to London, Mrs Jennings is 'disturbed that she could not make them choose their own dinners at the inn, nor extort a confession of their preferring salmon to cod, or boiled fowls to veal cutlets'. (*S & S, 160*) Mrs Jennings is behaving properly and kindly in the office of hostess, and it does seem rather rude of the sisters not to show more appreciation and interest; but this kind of high-minded indifference carries such a freight of authorial approval that their failure in politeness as guests is overlooked. On a later occasion Elinor behaves better. Mrs Jennings, in the goodness of her heart, brings a glass of Constantia wine for the suffering Marianne. Unwilling to disturb her sister, who has just consented to lie down to rest, and equally unwilling on this occasion to hurt Mrs Jennings' feelings, Elinor offers to drink the wine herself. That she acts out of unselfish consideration for another person, rather than for her own gratification, is unobtrusively but unmistakably signalled by her swallowing only 'the chief of it'. (*S & S, 198*)

Elizabeth Bennet's indifference to what she eats is conveyed when she replies to an enquiry from Mr Hurst that she prefers a plain dish to a ragout. This calls forth scorn in Mr Hurst, who is thereby censured not only for a taste for rich food but for talking about food at all (it is his only conversation with Elizabeth). Despite an abundance of energy and *joie de vivre* which must flow from health of body and mind, Elizabeth never betrays the slightest enjoyment of food . We might not expect her to join with Mr Collins in enumerating all the dishes at supper on the way back from Mrs Philips's, for that certainly would be vulgar and low; but neither will she take a daughterly interest in her mother's menu-making, escaping from such conversations as soon as she can, even when it is a question of what might please Darcy. In her attitude to food Elizabeth is perhaps better qualified to be a heroine than to be the mistress of a household.

The indifference to food of Catherine Morland is explicitly stated towards the end of *Northanger Abbey*. On her return home, her moping over Henry Tilney is mistaken by her mother for regret for the grander style of living at the Abbey. 'I did not quite like, at breakfast', says Mrs Morland, 'to hear you talk so much about the French bread at North-anger', to which Catherine replies, 'I am sure I do not care about the bread. It is all the same to me what I eat.' (*NA, 241*) This bears out what we have observed in her before, that she has been awed but not gratified by the magnificent table kept by the General. Catherine has a natural, healthy appetite – she feels hungry after a ball in Bath, and is not comfortable until she has appeased that hunger; she is hungry again on arrival at Northanger – but her tastes are simple. Her attitude to food is perfectly balanced, and she has achieved this, moreover, without giving the subject a moment's thought.

In *The Watsons* food is a repetitive motif, but the heroine Emma holds herself aloof from it – not consciously to display her superiority, but

simply as a fundamental of her nature. It is one way in which her greater
refinement than her sisters' is shown rather than told. Fanny Price has
already been discussed, but she does not starve herself throughout the
whole of *Mansfield Park*. Indeed, she is shown to have a healthy appetite
when happy, for example on the two-day journey with William from
Northamptonshire to Portsmouth, when 'a comfortable meal uniting
dinner with supper wound up the fatigues of the day'. (*MP, 376*) But she
is essentially indifferent to food. Even as a ten-year-old, on first arrival at
Mansfield Park, she cannot be consoled for the separation from her
home and family by a gooseberry tart.

This is promising for her status as heroine. The Bertrams might be
deceived by her tears and timidity into thinking she is insignificant, but
the reader, especially the reader familiar with Jane Austen's values, is
given this first clue to Fanny's innate refinement and strength of
character. That they are innate is spelled out very much later in the
novel, during the Portsmouth scenes, when Fanny is spared 'so horrible
an evil' as Henry Crawford's accepting her father's invitation to dinner:

> To have had him join their family dinner-party and see all their deficiencies
> would have been dreadful! Rebecca's cookery and Rebecca's waiting, and
> Betsey's eating at table without restraint, and pulling everything about as she
> chose, were what Fanny herself was not yet enough inured to, for her often to
> make a tolerable meal. *She* was nice only from natural delicacy, but *he* had been
> brought up in a school of luxury and epicurism. (*MP, 407*)

This seems to rule out Mansfield as the primary influence, yet only a few
pages later, it is given more weight:

> She was so little equal to Rebecca's puddings and Rebecca's hashes, brought to
> table as they all were, with such accompaniments of half-cleaned plates, and not
> half-cleaned knives and forks, that she was very often constrained to defer her
> heartiest meal, till she could send her brothers in the evening for biscuits and
> buns. After being nursed up at Mansfield, it was too late in the day to be
> hardened at Portsmouth; and though Sir Thomas, had he known all, might
> have thought his niece in the most promising way of being starved, both in
> mind and body, into a much juster value for Mr Crawford's good company and
> good fortune, he would probably have feared to push his experiment farther,
> lest she might die under the cure. (*MP, 413*)

Modern literary theory is very interested in finding whether Jane Austen
upholds or subverts (albeit perhaps unconsciously) the established social
system of her time, with all its injustices to modern eyes.[2] The question
whether Fanny's niceness is acquired or inborn is pertinent to such an

enquiry. If her niceness has been acquired at Mansfield, this argues for a reading which posits an effete nobility and gentry invigorated and reinvented by the values and attitudes of the class below. In Fanny's quick aptitude for acquiring the tastes that have formerly been confined to the upper classes, the bourgeoisie are shown to have the capability as well as the requisite energy to play their part in the leadership of their society. If, however, Fanny's delicacy is inborn, then a more conservative reading follows, in which a Cinderella figure ascends to the position from which she has been wrongfully excluded, and the old order goes on as before, fortified against attack from without by this recognition and admittance of one of its natural and most supportive members.

In favour of the first reading are Sir Thomas's reflections – all the more weighty because they come right at the end of the book – on the 'advantages of early hardship and discipline, and the consciousness of being born to struggle and endure'. (*MP, 473*) In favour of the second is the statement that Susan too has 'an innate taste for the genteel and well-appointed'. (*MP, 419*) These are not mutually exclusive statements, of course, but they do suggest differing interpretations of the class theme.

Whichever reading is preferred – and the fact that both are possible only proves the inexhaustible interest *Mansfield Park* continues to have for all ages and critical preoccupations – Fanny's delicacy with respect to eating is certainly established and approved. But it is characteristic of this novel's concern with the interplay between materiality and morality that its heroine is not so ethereal as to pretend to be able to do without food absolutely. In Portsmouth Fanny Price has to resort to such mundane objects as biscuits and buns to appease her irrepressible hunger. All art is selective and here Jane Austen gives a detail which she might have been expected to withhold. She makes one of her rare descents to the mundane in the interests of balance between the spiritual and the physical, for Fanny's temptation is concerned with both.

There is no high-flown ethereality in *Emma* either, for this is a novel replete with food. Of all the heroines Emma is the one who is most often concerned with food, simply by virtue of her position as housekeeper of Hartfield and lady bountiful of Highbury. But it is one of the points in this faulty heroine's favour that she is as indifferent to what she eats as she is indifferent to her own beauty. We never see Emma talking or thinking about food except in relation to other people.

By contrast, Anne Elliot in *Persuasion* has absolutely no dealings of any sort with food. (Which is not to say she is never present at a meal, but she is never shown speaking or thinking about any aspect of the subject.) This novel has fewer mentions of food than any other, reflecting the want of nourishment, for the soul and the emotions, of the inhospitable world which Anne inhabits. Under the circumstances her indifference to food has little opportunity, except negatively, of being manifest; her 'slender form' is the best proof of her abstemiousness.

Anne's slim figure is contrasted with that of her neighbour on the sofa, Mrs Musgrove, whose 'comfortable substantial size' is 'infinitely more fitted by nature to express good cheer and good humour, than tenderness and sentiment'. Here Jane Austen reverts to the notion of her youth, that the essential concomitant of feeling much is eating little. Against her own better judgement and knowledge of the world, it would seem, she succumbs for a moment to the potent dictates of sensibility, chiding herself for being irrational even as she writes. Mrs Musgrove has been indulging in 'large fat sighings' over the death of a son; the narrator remarks:

> Personal size and mental sorrow have certainly no necessary proportions. A large bulky figure has as good a right to be in deep affliction, as the most graceful set of limbs in the world. But, fair or not fair, there are unbecoming conjunctions, which reason will patronize in vain, – which taste cannot tolerate, – which ridicule will seize. (*P, 68*)

Jane Austen's last heroine, Charlotte Heywood of *Sanditon*, is able to demonstrate her simple tastes in food during the very comic scene in which Arthur Parker boils his cocoa and butters his toast; Charlotte, very decided in her preference of tea over cocoa, and toast with only 'a reasonable quantity of butter spread over it', is part amused and part horrified by her companion's strong dark cocoa and 'great dab' of butter put on the toast at the moment of its entering his mouth. (*MW, 418*)

'A good deal of Earthy Dross hung about him', is the rather strange phrase used of Arthur Parker. He is 'by no means so spiritualized' as his hypochondriac sisters – who are thin, whereas he is 'broad made and lusty'. (*MW, 413*) With the exception of a few comfortable middle-aged women like Mrs Musgrove and Mrs Jennings, whose size does indeed reflect their usual 'good cheer and good humour', all the fatness and certainly all the epicurism and gluttony in the novels belong to men.

When encountered in the younger male characters, greed is merely a matter of wrong priorities and self-indulgence, deplorable but relatively harmless. There is something almost endearing about the hearty appetite of Arthur Parker, perhaps because it is amusing to watch him outwit his sisters in getting hold of the good things he craves, perhaps because not only does he boil his cocoa and butter his toast for himself, rather than expecting a woman to do this for him, but he is eager to share his pleasures with his companion.

Charlotte Heywood, however, as a marriageable young woman who must rely on her wits to ensure her best chance of future happiness, is quite rightly less ready than the reader to indulge his foibles. For their attitude to food is one way in which the worth of the young men who approach them can be evaluated by the heroines. Mr Collins is a 'heavy young man' who relishes Mrs Philips's suppers and the dinners of Mrs Bennet and Lady Catherine; guilty of talking about these meals before, during and after them, he is condemned out of his own mouth as well as by the evidence of his figure. The same is true of John Thorpe, 'a stout young man' with 'an ungraceful form' who boasts of the amount of drinking done at Oxford. Alike in thinking well of themselves, neither man has any chance of succeeding with the heroine he courts.

There is no anti-hero in *Sense and Sensibility* for Elinor Dashwood to spurn, but Mr Palmer plays a like role in serving as contrast to the man she loves. Observing, at Cleveland, that the master of the house is 'nice in his eating', Elinor is 'not sorry to be driven by the observation of his Epicurism, his selfishness and his conceit, to rest with complacency on the remembrance of Edward's generous temper, simple taste, and diffident feelings'. (*S & S, 305*)

It is hardly necessary to say that none of the real heroes shows any interest in food, being the true counterparts of the heroines in this respect. Mr Knightley especially is the close counterpart of Emma, concerned as he is with food only in relation to other people. Mrs Bennet has hard work extracting any comment about her food from Mr Darcy; Edmund Bertram, returning to the Park from the Parsonage with his head full of Mary Crawford's attractions, does not attend as he ought to his Aunt Norris's enquiries about the dinner; Frederick Wentworth's only discourse about food is in relation to the habits on board ship, where he is keen to stress civilised standards. It is made plain that Henry Tilney evidently does not share his father's concern for good dinners. But only of Edward Ferrars is it actually stated that one of his virtues is 'simple taste'.

Emma is the exception to this quickness among the heroines in discounting as husband material any man who shows too much interest in food (though it is true she is judging for Harriet, not herself, when her judgement undoubtedly would be more discriminating). She is oblivious to the signs which should tell her of Mr Elton's essential selfishness and small-mindedness. Carried away by her own fancies, she registers but does not properly reflect upon his excessive eagerness for dining out, and is disappointed but not repelled to find him regaling Harriet with minute details of his dinner the night before:

> Mr Elton was speaking with animation, Harriet listening with a very pleased attention; and Emma . . . was beginning to think how she might draw back a little more, when they both looked around, and she was obliged to join them.
>
> Mr Elton was still talking, still engaged in some interesting detail; and Emma experienced some disappointment when she found he was only giving his fair companion an account of yesterday's party at his friend Cole's, and that she was come in herself for the Stilton cheese, the north Wiltshire, the butter, the cellery, the beet-root and all the dessert.
>
> 'This would soon have led to something better of course,' was her consoling reflection . . . . (*E, 89*)

Henry Crawford is another potential marriage partner against whom the charge of over-attention to what he eats is levelled: Fanny reflects that he has been 'brought up in a school of luxury and epicurism'. (*MP, 407*) But however this might be, and though good eating might well form part of the *menus plaisirs* which his sister cannot imagine him contracting, Henry has too much intelligence to allow any such weakness to show. There is certainly no evidence of it in his words or deeds during the action of the novel. Nor would it escape Mary's censure if she suspected any such tendency, beyond reasonable limits. We know how much she deplores its excesses both in her brother-in-law and in her uncle, the Admiral, whom she warns Henry against resembling. The charge against Henry may therefore be unfounded, a product of Fanny's sensitivity to the deficiencies of her Portsmouth home rather than a reflection of the truth. On the other hand possibly Fanny is intuiting a flaw which will manifest itself when youth is over. Having been self-indulgent all his life, and with no exertions necessary to earn a living, Henry may well lapse gradually into a man for whom food comes high on the list of pleasures. Indeed, the particularity of his own sister's warning suggests the reality of the danger: 'My dearest Henry, the advantage to you of getting away from the Admiral before your manners are hurt by the contagion of his, before you have contracted any of his foolish opinions, or learnt to sit over your dinner, as if it were the best blessing of life!' (*MP, 296*)

For the comfort and complacency of married life and middle age are likely to exacerbate any self-indulgence with respect to eating in the male. This is all the more reprehensible because a married man has the happiness of other people in his keeping. If the master of the house is irritable or demanding about his daily meals, it is his wife and children who will suffer. A harmless if unattractive foible in youth thus becomes a serious defect in a husband who cares more for the gratification of his appetite than for the peace and harmony of his home.

Mr Hurst, who lives 'only to eat, drink and play at cards', and Mr Palmer, who is 'nice in his eating', are two youngish married men who fall well below Jane Austen's standards for a husband – although, as their wives are vacant and silly, our feelings are not much engaged on their behalf. Mr Hurst and Mr Palmer are no more than cameo portraits, comic diversions for the reader and minor contributors to their respective heroines' education.

It is in the characters of General Tilney and Dr Grant that Jane Austen gives sustained critical attention to two men who, through love of eating, render the atmosphere in their homes unpleasant, thereby violating her principal rule of behaviour, that it is the duty of every individual to guard from unnecessary suffering those with whom he or she lives and associates. In these two characters, wealthy, powerful, middle-aged and male – everything that Marianne, Fanny and Jane are not – she attacks the excesses of patriarchy from the opposite angle, showing how those to whom much is given are liable – and able – to demand more. The amount of rich food that disappears down the throats of the Doctor and the General is in analogy to the amount of the world's goods and esteem that they expect and enjoy as of right. Nor is it only in eating, but in forcing others to dance attendance on their eating, that they delight in displaying their power. The huge appetites and selfish demands which these men impose upon their hapless families are as much a symptom as female self-starvation of a social system which Jane Austen regards as not always under such good regulation as it might be.

General Tilney has children and Dr Grant has a wife – and both have house-guests – to be made uncomfortable by their lack of self-control. Unlike Mr Hurst, both are intelligent men who ought to be capable of discerning that food is too trivial a matter to be worthy of their time and attention. Equipped with the learning and leisure for serious reflection, and mature in years, they ought to have acquired sufficient knowledge of themselves and their duty to get their feelings under better government. They are men of authority in their own homes, and some importance, even example, in their neighbourhoods, which should further act as a brake on their behaviour. That all these considerations weigh so little with them in comparison with the fleeting pleasures of the table lays them open to the severest censure.

Greed might be a more tolerable failing if the indulgence of it made its possessors cheerful and contented, like Mrs Jennings, who is fat and at ease with herself; she is not ashamed to recall her visit to Delaford with the words: 'Lord! How Charlotte and I did stuff the only time we were there!' (*S & S, 197*) But with the exception of Arthur Parker, who does relish his food, obsession with good eating seems to have the reverse effect on Jane Austen's male characters. It makes them irritable, hyper-critical and morose. General Tilney does not straightforwardly enjoy food, he has to make a perpetual fuss about it. Punctuality, formality, show, abundance and the best of everything are required at every one of his meals, at home or away, however inappropriate or unnecessary. His obsession with eating takes a dual path: the gratification of his own palate; and the acknowledgement, by other people, of the superiority of his table and taste.

When the Tilneys and Catherine Morland stop at Petty France on their way to Northanger from Bath, they have to 'eat without being hungry' (it is only two hours since they had an ample breakfast); and the meal itself, including loitering about waiting for it to be cooked, wastes another two hours. Instead of being content, like the Bennet sisters at the George, with 'such cold meat as an inn larder usually affords', or like Willoughby at Marlborough hastily swallowing some cold beef and porter so that the journey can be quickly resumed, General Tilney must order a meal to be specially prepared. This is done without any defer-ence to the wishes of the rest of the party, for he never consults his children's wishes and makes only nominal obeisance to Catherine's. The interval at Petty France is tedious and uncomfortable to them, but even to himself it does not appear to bring any pleasure. 'His discontent at whatever the inn afforded, and his angry impatience at the waiters, made Catherine grow every moment more in awe of him, and appeared to lengthen the two hours into four.' (*NA, 156*)

Though he has already eaten well twice that day, on the first evening at Northanger his excessive concern with punctuality leads him into an unforgivable breach of manners. As Catherine and Eleanor descend from dressing, 'General Tilney was pacing the drawing-room, his watch in his hand, and having, on the very instant of their entering, pulled the bell with violence, ordered "Dinner to be on table *directly*".' (*NA, 165*) Strict punctuality at meals might proceed from greed or from tyranny; in General Tilney Jane Austen shows how closely connected the two defects are, or can be, in a man. Avid for the consumption of food, he also seeks to consume and destroy the autonomy of all who come under his sway. He is so used to exercising complete power over his children, his servants, and presumably once his regiment, that in his anger he forgets what is due to a guest, though later 'recovering his politeness'.

The General is frequently guilty of what Darcy would call 'the indirect boast' in his often-expressed and quite ludicrous fears that his table has nothing to tempt Catherine's appetite. Though ostensibly and ostentatiously so desirous of her comfort, he greatly diminishes it by his excessive attentions and the bullying way in which he extracts praise from her.

In what he says about eating, and all the paraphernalia that goes with that activity, he is untruthful and insincere. He professes to be 'careless' about his surroundings when he dines, though the dining-parlour at Northanger is enormous and 'fitted up in a style of luxury and expense'; and to be 'without vanity of that kind' in the choice of china, though the 'elegance' of his is sufficient to force itself on Catherine's notice. (*NA, 175*) Having taken Catherine on a tour of 'a village of hot-houses' and 'a whole parish at work' in the kitchen gardens, 'he then modestly owned that, "without any ambition of that sort himself – without any solicitude about it – he did believe them to be unrivalled in the kingdom. If he had a hobby-horse, it was *that*. He loved a garden. Though careless enough in most matters in eating, he loved good fruit – or if he did not, his friends and children did".' (*NA, 178*) This last phrase is quite wonderfully hypocritical. How much of what he says does the General himself believe?

One of Jane Austen's skills is to find a voice and a distinctive syntax for each of her characters, and to carry it on consistently, without the least hint of caricature. Consider the phrases General Tilney uses when made voluble by his favourite subject. 'Vanity of that kind' is echoed by 'ambition of that sort'; and having declared of his garden that, 'If he had a hobby-horse, it was *that*', once indoors he avers, 'If he had a vanity, it was in the arrangement of his offices'.

The money and labour that are expended at Northanger to produce dinner for three or four people each day are out of all proportion. Having marvelled at the hot-houses and kitchen gardens, and the number of outdoor servants, Catherine is taken into the kitchens.

> The General's improving hand had not loitered here: every modern invention to facilitate the labour of the cooks, had been adopted within this, their spacious theatre . . . The purposes for which a few shapeless pantries and a comfortless scullery were deemed sufficient at Fullerton, were here carried on in appropriate divisions, commodious and roomy. The number of servants continually appearing, did not strike her less than the number of their offices. (*NA, 183–84*)

The General's claim that the purpose of his improvements has been to soften the labours of his servants is as little to be believed as his assertion that the hot-house fruit is grown for his children's benefit. The extent to which he dominates his children is particularly well illustrated in the excursion to Henry's parsonage at Woodston. The General expressly says to his son, 'You are not to put yourself at all out of your way. Whatever you may happen to have in the house will be enough. I think I can answer for the young ladies making allowance for a bachelor's table.' (*NA, 210*) When, therefore, Henry sets off to Woodston two days earlier than he would otherwise have gone, Catherine asks him why.

> 'Why! – How can you ask the question? – Because no time is to be lost in frightening my old housekeeper out of her wits – because I must go and prepare a dinner for you to be sure.'
> 'Oh! not seriously!'
> 'Aye, and sadly too – for I had much rather stay.'
> 'But how can you think of such a thing, after what the General said? When he so particularly desired you not to give yourself any trouble, because *anything* would do.'
> Henry only smiled. 'I am sure it is quite unnecessary upon your sister's account and mine. You must know it to be so; and the General made such a point of your providing nothing extraordinary: – besides, if he had not said half so much as he did, he has always such an excellent dinner at home, that sitting down to a middling one for one day could not signify.'
> 'I wish I could reason like you, for his sake and my own. Good bye.' (*NA, 211*)

Catherine is forced to accept that Henry understands his father best. When they do sit down to dinner at Woodston, after a day in which the General has been gratified by the apparent success of his schemes for the match between the two young people, Catherine 'could not but observe that the abundance of the dinner did not seem to create the smallest astonishment in the General; nay, that he was even looking at the side-table for cold meat which was not there. His son and daughter's observations were of a different kind. They had seldom seen him eat so heartily at any table but his own; and never before known him so little disconcerted by the melted butter's being oiled.' (*NA, 215*)

It is one of the triumphs of Jane Austen's art that she never repeats a character. Though General Tilney and Dr Grant are ultimately alike in their epicurism, hypocrisy and carelessness of other people's feelings, each has developed these unpleasant characteristics in his own dist- inctive way. One of the most fundamental differences between them is that Dr Grant is idle where General Tilney is active and officious – as a result of which, among other things, Dr Grant is stout while the General still has a fine figure. In these two portraits Jane Austen shows how apparently very different styles of men can use food to manipulate and tyrannise over their immediate family.

Dr Grant is very justly described by his acute sister-in-law after she has been living in his house for a month:

'Though Dr Grant is most kind and obliging to me, and though he is really a gentleman, and I dare say a good scholar and clever, and often preaches good sermons, and is very respectable, *I* see him to be an indolent selfish bon vivant, who must have his palate consulted in everything, who will not stir a finger for the convenience of any one, and who, moreover, if the cook makes a blunder, is out of humour with his excellent wife.' (*MP, 111*)

From the point in this sentence where Mary begins to give her own observations, these are all heavy charges, but it is in the last phrase that the weight of condemnation falls. For Jane Austen, morality is not only a matter of personal responsibility between an individual and his conscience or his Maker; it is more social than that, it is a matter of how the conduct impinges on the lives of other people. Even were Mrs Grant *not* an excellent wife, it would be Dr Grant's duty to restrain his own feelings out of consideration for hers; as it is, she could not be more forbearing and cheerful, or more attentive to his wishes; she certainly gets from him less than her desserts, but at least she has the satisfaction of knowing her own conjugal manners are beyond reproach.

Of course it might be better for her husband's soul were he to be brought up short by a gentle remonstrance on her part. By getting away with behaving badly he falls into the habit of doing so, and is perhaps unaware of how unjust he is to her at times (not that that is any excuse, particularly in a clergyman). His irritability having been humoured, he is incapable of constraining it even when he has guests in the house. If a man owes one kind of duty to his wife, he owes a lesser but still important duty to those under his roof. Glad though he is to have Mr and Miss Crawford as his guests (characteristically because it gives him the excuse of opening a bottle of claret each day that Mr Crawford stays, and the opportunity of sitting over the wine with another gentleman after the ladies have withdrawn, a masculine pleasure denied the man who dines alone with his wife) – glad though he is of their company, he is guilty of making them uncomfortable by the uncontrolled gloom into which a bad dinner throws him.

Using two similar episodes, Jane Austen repeats but intensifies Dr Grant's offences. In the first instance, the Crawfords walk up to the Park after dinner on a starlit August night to escape the atmosphere at the

Parsonage. As Mary describes it, 'Henry and I were partly driven out this very evening, by a disappointment about a green goose, which he [Dr Grant] could not get the better of. My poor sister was forced to stay and bear it.' (*MP, 111*) To make your guests feel so uncomfortable that they seek refuge elsewhere, to oblige your wife to listen to an evening-full of complaint, and all because of one disappointing edible, is very bad.

Distress to an even greater number of people ensues from a similar incident (and another bird) two months later. On the evening of the first (and last) regular rehearsal of the first three acts of *Lovers' Vows* at Mansfield, Mrs Grant fails to turn up with the Crawfords. 'Dr Grant, professing an indisposition, for which he had little credit with his fair sister-in-law, could not spare his wife. "Dr Grant is ill," said she, with mock solemnity. "He had been ill ever since he did not eat any of the pheasant today. He fancied it tough – sent away his plate – and has been suffering ever since".' (*MP, 171*) This time, not only is Mrs Grant subjected to another miserable evening, but Dr Grant's selfishness inconveniences the entire cast of the play, and indeed would have made the rehearsal impossible had not Fanny been prevailed upon to stand in. Fanny herself is perhaps the worst sufferer on the occasion, despite the fact that she would seem to have so little connection with anything Dr Grant may choose to do in his own home. But this is how it is with selfish behaviour, Jane Austen demonstrates: the perpetrator does not take the trouble to imagine how far the consequences of his action may spread.

That the rehearsal should not be taking place at all if of course no justification, for Dr Grant has never, in his role as clergyman of the parish, advised caution to the young people. He can have no moral disapprobation for theatricals, or his wife would not have become involved. His spurious indigestion is not a sly attempt to save them from sin.

A goose, a pheasant and a turkey – Dr Grant's character is revealed to us through poultry. One of Mrs Grant's home-reared turkeys has been killed just the right number of days ahead for it to hang and acquire full flavour for Sunday's dinner, when Dr Grant will appreciate it more 'after the fatigues of the day'. (He does virtually nothing on the other six days of the week.) But the weather turns warmer than Mrs Grant had calculated on for November, and the turkey has to be cooked before Sunday. As it happens, Mrs Grant makes a little dinner-party of it and Dr Grant is all good humour; but meanwhile Mrs Grant has to contend with some uneasiness. For the trouble with a moody companion is that the moods have always to be anticipated though they might not always appear. With a few economical touches, and without the slightest complaint on Mrs Grant's part (for that would be a breach of decorum, and therefore inconsistent with her character), her sufferings as a wife are suggested. The unusual occurrence of a sensible woman talking in company about food – and reverting to the subject later – shows the disturbance of her mind. It is notable too that she takes care to break the news of the turkey's fate to her husband while there are other people present to restrain any remonstrance he might otherwise have made.

I will return to this extraordinarily rich passage, which serves not only to illustrate the respective characters of the Grants and of their marriage, but to contrast the attitudes towards housekeeping (and therefore the moral worth) of the two sisters, in a later chapter. Before leaving it here two things remain to be said. The first is that, besides doing all this, the incident forwards the plot by introducing the dinner which brings Henry and Fanny together, and which therefore brings Fanny the test of her life (hitherto she has been little more than a bystander). The second returns to Dr Grant's character and the touch of hypocrisy which his answer to his wife's confession about the turkey displays. We have not, hitherto, heard Dr Grant *speak* about food, except to quarrel with Mrs Norris over the apricot, for most of his ill humour has come to us by report. That is artistically correct, for it is the effect of his ill humour on others which matters most about his part in the novel, especially as the heroine Fanny is not often in proximity to him. But Jane Austen knows her portrait is incomplete without allowing him to reveal the true proportions of his insincerity, or self-delusion, in direct speech. The repetition at the beginning of his answer is masterly, suggesting an impatience with the subject which is of course very far from being his true feeling:

> 'Very well, very well,' cried Dr Grant, 'all the better. I am glad to hear you have anything so good in the house. But Miss Price and Mr Edmund Bertram, I dare say, would take their chance. We none of us want to hear the bill of fare. A friendly meeting, and not a fine dinner, is all we have in view. A turkey or a goose, or a leg of mutton, or whatever you and your cook choose to give us.' (*MP*, 215)

It must give every reader satisfaction that Dr Grant's death (which frees the living of Mansfield for Fanny and Edmund so opportunely) is the direct consequence of his greed. The satisfaction is doubled when one contemplates that this great event in Dr Grant's history is given no more than seventeen words ('when Dr Grant had brought on apoplexy and death, by three great institutionary dinners in one week . . . ') in the middle of one of the longest sentences in the book, 102 words altogether, devoted mainly to the destiny of his sister-in-law Mary Crawford. (*MP, 469*)

Mrs Grant's satisfaction is unknowable. But Tom Bertram had predicted from the very first sight of Dr Grant that 'he was a short-neck'd, apoplectic sort of fellow, and, plied well with good things, would soon pop off'. (*MP, 24*) If Tom can see it, so perhaps can Mrs Grant. The good things have not been wanting.

Chapter Five

The Sweets of Housekeeping

Food itself is morally neutral in Jane Austen. If eating is a suspect activity because it gratifies the self, to provide food for other people is commendable. Charitable giving to the poor is perhaps the most obvious example of such provision, but it is a part of life largely ignored by Jane Austen outside of *Emma*. This is not because Jane Austen thinks charity unimportant, but rather because she finds little in it to exercise her powers of discrimination. Charity is one-sided; to practise it is an obligation upon the classes of whom she writes. It therefore lacks not value but subtlety for her. Much more interesting, much more fruitful for her art, are the ways in which people form and keep the social contracts which they enter into with one another in their own homes.

There are two situations in which her characters might contract to be providers of food: as a housekeeper, or as a host. The housekeeper's commitment is usually for life, the host's freshly entered into with each invitation issued. It is in how judiciously, generously and unobtrusively the duties attaching to these respective offices are performed that Jane Austen finds rewarding material for her psychological and moral insights.

This chapter will look at the domestic establishments in some of Jane Austen's fictional houses, at the good and bad housekeepers among her characters, and at the contribution which the theme of housekeeping makes to the meaning and structure of some of the novels. The parallel theme of hospitality will be examined in the following chapter.

The term housekeeper requires a little explanation. In her correspondence Jane Austen occasionally uses the word of herself and other women of her class. She certainly understood it to mean the person, be it mistress or servant, who has the direction of a household in her hands. In the novels it is applied only twice to a gentlewoman – by Mrs Morland to her daughter Catherine and by the narrator to the elderly Miss Dashwood who dies before the action of *Sense and Sensibility* begins. This shows the fluidity of the term, since almost certainly there was a paid housekeeper too at Norland, though probably not (after Henry's marriage) at Woodston Parsonage. Much more regularly in the fiction the word is used to refer to the female upper servant who administered household affairs and superintended the work of the maids, and who is often prominent enough in the narrative (and in the life of the family) to be named. Longbourn has Mrs Hill, Pemberley Mrs Reynolds, Sotherton Mrs Whitaker, Donwell Mrs Hodges, and so forth.

Not every mistress of an establishment in Jane Austen's novels, however, is able to afford a housekeeper to take over her cares. Many of them have to be their own housekeepers in the fullest sense. It is worth remarking that if the great divide among Jane Austen's male characters is between those who enjoy an unearned income and those who have to work at a profession, her married women are correspondingly distinguished between those who have no choice but to take an active part in the management of their households and those who, having initially laid down the ground rules, need have little more involvement than an early-morning consultation with the servant housekeeper about the menus for the day. Even so the mistress of the house is ultimately responsible for its smooth running. In this more limited sense she may be said to be a housekeeper, though without the additional duty which belongs to her poorer sisters of making a modest income go as far as possible.

It is of course financial circumstances, not taste and aptitude, which determine on which side of the labour divide a woman's life will fall. It behoves her therefore to choose a husband whose home and income will establish her in a position suitable to her abilities. Elizabeth Bennet understands this when she relinquishes Wickham because of his poverty, long before anything else is known against him. In rejecting Mr Collins, and later in visiting his home, she has not a moment's regret for the pleasures of housekeeping in a parsonage which Charlotte is able to enjoy 'whenever Mr Collins could be forgotten'. It is not extravagance in Elizabeth (as a married woman she saves from her allowance in order to send occasional gifts to Lydia) but impatience with the details of housekeeping which prompt her to avoid a situation which would involve her too much with food. She is 'above' either economy or show; that is why she will not take an interest in her mother's menus.

Mary Crawford is another young woman who knows she has no turn for housekeeping, even though, unlike Elizabeth's, her heart leads her in an inconvenient direction, and she has a much greater struggle in knowing what to do. It may be thought that *every* woman would prefer leisure to care. Not so. Both Lady Catherine de Bourgh and Mrs Norris, in their different spheres, have insufficient real duties to absorb their energies, and as a consequence bustle about criticising and interfering in other people's homes. Both would be better members of society had life given them real, everyday difficulties to contend with.

The most admirable women are adaptable to either mode of living. One feels that Elinor Dashwood would be as faultless in the role of great lady as she is in that of a (relatively) poor parson's wife. Her mother has set her an excellent example. Undoubtedly Mrs Dashwood enjoyed the services of a housekeeper at Stanhill and Norland but, after twenty years' marriage in comfortable circumstances, she must suddenly become her own housekeeper at Barton, a role she accepts without complaint and fulfils, as far as we are permitted to see, with competence and grace.

The 'two maids and a man' with whom the Dashwood women are 'speedily provided from amongst those who had formed their establishment at Norland' – the 'speedily' implying that anyone who has worked for Mrs Dashwood is happy to follow her even to a humble cottage three counties away, probably never to see their own relations again – correspond to the Austens' own establishment in Bath. 'We plan having a steady Cook, & a young giddy Housemaid, with a sedate, middle aged Man, who is to undertake the double office of Husband to the former & sweetheart to the latter. – No children of course to be allowed on either side', Jane had joked to Cassandra. (*L, 99*) Though there is a cook at Barton Cottage, it would seem that as at Chawton it is the daughters of the house who make breakfast, from the circumstance of Edward's not expecting them to walk with him to the village before that meal. The Dashwoods' manservant is Thomas, whose duties include waiting at table and running errands – perhaps shopping – in Exeter, four miles away.

The other modest establishment in *Sense and Sensibility* is that of which Edward Ferrars is to be master. In varying guises it is projected several times in the course of the narrative. When his engagement to Lucy Steele is first made public, Mrs Jennings quickly decides what their income and style of life will be:

> There is no reason on earth why Mr Edward and Lucy should not marry; for I am sure Mrs Ferrars may afford to do very well by her son, and though Lucy has next to nothing herself, she knows better than anybody how to make the most of everything; and I dare say, if Mrs Ferrars would only allow him five

hundred a-year, she would make as good an appearance with it as anybody else would with eight. Lord! How snug they might live in such another cottage as yours – or a little bigger – with two maids and two men; and I believe I could help them to a housemaid, for my Betty has a sister out of place, that would fit them exactly. (*S & S*, 260).

But after Edward's mother throws him off and he decides to be ordained without seeming to have any chance of preferment, Mrs Jennings changes her picture to keep pace with the change in his income:

Wait for his having a living! – aye, we all know how *that* will end; – they will wait a twelvemonth, and finding no good comes of it, will set down upon a curacy of fifty pounds a-year, with the interest of his two thousand pounds, and what little matter Mr Steele and Mr Pratt can give her. – Then they will have a child every year! and Lord help 'em! how poor they will be! – I must see what I can give them towards furnishing their house. Two maids and two men indeed! – as I talked of t'other day. – No, no, they must get a stout girl of all works. – Betty's sister would never do for them *now*. (*S & S*, 277).

The next stage in Edward's fluctuating fortunes is the presentation, by Colonel Brandon, of the living of Delaford, worth £200 p.a. The Colonel considers that this will do no more than make him comfortable as a bachelor and will not afford the means to marry. Mrs Jennings and Elinor disagree, and Elinor has a vision of Edward and Lucy in their parsonage, she 'the active, contriving manager, uniting at once a desire of smart appearance, with the utmost frugality, and ashamed to be suspected of half her economical practices'. (*S & S*, 357) This is on an income of £300 (for Edward's fortune brings in £100 p.a.). When Lucy's perfidy releases Edward to propose instead to Elinor, his projected income rises to £350, for Elinor also has £1,000 to bring in £50 interest. However, 'they were neither of them quite enough in love to think that three hundred and fifty pounds a-year would supply them with the comforts of life'. (*S & S*, 369) Rather than descend to the 'economical practices' for which she would criticise Lucy, Elinor prefers not to marry. But her wishes are moderate. When Mrs Ferrars relents and gives Edward the sum of £10,000 which will bring in precisely the additional £500 p.a. which Mrs Jennings first predicted for him, yielding a total income of £850 p.a., and with a glebe farm to supply at least some of their food, Edward and Elinor settle to a comfortable if hard-working and economical life. Most importantly, perhaps, it is an honest and independent life; Elinor's critical vision of Lucy had included her scrounging and sponging off Colonel Brandon and other wealthy friends.

Jane Austen's nieces Elizabeth (born 27 January 1800) and Marianne
(born 15 September 1801), daughters of Edward Austen, afterwards Knight
(Jane Austen Memorial Trust)

All the other households in *Sense and Sensibility* are supported by comfortable incomes: Norland, Barton Park, Cleveland, Delaford and the London home of Mrs Jennings. All have their servant-housekeepers. As *mistress*-housekeepers, Mrs Jennings is contrasted with her daughter, Mrs Palmer. Each is shown returning to her home after a lengthy period of absence. Mrs Jennings immediately involves herself in domestic affairs. Apologising to Colonel Brandon for some delay in receiving him, she gives a vivid picture of her activity: 'I have been forced to look about me a little, and settle my matters; for it is a long while since I have been at home, and you know one has always a world of little odd things to do after one has been away for any time; and then I have had Cartwright to settle with – Lord, I have been as busy as a bee since dinner!' (*S & S, 163*).

Charlotte Palmer's chief business with her housekeeper, on first arrival at Cleveland, is to show her the new baby; that done, she spends the next few hours irresponsibly

> in lounging round the kitchen garden, examining the bloom upon its walls, and listening to the gardener's lamentations upon blights, – in dawdling through the green-house, where the loss of her favourite plants, unwarily exposed, and nipped by the lingering frost, raised the laughter of Charlotte, – and in visiting her poultry-yard, where, in the disappointed hopes of her dairy-maid, by hens forsaking their nests, or being stolen by a fox, or in the rapid decease of a promising young brood, she found fresh sources of merriment. (*S & S, 303*)

The contrast between herself and her mother may be attributable to the younger woman's never having known necessity. Though Mrs Jennings now has all the money and all the servants she could want, she perhaps betrays a lowly start in life by the very great interest that she takes in the details of other people's housekeeping as well as her own. This curiosity is not mere impertinence, equivalent to Nancy Steele's nosiness about other people's clothes and 'beaux' – for all Mrs Jennings's remarks, whatever their vulgarity, are characterised by common sense and goodwill. Her predictions about Edward and Lucy, given above, are one example. Another is her recollection of her only visit to Colonel Brandon's home at Delaford, which she reverts to twice in the novel. The description of the place which she gives to Elinor will be analysed in a later chapter. Here it is sufficient to say that she focuses not on its aesthetic qualities, but on its ample provision of food: fruit trees, stewponds and the proximity of a butcher. Later she mentions having questioned the housekeeper as to the number of beds that could be made up there (the answer is fifteen). To elicit domestic details from a servant is not very honourable conduct – the servant is often flattered by the attention, and at any rate can hardly refuse to answer questions about matters that should be the private concerns of her master or mistress. Those who indulge in this practice – Mrs Norris is another – betray minds that run very much on the same level as the servant-housekeepers themselves. But while a fascination for the details of housekeeping is slightly unworthy, and is something to which the heroines and the most refined older women would never sink, Jane Austen refuses to condemn it altogether, knowing that domestic comfort depends upon a proper interest being shown in such minutiae by the mistress of the house.

At the beginning of *Pride and Prejudice* we are told that the business of Mrs Bennet's life is to get her daughters married – but its everyday business is certainly to provide a good table. The subject is always on her mind. Unlike Mrs Jennings, however, her preoccupation arises not from a motherly instinct to nourish all under her roof, but from feelings very much less commendable.

There are three things in which, as a housekeeper, Mrs Bennet prides herself, and which she is anxious that everybody should acknowledge. First, that her daughters have no household work to do. When Mr Collins comes to Longbourn, he admires the dinner and begs to know 'to which of his fair cousins, the excellence of its cookery was owing. But here he was set right by Mrs Bennet, who assured him with some asperity that they were very well able to keep a good cook, and that her daughters had nothing to do in the kitchen.' (*P & P*, 65) Perhaps at this stage it has not crossed Mrs Bennet's mind that Mr Collins might be looking for a wife, and it would not be unreasonable for him to want one who can cook. Earlier she has aimed the same shaft more appropriately, though more mean-spiritedly, at Bingley. During a visit to Netherfield, Elizabeth tries to distract her mother from arguing with Darcy by asking whether Charlotte dined at Longbourn the previous day. Mrs Bennet replies in the negative, adding, 'I fancy she was wanted about the mince pies. For my part, Mr Bingley, *I* always keep servants that can do their own work; *my* daughters are brought up differently.' (*P & P*, 44)

Her earlier spat with Darcy consists of his assertion that 'in a country neighbourhood you move in a very confined and unvarying circle' and her offended refutation, which reaches its climax in 'I know we dine with four and twenty families'. To everybody present this is highly hilarious, and even Bingley can hardly 'keep his countenance'. This is the second aspect of her housekeeping in which Mrs Bennet takes pride. It *is* an impressive number, but is one of those things that people secure in their social position do not mention.

Her remark may be inspired by a similar boast Jane Austen may often have heard made by her unloved aunt, Mrs Leigh Perrot. In a letter written in her extreme old age, long after Jane's death but reminiscing about the period when Jane would have been a child, Mrs Leigh Perrot described her household at Scarlets in Berkshire to James Edward Austen-Leigh, to whom she was thinking of leaving the property:

> First let me tell you that your excellent Uncle & myself, although we lived much more for company than for ourselves, by choice, yet we never had half the Income which you now have, nor were we ever in debt – dining with thirty families, & frequently with our house filled, a housekeeper was necessary, as well as a tolerable cook, and a housemaid. These were our only females. We had an excellent footman, coachman & gardener, with a boy whose business it was to weed, work in the garden, but even when we were alone, he always came in to wait at table, that he might be less awkward in company.[1]

It is becoming clear that all Mrs Bennet's pride in her housekeeping is to do with the impression she is making on other people – and that it arises from her own sense of social inferiority. She has married 'up', as comparison with her sister Mrs Philips attests, and she uses food to force other people to acknowledge her right to her position. Her third boast is that she always keeps a good table. Chapter Thirteen begins with this exchange:

> 'I hope, my dear,' said Mr Bennet to his wife, as they were at breakfast the next morning, 'that you have ordered a good dinner today, because I have reason to expect an addition to our family party.'
> 'Who do you mean, my dear? I know of nobody that is coming I am sure, unless Charlotte Lucas should happen to call in, and I hope *my* dinners are good enough for her. I do not believe she often sees such at home.' (*P & P, 61*)

Poor Charlotte Lucas seems to come in for a lot of displaced aggression. It is psychologically interesting that this remark is echoed, much later in Jane Austen's work, by another social climber, Mrs Elton, talking in a similarly patronising tone about Jane Fairfax:

> 'We live in a style which could not make the addition of Jane Fairfax, at any time, the least inconvenient. – I should be extremely displeased if Wright were to send us up such a dinner, as could make me regret having asked *more* than Jane Fairfax to partake of it. I have no idea of that sort of thing. It is not likely that I *should*, considering what I have been used to. My greatest danger, perhaps, in housekeeping, may be quite the other way, in doing too much, and

being too careless of expense. Maple Grove will probably be my model more that it ought to be . . . ' (*E, 283*)

Mrs Bennet and Mrs Elton have much in common as housekeepers, for Mrs Bennet is also careless of expense, concerned only to create a good show. 'My dinners' are designed not to give pleasure or health, but to impress superiors and to subordinate inferiors. She has lost Mrs Jennings's good sense of what food should be for, and resorts to it to manipulate others. She plans her meals 'to do credit to her housekeeping'; she thinks only in terms of credit, that is what *she* can get out of the transaction.

It now occurs to her that Mr Bingley might be the unexpected visitor, and she bursts out, 'But – good lord! how unlucky! there is not a bit of fish to be got today. Lydia, my love, ring the bell. I must speak to Hill, this moment.' We know from the text that this is Monday, when fish cannot be bought because there has been no catch the previous day. In such minor domestic detail the world of *Pride and Prejudice* is anchored in the real world. At the same time, and in such brief and apparently insignificant sentences, Jane Austen manages to convey a great deal of information about character. Mrs Bennet is so ill-judging that she imagines Mr Bingley's love for Jane will be affected by the presence or absence of fish on the table. She is also so careless of her husband's comfort that she would interrupt breakfast and summon Hill, the housekeeper, to an immediate conference in the room in which the family are eating, instead of waiting until the meal is finished. Nor can she even do something as simple as ringing the bell quietly and without fuss, but must get another person to do it for her, creating as much turmoil as she can. This turning to Hill in every moment of panic shows up her fundamental inadequacy; later in the novel she will be seen to be pathetically dependent on Hill. Mrs Bennet's claims to household competence in fact rest on very little, for not only does she have servants to carry all the burden, but she fails to perform her own principal duty, to spend the family income judiciously. She is too fond of show, and has 'no turn for economy'. (*P & P, 308*)

Contrasted with Mrs Bennet is Charlotte Lucas, or Charlotte Collins as she becomes. Mrs Bennet dimly perceives the contrast, though without drawing the conclusion that there is anything to blame in herself. Elizabeth has just returned from visiting the newly-married pair:

'Well, Lizzy,' continued her mother soon afterwards, 'and so the Collinses live very comfortable, do they? Well, well, I only hope it will last. And what sort of table do they keep? Charlotte is an excellent manager, I dare say. If she is half as sharp as her mother, she is saving enough. There is nothing extravagant in *their* housekeeping, I dare say.'

'No, nothing at all.'

'A great deal of good management, depend upon it. Yes, yes. *They* will take care not to outrun their income. *They* will never be distressed for money. Well, much good may it do them! And so, I suppose, they often talk about having Longbourn when your father is dead. They look upon it quite as their own, I dare say, whenever that happens.' (*P & P, 228*)

There is poetic justice in the formerly-patronised Charlotte Lucas turning into the Charlotte Collins who will one day have the power to turn Mrs Bennet out of her house. Not that we ever see Charlotte gloating. What we do see – and are asked to admire – in her is an honest relish at having a house of her own to run. Elizabeth vouches for her not being extravagant, but neither is she penny-pinching: Lady Catherine, after all, considers Charlotte's joints of meat to be too large for her family (meaning her household; no young olive branches have yet appeared). Charlotte performs her duties to perfection, without snobbery or show of any kind and, what is more, with uncomplaining cheerfulness. Her house is neat and well-ordered; and 'when Mr Collins could be forgotten, there was really a great air of comfort throughout, and by Charlotte's evident enjoyment of it, Elizabeth supposed he must often be forgotten'. (*P & P, 157*) That is Elizabeth's assessment on first being shown round the house and, after a six weeks' residence in it, she takes leave with the feeling that Charlotte 'did not seem to ask for compassion. Her home and her housekeeping, her parish and her poultry, and all their dependent concerns, had not yet lost their charms'. (*P & P, 216*) Charlotte embodies that essential virtue in Jane Austen, contentment with her lot. To find happiness where one can, and to avoid creating unhappiness in those around one, are moral imperatives for Jane Austen. These Charlotte admirably attains (unlike, say, that other young wife, Mary Musgrove). Not the least of Charlotte's perfections as a housekeeper is her sense of proportion, so that, despite her own interest in the subject, she does not obtrude it on Elizabeth.

As a consequence we, as readers, know rather fewer details about the domestic arrangements at Hunsford Parsonage than the mistress's own interest in these matters might justify us in expecting. Some of what we do know comes from Lady Catherine's interference. After dinner at Rosings, when the ladies are alone, 'she enquired into Charlotte's concerns familiarly and minutely, and gave her a great deal of advice, as to the management of them all; told her how everything ought to be regulated in so small a family as hers, and instructed her as to the care of her cows and her poultry'. (*P & P, 163*) So this is another parson's wife who keeps cows – presumably in the two meadows which form Hunsford glebe. There is also a suggestion of pigs (Elizabeth makes a joke about them getting into the garden). The garden is said to be large, and Mr Collins works in it himself, almost certainly cultivating produce for the table.

When Lady Catherine calls at the Parsonage, 'nothing escaped her observation . . . . She examined into their employments, looked at their work, and advised them to do it differently; found fault with the arrangement of the furniture, or detected the housemaid in negligence', (*P & P, 169*) which certainly suggests there is only one housemaid. Has Charlotte a cook? If it were not for our knowing that she has been brought up able to cook, we might not even ask the question, for she would be unique in Jane Austen's fiction as a gentlewoman doing her own cooking – even the Watson sisters only superintend, direct and scold, spending half the morning in the kitchen when a special visitor is expected. In Charlotte's case, the evidence on one side is that she is never shown cooking (but then, how would we ever have known that Charlotte cooked at Lucas Lodge, if it were not for Mrs Bennet's spiteful comments?); and on the other, that Charlotte never accompanies Elizabeth on her morning walks at Hunsford, which suggests she is too busy; that Lady Catherine is never invited back to dinner; and that 'the style of living of the neighbourhood in general, was beyond the Collinses' reach'. This seems to put them at a lower level that the Grants at Mansfield Parsonage, who regularly invite their neighbours from the mansion house to dine. But we know that the stipend at Mansfield is £1,000 p.a., a sum on which a couple without any children can live a very comfortable life.

Mansfield Park is another novel in which the discussion of housekeeping plays an important part, and which includes portraits of a variety of housekeepers. Three contrasts are set up: between Mrs Price and Mrs Norris; between Mrs Norris and Mrs Grant; and between Mrs Grant and Mary Crawford. Two of the pairs are sisters, and the other pair are linked by having (at different periods) the same house to run.

This patterning is made more significant by the fact that Fanny is related to the first pair, and is eventually to be mistress of the same house as the third. These contrasts represent therefore her inheritance and her destiny, inviting us to consider how she will measure up to and follow those who have gone before. Only the contrast between Mrs

Grant and Mary Crawford seems to have no direct relationship to Fanny, but in fact it serves to make explicit the respective qualifications of Fanny and Mary to be Edmund's wife. The pattern can be seen therefore to be a very important one to the meaning of *Mansfield Park*, so important that it elicits Jane Austen's only direct comparison, anywhere in the fiction, between different women in their roles as housekeepers:

> Of her two sisters, Mrs Price very much more resembled Lady Bertram than Mrs Norris. She was a manager by necessity, without any of Mrs Norris's inclination for it, or any of her activity. Her disposition was naturally easy and indolent, like Lady Bertram's; and a situation of similar affluence and do-nothing-ness would have been much more suited to her capacity, than the exertions and self-denials of the one, which her imprudent marriage had placed her in. She might have made just as good a woman of consequence as Lady Bertram, but Mrs Norris would have been a more respectable mother of nine children, on a small income. (*MP, 390*)

The assessment is the narrator's own, rather than Fanny's possibly faulty judgement, for it is immediately followed by the statement that 'Much of all this, Fanny could not but be sensible of '. It is the only place in the book where Mrs Norris receives a shred of credit, and convinces by pointing out the potential for good in her bad qualities, rather than a stray good quality which happens to mitigate the bad ones.

The passage underlines Jane Austen's concern, especially insistent in the case of women's choosing their destiny with marriage, that duties should be matched to abilities. By her choice of partner Fanny Ward rashly sets up a family unit which combines low income with bad management, to the inevitable future misery of the unborn children of the union. The innocent will suffer, and it is for this Mrs Price is held culpable and treated harshly from the very first chapter. That she herself suffers the consequence of her folly is no more than her just deserts, but having chosen her path in life she should not wonder when the results turn out just what anybody might have foreseen. In such circumstances her plain duty is to exert herself, not to fret or repine.

With consistency of characterisation, the lack of intelligence and foresight which led Mrs Price into her predicament also define her conduct as a housekeeper. The Portsmouth household is not the poorest in Jane Austen's fiction, but it is unquestionably the most ill-managed. Mrs Price has two servants to help her, whereas the Bateses have only one. (Mrs Smith in *Persuasion* is unique in Jane Austen in having no personal servant at all, but as she lives in lodgings – miserable enough, it is true – her meals are provided by her landlady.) The fact is that, because of the large number of children in the Portsmouth house, Rebecca and Sally have more to do between them than the Bateses' Patty or the Watsons' Nanny and Betty (and how characteristic these diminutives are of the humbler domestic establishments in the novels).[2]

As Fanny sees, Mrs Price cannot manage and direct such help as she can afford, and the servants take advantage of her weakness, shouting out their excuses from the kitchen. Mrs Price is condemned as 'a dawdle' and 'a slattern', 'whose house was the scene of mismanagement and discomfort from beginning to end'.

> Her days were spent in a kind of slow bustle; always busy without getting on, always behindhand and lamenting it, without altering her ways; wishing to be an economist, without contrivance or regularity; dissatisfied with her servants, without skill to make them better, and whether helping, or reprimanding, or indulging them, without any power of engaging their respect. (*MP, 389*)

Almost the first speech which Mrs Price utters on the arrival of William and Fanny is a good specimen of the helpless and self-pitying attitude which characterises her as provider of food and comfort. Although she has been watching out for the travellers for half an hour, time which she could have spent more usefully making sure some refreshment was ready, when they do arrive she can only plague them with questions, make excuses and lament:

> 'And when did you get anything to eat? And what would you like to have now? I could not tell whether you would be for some meat, or only a dish of tea after your journey, or else I would have got something ready. And now I am afraid Campbell will be here, before there is time to dress a steak, and we have no butcher at hand. It is very inconvenient to have no butcher in the street. We were better off in our last house. Perhaps you would like some tea, as soon as it can be got.' (*MP, 379*)

It is a further half an hour before the tea things arrive, and then only thanks to Susan. In the course of the following three months, hashes, puddings, toasted cheese and bread and butter are the only foods ever mentioned in the Portsmouth house. Tea with town milk is the constant drink, except for Mr Price's evening rum and water.

Mrs Price, then, is firmly established as the worst housekeeper in the novel. But the sister to whom she is compared is by no means the best. Mrs Norris carries the opposing qualities of activity, minuteness and economy too far. Farther, that is, than her particular circumstances render appropriate. Had she really been the mother of a large family on a small income her methods would have some merit, though there would have been as little emotional comfort in her home, probably, as in Mrs Price's. As it is, the 'very strict line of economy' which 'was begun as a matter of prudence', when children remained a possibility, 'soon grew into a matter of choice' when no children arrived to occupy her head and heart. (*MP, 8*) Economy and contrivance have become for Mrs Norris an end in themselves. Subverted in this way, they cease to have the only justification possible, that of increasing the comfort of other people; instead they are a source of gratification to herself, occupying time and effort which ought to be better employed and, what is worse, actually making those around her *un*comfortable.

In all these moral shortcomings she is the counterpart of Dr Grant, notwithstanding that their offences could hardly be farther apart. His greed and her parsimony equally preclude that knowledge of themselves and their duty to others which for Jane Austen is the indispensable virtue. The narrator tells us, 'Dr Grant and Mrs Norris were seldom good friends; their acquaintance had begun in dilapidations and their habits were totally dissimilar'.[3] (*MP, 55*)

After her husband's death, Mrs Norris leaves Mansfield Parsonage for the White house, deliberately choosing 'the smallest habitation which could rank as genteel among the buildings of Mansfield parish'. Her claims to her sister that she has 'barely enough to support me in the rank of a gentlewoman, and enable me to live so as not to disgrace the memory of the dear departed' are contraverted by our access to her private thoughts; she has already secretly 'consoled herself for the loss of her husband by considering that she could do very well without him, and for her reduction of income by the evident necessity of stricter economy'. (*MP, 23*) To meanness she adds hypocrisy and cant: 'If I can but make both ends meet, that's all I ask for', she says, to which Lady Bertram replies, 'Sir Thomas says you will have six hundred a year'. Mrs Norris won't give up the point:

> 'Lady Bertram, I do not complain, I know I cannot live as I have done, but I must retrench where I can, and learn to be a better manager. I *have been* a liberal housekeeper enough, but I shall not be ashamed to practise economy now. My situation is as much altered as my income. A great many things were due from poor Mr Norris as clergyman of the parish, that cannot be expected from me. It is unknown how much was consumed in our kitchen by odd comers and goers. At the White house, matters must be better looked after.' (*MP, 30*)

It is highly unlikely that *anything* was consumed in Mrs Norris's kitchen by odd comers and goers, if the way she chases young Dick Jackson away from the servants' quarters at the Park, where it happens to be dinner-time, is any indication. 'The boy looked very silly and turned away without offering a word, for I believe I might speak pretty sharp; and I dare say it will cure him of coming marauding about the house for one while – I hate such greediness.' (*MP, 142*)

She is even prepared to carry the 'two bits of deal board' to his father herself in order to deprive the boy of any reason to remain – undignified and unladylike behaviour. And what was she doing near the servants' hall door anyway, 'looking about me in the poultry yard'? She makes very free with the domestic arrangements at the Park, usurping Lady Bertram's position. Perhaps Lady Bertram would have been a less indolent mistress of Mansfield Park had her sister not always been by to make every decision for her. Mrs Norris's officiousness is demonstrated again and again in the novel, in matters little and great. When Sir Thomas returns rather earlier than expected from his hazardous voyage:

> Mrs Norris felt herself defrauded of an office on which she had always depended, whether his arrival or his death were to be the thing unfolded; and was now trying to be in a bustle without anything to be in a bustle about, and labouring to be important where nothing was wanted but tranquillity and silence. Would Sir Thomas have consented to eat, she might have gone to the house-keeper with troublesome directions, and insulted footmen with injunctions of dispatch; but Sir Thomas resolutely declined all dinner; he would take nothing, nothing till tea came – he would rather wait for tea. Still Mrs Norris was at intervals urging something different, and in the most interesting moment of his passage to England, when the alarm of a French privateer was at the height, she burst through his recital with the proposal of soup. 'Sure, my dear Sir Thomas, a basin of soup would be a much better thing for you than tea. Do have a basin of soup.'
>
> Sir Thomas could not be provoked. 'Still the same anxiety for everybody's comfort, my dear Mrs Norris,' was his answer. 'But indeed I would rather have nothing but tea.'
>
> 'Well, then, Lady Bertram, suppose you speak for tea directly, suppose you hurry Baddeley a little, he seems behind hand tonight.' She carried this point, and Sir Thomas's narrative proceeded. (*MP, 180*)

On the occasion of the ball, when the servants might be thought to have enough to do, she must quarrel with the housekeeper about supper. Her relations with servants are reprehensibly familiar. If she is not speaking sharply, or interfering with their work, then she is fussing about their health (to put them under an obligation to her) or flattering them out of confidences and gifts. The servants at the Park, who know her only too well, have her measure (the one moment in all Jane Austen's fiction when a servant is allowed to betray any personal feeling is the half smile with which Baddeley assures Mrs Norris that it is Fanny, not she, whom Sir Thomas has sent for – Mr Crawford having arrived to pay his suit).

Servants elsewhere are more easily deceived by her flattery. Like Mrs Jennings, but in a far more acquisitive and mean-spirited way, Mrs Norris gravitates towards the servant-housekeeper of any house she visits. During the day at Sotherton:

> Whatever cross accidents had occurred to intercept the pleasures of her nieces, she had found a morning of complete enjoyment – for the housekeeper, after a great many courtesies on the subject of pheasants, had taken her to the dairy, told her all about their cows, and given her a receipt for a famous cream cheese; and since Julia's leaving them, they had been met by the gardener, with whom she had a most satisfactory acquaintance, for she had set him right as to his grandson's illness, convinced him it was an ague, and promised him a charm for it; and he, in return, had shewn her all his choicest nursery of plants, and actually presented her with a very curious specimen of heath. (*MP, 104*)

In addition to the heath, she comes away with – 'sponges' is her niece Maria's term – a cream cheese and four pheasant's eggs from Sotherton, pressed on her, she claims, by the housekeeper, Mrs Whitaker, with tears in her eyes. How much information she has obtained through her 'gossip' and flatteries is unknown, but its nature may be guessed by her effusion: 'That Mrs Whitaker is a treasure! She was quite shocked when I asked her whether wine was allowed at the second table, and she has turned away two housemaids for wearing white gowns.' (*MP, 106*) The second table, of course, is the servants' table. The Sotherton establishment is large, though it exists to serve just two people, Mr Rushworth and his mother. With a large staff beneath her, and a mistress newer to the house than herself (Mrs Rushworth has learnt about the family portraits and so forth from her), Mrs Whitaker is a person of some consideration – and probably, a great deal more sense than her mistress.

It must be through enquiries of servants, or perhaps a chain of servants, methods anyway that ought to have been beneath her, that Mrs Norris learns the private domestic details of her successors at the Parsonage. The neighbourhood generally are pleased with Dr and Mrs Grant but 'They had their faults, and Mrs Norris found them out':

> The Dr was very fond of eating, and would have a good dinner every day; and Mrs Grant, instead of contriving to gratify him at little expense, gave her cook as high wages as they did at Mansfield Park, and was scarcely ever seen in her offices. Mrs Norris could not speak with any temper of such grievances, nor of the quantity of butter and eggs that were regularly consumed in the house. 'Nobody loved plenty and hospitality more than herself – nobody more hated

pitiful doings – the parsonage she believed had never been wanting in comforts of any sort, had never borne a bad character in *her time*, but this was a way of going on that she could not understand. A fine lady in a country parsonage was quite out of place. *Her* store-room she thought might have been good enough for Mrs Grant to go into.' (*MP, 31*)

The Grants offend her by choosing to introduce a large new dining-table – 'wider, literally wider, than the dinner table here', says Mrs Norris at the Park – into the Parsonage, instead of taking the one she wanted to sell them. Affronting both her avarice and her frugality, this is a grievance never to be forgiven or forgotten. Three years later, she 'could never behold either the wide table or the number of dishes on it with patience', and always contrives 'to experience some evil from the passing of the servants behind her chair, and to bring away some fresh conviction of its being impossible among so many dishes but that some must be cold'. (*MP, 239*) On another occasion, she vents her rage at Fanny's being invited with Edmund to dine at the Parsonage, in the sarcasm that though the party is to consist of only five, an inelegant number she is surprised Mrs Grant can tolerate at her table, 'you will have dinner enough on it for ten I dare say'. (*MP, 221*)

Mrs Grant is a minor character but she has two of the qualities most prized by Jane Austen: she consistently endeavours to promote the comfort and happiness of those around her; and she is contented with her lot. Her only deficiency, if there be one, is a lack of gravitas underpinning her cheerful and obliging manners. That the people she loves are enjoying themselves is sufficient for her; she makes little or no attempt to check the greed and indolence of her husband, or the flirtatious licence of Henry, or the theatrical schemes of the young people in general – although it is hard to see how she could affect any of these without making herself unpleasant. Her fault is not only wanting too much to be liked, but simply failing to perceive dubious morality.

As a housekeeper, however, she is very attractive. Since there is no hint of the Grants having insufficient income to support their style of living, their generous table, their 'elegant and plentiful' dinners, are far more agreeable than Mrs Norris's economies. As well as all that butter and all those eggs, they eat turkey, pheasant, goose; and apricot tarts and preserves; and they drink claret. This is very different fare from that at Portsmouth; it is as rich as the soup, venison, gooseberry tart, cake and madeira of the Park itself; but, appropriately, there is no food of any kind mentioned in connection with the White house, or the Parsonage in Mrs Norris's day, with which to compare it.

Though Mrs Grant is accused of rarely going into the 'offices', this is only in comparison with the 'officiousness' of her predecessor; she evidently has the house running smoothly and the servants under good order. The only shortcoming is that the cook (despite having as high wages as the one at the Park) sometimes makes a blunder. Since Mrs Grant herself has to bear the worst consequences of this – her husband's irritability – there is presumably nothing she can do to prevent its happening occasionally; lack of refrigeration and of accurate temperature control in cooking methods must have made the production of 'elegant and plentiful' dinners a chancy business even for the most experienced of cooks.

There seem plenty of servants at the Parsonage: the cook and the gardener, Robert, the unspecified 'civil servant' who is sent out to invite Fanny indoors when she is caught in the rain, and the 'maids' who help her change her wet clothes. Perhaps Robert also waits at table, but if so not alone, for it is the passing of *servants* behind her chair that Mrs Norris objects to when dining with the Grants. Mary Crawford brings her own maid with her. From the Parsonage windows she can see two farmyards, one of which must be the glebe. Dr Grant has a bailiff, a stable, carriage and horses, and a pony for a servant to use to fetch his letters from the post; and though the village has neither nurseryman nor poulterer (two completely urban concepts) it does have a miller and a butcher. The Grants, indeed, seem to have every comfort about them and to want for nothing.

Mrs Grant acts as her own housekeeper, and seems to take just the right degree of involvement in the domestic economy of Mansfield Parsonage. Under her management the house appears to be not only well-provisioned, but cared for, comfortable and pretty inside and out. There is a hint of the fashionableness of Uppercross Cottage and of the Musgrove daughters' attempts to modernise Uppercross House itself in the way Mrs Grant soon after her arrival fills – or rather, more than fills – her favourite sitting-room with pretty furniture, and has the window 'cut down to the ground' to open on to the lawn. She lays out a shrubbery and gravel walk, with a taste which Fanny herself admires, and she makes a choice collection of plants and poultry.

But her plants and her poultry, and her pretty furniture, are not enough to fill up her heart, and, since 'hers must be a desperate dull life with the Doctor', as Tom not unjustly puts it, she has a great deal of love to bestow on her sister, and sociable and neighbourly attention on others around her. Her wifely duties are her priority. The 'little rubs and disappointments' she experiences as the wife of a selfish man are passed over with exemplary forbearance; but only when the Doctor is particularly out of humour is she prevented from playing a fuller part in the society of Mansfield. Her domestic cares do not prevent her, for example, from very kindly spending the whole day with Lady Bertram when the others go to Sotherton. (Dr Grant joins them for dinner; he cannot be left to dine alone even for one day.)

As Mrs Grant says in defence of marriage, 'if one scheme of happiness fails, human nature turns to another . . . we find comfort somewhere . . . .' (*MP, 46*) This may not always be true of human nature generally, but she is aptly describing herself. Though her own marriage is hardly the happiest on earth, she finds comfort where she can, the most durable source being her housekeeping. But this admirable Jane Austen character knows the importance of balance. Housekeeping, for all the pride and pleasure she takes in it, is not the chief occupation or justification for her existence, or the only subject for which she cares enough to talk about.

Mrs Grant indeed could be a portrait of an older Mrs Collins, one who has had no children and has gradually increased in worldly prosperity. Both women have married men with faults of character, and if the women have a fault themselves it is for making such a marriage without affection (unless Mrs Grant was truly 'taken in'). Neither was a beauty in her youth and each is thankful for a comfortable home; in return they play a full part in making that home comfortable for their husbands, whom they treat with admirable forbearance. Finding happiness in house and garden, parish and poultry, they do not allow their own tempers to be soured by the proximity of trying companions (the trial being all the greater in that a clergyman is always at home, and that home not a large one).

Fanny has no difficulty (though great pain) in understanding which woman, out of her aunts and her mother, would make the better mistress of a large family on a small income. Neither can her good sense doubt, though we are never given her thoughts on the subject, which of her two predecessors at Mansfield Parsonage makes a better model for her to follow in her own housekeeping there. Fanny will only be happier than Mrs Grant in having a good-tempered husband, and one who does not demand those 'elegant and plentiful' dinners every day. (But will Edmund, however sincerely attached to Fanny, ever be able completely to vanquish, in his own sitting-room, the vision of Mary seated in front of those French windows playing the harp?) Otherwise it is Mrs Grant whose place and role she will succeed to – with the difference that if Fanny has a large family, she will exercise some (not too much) of Mrs

Norris's care. By the end of the novel we cannot doubt that Fanny has observed enough of different styles of housekeeping, and observed with intelligent assessment, to know the best way to conduct her own household affairs.

As a *potential* wife and mistress of a parsonage, Fanny is contrasted throughout the book with her serious rival for Edmund's affection, Mary Crawford. Their views on almost everything are unalike, as appears at different times in conversation or action. Mary's indifference to farming – the precursor to housekeeping, of course – is twice made plain. On the journey to Sotherton she does not share any of Fanny's interest in 'the difference of soil, the state of the harvest' or 'the cattle'. (*MP, 80*) She has no conception of the importance of getting in the hay while it is fine, attempting to hire a wagon to convey her harp just when all the vehicles available are most needed for more serious purposes. (She can speak very amusingly about it, however, admitting to having 'offended all the farmers, all the labourers, all the hay in the parish'.) (*MP, 58*)

A similarly cavalier attitude is evinced by her brother, in discussing possible improvements to Edmund's living at Thornton Lacey. While Edmund, with admirable balance between aesthetic considerations and the practical necessities of life, intends to move the farm-yard, Henry Crawford advocates clearing it away entirely. How the nation would ever be fed if the Crawfords had the management of the countryside is a question they certainly could not answer themselves.

To be plausibly presented, Mary's attitude toward housekeeping – a subject she rarely thinks about and does not want to have to think about very much, even when married – has to be revealed in just one exchange between her sister and herself. Mrs Grant is deploring the warmth of the weather for November, as an unexpected frost will take Robert by surprise and lose the tender plants which he is leaving out: 'and what is worse, cook has just been telling me that the turkey, which I particularly wished not to be dressed till Sunday, because I know how much more Dr Grant would enjoy it after the fatigues of the day, will not keep beyond tomorrow'. Edmund and Fanny are with the sisters, and Mary's reply is aimed partly at him:

> 'The sweets of housekeeping in a country village!' said Miss Crawford archly. 'Commend me to the nurseryman and the poulterer.'
> 'My dear child, commend Dr Grant to the deanery of Westminster or St Paul's, and I should be as glad of your nurseryman and poulterer as you can be. But we have no such people in Mansfield. What would you have me do?'

'Oh! you can do nothing but what you do already; be plagued very often and never lose your temper.'

'Thank you – but there is no escaping these little vexations, Mary, live where we may; and when you are settled in town and I come to see you, I dare say I shall find you with yours, in spite of the nurseryman and the poulterer – or perhaps on their very account. Their remoteness and unpunctuality, or their exorbitant charges and frauds will be drawing forth bitter lamentations.'

'I mean to be too rich to lament or to feel anything of the sort. A large income is the best recipe for happiness I ever heard of. It certainly may secure all the myrtle and turkey part of it.' (*MP, 214*)

The ensuing conversation between Edmund and Mary on the subject of incomes, large and otherwise, is appropriately 'sorrowful food for Fanny's observation'. (Fanny perhaps lives too much upon metaphorical food, a point which I shall take up later.) Her antagonism to a marriage between Edmund and Mary finds many justifications, including the one suggested here and voiced at Portsmouth when, on receiving a letter from Edmund which shows him on the verge of proposing to Mary, she cries, 'He will marry her, and be poor and miserable'. (*MP, 424*)

Edmund's income in fact will be considerably larger if he marries Mary than Fanny, since the former's fortune will bring in £1,000 a year – as much again as the stipend at Mansfield – and of course, Fanny herself has nothing. Fanny's only meaning in this outburst, if reason is to be looked for at all in her unhappiness, is that Mary will be so extravagant, in housekeeping and other matters of expenditure, especially perhaps in demanding a house in town, that their income will not suffice for their wants.

But if Mary knows that she has no taste or aptitude for housekeeping, she is right to avoid putting herself in a position where if she neglects her duties her family must suffer and if she attends to them she herself will be miserable. To do otherwise, to put love and attraction above cool-headed assessment of the consequences, would be to fall into the same error, albeit in lesser degree, as Mrs Price.

Jane Austen thus brings the linked pairs, the patterning, full circle. In the centre of the circle, observing the women about her and fitting herself for her own destiny, is Fanny Price.

This has been an almost wholly female chapter. As the narrator of *Persuasion* remarks of 'the little social commonwealth' of Uppercross, while the men have their own concerns of sport and politics, 'the females were fully occupied in all the other common subjects of house-keeping, neighbours, dress, dancing and music'. (*P, 43*) In Jane Austen's own life, a shared interest in housekeeping helped to establish a network between women – women neighbours or relations from different branches of the family.[4] Exchanging recipes and remedies, sending gifts of food, discussing the minutiae of the subject was mutually supportive and defining of women's special role. In the novels, this positive aspect is largely missing. If one woman takes an interest in another's housekeeping, it is usually either to criticise or to be inquisitive, as we have seen. Housekeeping in the novels has become unpleasantly competitive, too often a matter of status and show, whether economy or abundance is what is being shown.

Amusingly enough, the only friendly exchange of a recipe in any of the novels takes place between two men, when Mr Elton jots down (with the bit of pencil which Harriet later spirits away) instructions for making spruce beer given by Mr Knightley. But if Jane Austen's women are too often deficient as housekeepers, and if we miss in her a sense of female solidarity in this respect, it is because the heroines must learn from the mistakes of their elders in order to choose wisely the sphere in which the rest of their lives will be lived.

Only Anne Elliot, of all the heroines, marries without knowing where she is to live. What matters to Anne is trust in Providence and forming a home as unlike her father's as possible. Appropriately, and despite the remark about the women of Uppercross, *Persuasion* has in fact less to say than any of the novels about housekeeping. But it has a great deal to say about hospitality, that relationship with the giving and sharing of food in which men too can play a part, often the decisive part in their circle. A consideration of hospitality enables Jane Austen to focus her moral scrutiny on both men and women, on partnerships, on whole communities even. It is to this I now turn.

Chapter Six

Town and Country Hospitality

'Old fashioned notions – country hospitality – we do not profess to give dinners – few people in Bath do – Lady Alicia never does.' (*P, 219*) These are the arguments with which Elizabeth Elliot convinces herself that the Musgroves need not be asked to dine with them in Bath. As so often in Jane Austen's art, this little insight into the way Elizabeth's mind works conveys more than one kind of intelligence to the reader. Elizabeth's personality is developed and exposed, and we delight in her self-deluding meanness of spirit. But beyond that, the changing habits and expectations of the society to which the Elliots and Jane Austen both belong, are held up for serious appraisal.

In considering hospitality in Jane Austen's fiction, I want, like her, to keep both these ideas in play: to observe how she uses the subject both to illustrate individual character and to comment on the values and manners of the age. This is why it is most useful to examine the texts in the order in which they were written, or at least within the two broad divisions of Steventon and Chawton novels.[1] More than any other kind of relationship to food, hospitality reflects the underlying assumptions of society, assumptions which can and do shift with time. Social forms which once served society well by regulating and polishing behaviour for the better comfort of all can become ossified, empty and oppressive to the individual. Change may be necessary, but change must be motivated by good feeling and concern for others, not by desire to create an impression. Elegance and propriety are always desirable, because they smooth over any social disharmony, but they should be accompanied by real generosity of spirit; and where there *is* such generosity, want of elegance and propriety may be excused. Throughout her writing career Jane Austen kept her eye firmly on the way her society was moving as manifested in its ideas of hospitality.

All her novels, and fragments of novels, have necessarily something to say about this everyday aspect of life, where the domestic and the social intersect. Much of the action of her plots arises from one set of people inviting another set into their house, for a meal or an extended visit. Since so much hospitality is given, the spirit in which it is given must often come under scrutiny. In certain novels the subject is dwelt on more intensively than in others, attaining, by the repeated drawing of this thread to the surface, the significance of a unifying theme. It is no coincidence that the narratives in which this happens tend to be those whose heroines are portrayed as most beset and least supported by the system of social intercourse within which their days are passed. *Sense and Sensibility* and *Persuasion* are pre-eminently such novels. The fact that their dates of composition are separated by some twenty years not only enables us to trace both the shifts and the continuities in social behaviour during Jane Austen's lifetime, but indicates her abiding interest in the subject.

Caroline Austen relates an anecdote of one of Jane Austen's Steventon neighbours, John Harwood, of Deane House. The recent death of his father had brought to light extensive and unsuspected debts; determined to clear them off, but to also retain Deane House, he was living there in the strictest economy with his elderly mother and aunt. (Jane Austen refers to this circumstance in one of her letters, regretting that he would now be unable to marry her friend Elizabeth Heathcote, who was widowed with a small son.) Another misfortune befell when the impoverished curate of Overton, Mr Dennis, died suddenly while visiting Deane House; his widow was sent for, and the shock brought on the birth of her baby in the house. In a fine illustration of true country hospitality and gentlemanly behaviour, Caroline continues,

> Mrs Dennis remained at Deane the full time that could be thought necessary for her recovery, and was most carefully attended to. It was surmised she had never known so much comfort before, and it was quite certain that she could not have had it in her home at Overton. Nothing was spared for her. Tho' poverty was in the house, she, the guest, was not to feel it. One day there was a question about wine. A little had been used at the funeral, and a very few bottles of white wine were all that remained of the old store; wine was never thought of now in the family except on very particular occasions. Mrs Anna Harwood made the not unreasonable suggestion that beer caudle should be sent up to Mrs Dennis; it was equally wholesome and some people preferred it. But the master of the house was in the room, and when he comprehended what the ladies were talking about he positively ordered that as long as there was a drop remaining Mrs Dennis should have wine in her gruel.[2]

It was against such standards of behaviour, termed by Caroline Austen 'old-world', that Jane Austen was to measure not only the characters she created herself, but the society in which they had their being. As with so many of the ideas that were to engage her attention throughout the whole of her writing career, she began by mocking the excesses not of life but of books. Among the conventions of sensibility current in the novels of her youth was an unquestioning and exaggerated hospitality to complete strangers. So, in her burlesque fragment 'Evelyn', Mr Gower knocks on the door of a family unknown to him and is shown upstairs to the lady of the house, who exclaims:

> 'Welcome best of Men – Welcome to this House, and to everything it contains. William, tell your Master of the happiness I enjoy – invite him to partake of it. – Bring up some Chocolate immediately; Spread a Cloth in the Dining Parlour, and carry in the venison pasty. In the mean time let the Gentleman have some sandwiches, and bring in a Basket of Fruit. Send up some Ices and a bason of Soup, and do not forget some Jellies and Cakes.' [And on her husband's joining her] The Chocolate, The Sandwiches, the Jellies, the Ice and the Soup soon made their appearance, and Mr Gower having tasted something of all, and pocketed the rest, was conducted into the dining parlour, where he ate a most excellent Dinner and partook of the most exquisite Wines, while Mr and Mrs Webb stood by him still pressing him to eat and drink a little more. (*MW, 182*)

From this beginning the Webbs go on to give the stranger their house, grounds, daughter and £10,000.

Comic exaggeration of this kind gives way to more credible and consistent, if somewhat schematic, character-drawing in *Sense and Sensibility*. Mrs Jennings is as hospitable as she is well-organised domestically, urging Marianne to name her own supper, pressing on her all the delicacies her larder can afford and, in her indignation at Mrs Ferrars' treatment of Edward, longing to offer him bed and board at her own house. Her benevolence extends to Betty's sister, for whom she is looking out for a good 'place'.

Neither of Mrs Jennings's daughters equals her in warmth of heart, but whatever Charlotte Palmer's giddiness as a housekeeper or her husband's affected taciturnity, they are not actually inhospitable. The Palmers not only make the Dashwood sisters 'feel themselves welcome' at Cleveland, but most generously give up their house to Marianne and her attendants for the duration of her illness. Indeed, if the ultimate in hospitality is to make your home a temporary hospital for any person who chances to fall ill there (as John Harwood did at Deane), then the Palmers attain a degree of unselfish excellence matched elsewhere in the novels only by Mr Bingley in *Pride and Prejudice*, the Harvilles in

Persuasion and the Heywoods in *Sanditon*. (Mr Bingley's merit is perhaps the least in that he is in love with his patient at Netherfield, Jane Bennet.)

The daughters and sons-in-law of Mrs Jennings are two couples drawn in bold strokes for maximum contrast among themselves. These four characters – the Palmers and the Middletons – are created somewhat in the Dickensian style: each has a leading characteristic, which appears whenever they do, and each is meant to be funny. They are 'gallery' characters, a method Jane Austen took not of course from Dickens but from her predecessor Fanny Burney, whose heroines similarly educate themselves by encountering a succession of grotesques. It was a method which Jane Austen gradually came to discard as she sought greater truth to nature for her people.

The Middletons are as ill-assorted a couple as the Palmers (and just as implausible *as* a couple); but, like the Palmers, their respective better qualities combine together to make a reasonable quantity of good humour and good breeding with which to welcome guests. Sir John and Lady Middleton live 'in a style of equal hospitality and elegance. The former was for Sir John's gratification, the latter for that of his lady.' (*S & S, 32*) That is, he loves parties and people, and she enjoys keeping a good table; he wants to make happy as many people as possible, and she simply wants people to admire the abundance and elegance of her arrangements. To satisfy these separate yet complementary desires: 'They were scarcely ever without some friends staying with them in the house, and they kept more company of every kind than any other family in the neighbourhood.'

In assessing the relative merits and motivation of the Middletons, Jane Austen is in no doubt that 'Sir John's satisfaction in society was much more real'. That is, he enjoys it for its own sake, not because it panders to his vanity. The distinction is important – if not very subtle – because it illustrates the fact that hospitality can be offered both for selfish and for selfless reasons. But while Sir John's good feelings may, to a degree, excuse the coarseness of his manners, sometimes 'the tranquil and well-bred direction' of Lady Middleton, however unfeeling, is a welcome respite from her husband's heartier style of hospitality. (*S & S, 143*)

Sense and Sensibility is a highly social novel, much concerned with the obligations of host and guest. There are several reasons for this, the most obvious being Sir John's own character, his unremitting attempts to collect people together, and his assumption that nobody can ever like being on his or her own. Treated as high comedy whenever it appears, this leading characteristic obviously has considerable influence over the mechanics and development of the plot. Incongruous characters get

After dinner, from *Mrs Hurst Dancing* (*c.* 1815)
(© *Neville Ollerenshaw 1981; reprinted by
permission of Neville Ollerenshaw and
Victor Gollancz Ltd*)

thrown together and suffer the consequences of being unable to escape one another because of Sir John's misplaced zeal.

To acknowledge the influence of Sir John on the plot without enquiring more deeply, however, would be to approach the creation of character from the wrong direction. It would be more penetrating to say that, because she has certain points she wants to make about the subject of hospitality, Jane Austen creates a character whose habits and inclination give her scope for making them. Here, at the outset of her literary career, and still much exercised by the opposition of self and society which is the fundamental subject-matter of the novel of sensibility, she sets up her most demanding, stultifying, shallow social framework (until *Persuasion*) in order to test her heroines to the utmost.

In Jane Austen's youth the highly polished, ceremonial and formal social arrangements of the eighteenth century prevailed, but tempered in country neighbourhoods by the remains of a still older, less exclusive hospitality which reached right back to monastic days – monasteries of course being the first 'hospitals' of all. In both religious houses and country manors, there was a tradition of succour for all comers and of all degrees of people sitting down to break bread together in one great hall. Though this had long passed away, country hospitality at its best retained something of its informing Christian spirit (as exemplified in John Harwood of Deane), but overlaid with the greater elegance and decorum of eighteenth-century manners.

Originating in London and Bath, and always at its most extreme there, polite behaviour was not just a matter of empty forms, it was a necessity when people began to spend their leisure hours in proximity to one another. The polish acquired in these two fashionable centres was carried back and disseminated among the country gentry. It was also taught in the conduct books which proliferated for the purpose. From the varieties of behaviour warned against in these conduct books, it is evident that offensive and disgusting habits had been tolerated until quite recent times.[3] Although the niceties of etiquette could sometimes be carried too far, especially in high society in London, most of the improvements were genuine, and genuinely needed.

One of the notable aspects of hospitality during the last quarter of the eighteenth century, when Jane Austen was growing to maturity and writing her first novels, was the sheer frequency of it – not just in London where visiting was easy, but in country neighbourhoods where there were bad roads, dark nights and long distances to contend with. The old hospitality had met the needs of travellers called by business of one kind or another to take to the road; but now people left their own firesides for their neighbours' with no other purpose than the pleasures and rewards of social intercourse. We have seen how Mrs Bennet boasts of dining with four-and-twenty families, and Jane Austen's aunt Mrs Leigh Perrot with even more. At Steventon the Austens not only mixed on equal terms with the neighbouring gentry, but attended balls at Hurstbourne and Hackwood, the respective homes of Lord Portsmouth and Lord Bolton. Every provincial centre had its monthly assemblies through the winter, where country families could meet and dance, exchange news and find marriage partners; the Austens' was at Basingstoke and the Bennets' at Meryton.

When Mr Bingley has been at Netherfield just two weeks, Jane Bennet, beside dancing with him at the Meryton assembly, has already dined in company with him four times. During the Gardiners' week-long visit to Longbourn, they do not sit down once to a purely family dinner. Before the explosion in middle-class numbers, English society was divided quite simply into the leisured minority and the rest; it became a convention that the minority in any locality must mix socially, whether or not they were personally congenial to one another. Hence new families (of the right social standing) would be automatically visited on coming into the neighbourhood, as are the Bingleys and the Grants. Very often, as in *Sense and Sensibility*, people seemed to meet for no higher purpose than 'for the sake of eating, drinking, and laughing together, playing at cards, or consequences, or any other game that was sufficiently noisy'. (*S & S, 143*) Underlying this was not infrequently the quest for eligible marriage partners for the rising generation. The entire oeuvre of Jane Austen is founded on this development in eighteenth-century life.

Barton in Devon would seem as remote a setting as any in Jane Austen, but an amazing amount of socialising goes on there. In summer Sir John Middleton is 'for ever forming parties to eat cold ham and chicken out of doors'; in late autumn he plans an expedition with open carriages and cold provisions to Whitwell; in winter he gives regular balls at the Park; and for him Christmas can only be marked by indulging in 'a more than ordinary share of private balls and large dinners'. (*S & S, 33, 152*) He never calls in at Barton Cottage without inviting its inhabitants either to drink tea at the Park that evening, or dine with them the following day, or often both. Nor is his the only moving spirit, for in apologising for securing only two complete strangers to meet the Dashwoods at their first dinner at the Park, he reveals that 'he had been to several families that morning in hopes of procuring some addition to their number, but it was moonlight and every body was full of engagements'. (*S & S, 33*)

Sir John's distinction between drinking tea (which, it will be remembered, occurred *after* dinner, and implied a visit to last the evening) and dining is evidently motivated only by the amount of notice required. Not, probably, that he is thinking of the convenience of the Park, for the lavish arrangements there are capable at any time of accommodating additional dinner guests. But the Dashwoods' own dinner would be in preparation; they require twenty-four hours' notice of dining out. No such consideration governs the similar distinction made by Lady Catherine de Bourgh in her invitations to the Collinses and their guests at Hunsford. They are invited to dinner when Lady Catherine cannot get anybody else but, once her nephews come to stay, the Hunsford party are asked only to drink tea. However, Mrs Philips's invitation to her nieces to drink tea, play cards and eat supper, but not to dine with the officers, can be motivated only by the shortage of space in her dining-room. This may be the case too at the Coles', but nobody seems to find it odd or insulting that the dinner guests include 'the male part of Mr Cox's family' and that 'the less worthy females' – of the *same family* – 'were to come in the evening, with Miss Bates, Miss Fairfax and Miss Smith'. (*E, 214*)

Lady Catherine does not mind whom she insults. Her entire performance as a hostess is despicable. Her only pleasure in guests is the presence of somebody to lecture and impress. To be sure her dinners are 'exceedingly handsome' and include some dishes which are a novelty to the company – French dishes, perhaps – and there is an abundance of servants and articles of plate. But nothing is said or done to put guests at their ease, and every act of condescension or generosity – such as sending them home in her carriage – is made in order to confer obligation, costing Lady Catherine no trouble. Her hospitality is compared with her nephew's: at Pemberley he is truly considerate of the feelings and comfort of Elizabeth and the Gardiners. Meanwhile on Elizabeth's home ground, the cold propriety of the Bingley sisters at Netherfield, counteracted but not amended by their brother's real kindness; the vulgarity of Mrs Philips with her 'little bit of hot supper'; the strutting provincialism of Sir William Lucas; and Mrs Bennet's own much-vaunted dinners, with always those four-and-twenty families in the background, add up to a picture of unremitting hospitality perpetually falling short of either good manners or good feeling.

Both *Pride and Prejudice* and *Sense and Sensibility* portray country gentry who accept as a way of life that the majority of their evenings are to be devoted to socialising. But only in *Sense and Sensibility* are the obligations found persistently irksome – by Marianne, and (though she complains less) by Elinor. In their country society, Marianne finds 'impertinence, vulgarity, inferiority of parts', and Elinor finds 'insipidity'. (*S & S, 127, 143*) The case is even worse when the sisters get to London. In the parties there the company all suffer from 'want of sense, either natural or improved – want of elegance – want of spirits – or want of temper'. (*S & S, 233*) When they go out in the evening Elinor and Marianne are subjected not only to these intellectual and emotional deficiencies, but to the physical discomforts of 'heat and inconvenience' caused by being part of a crowd. On two occasions Marianne nearly faints.

Time-wasting and pointless though country hospitality may often be, this novel seems to say, hospitality given in London, even by the same people, is worse, because greater snobbery and ceremony govern the proceedings. A direct comparison is drawn between the two when the Middletons give their first evening invitations after their arrival in town:

> Sir John had contrived to collect around him, nearly twenty young people, and to amuse them with a ball. This was an affair, however, of which Lady Middleton did not approve. In the country, an unpremeditated dance was very allowable; but in London, where the reputation of elegance was more important and less easily attained, it was risking too much for the gratification of a few girls, to have it known that Lady Middleton had given a small dance of eight or nine couple, with two violins, and a mere side-board collation. (*S & S, 171*)

Equally attentive to appearances as a hostess is Fanny Dashwood. In London Fanny and Lady Middleton gravitate together as kindred spirits in cold-hearted elegance. 'The Dashwoods were so prodigiously delighted with the Middletons, that though not much in the habit of giving anything, they determined to give them – a dinner'. (*S & S, 230*) When this great occasion takes place: 'The dinner was a grand one, the servants were numerous, and everything bespoke the Mistress's inclination for show, and the Master's ability to support it.' (*S & S, 233*) What is lacking is any attention to the feelings of the guests. Later, Fanny exercises her utmost ingenuity to avoid inviting her husband's sisters to stay under her roof.

Fanny has already shown her want of truly hospitable feelings in her ungracious treatment of her in-laws during their six-months residence at Norland after her arrival there as mistress. Her attitude in this early part of the novel is contrasted with the warmth of the elder Mrs Dashwood's invitation to Edward to visit them at Barton, and her plans for extending Barton Cottage for the better accommodation of 'such parties of our friends as I hope to see often collected here'. (*S & S, 29*)

Mrs Dashwood's generosity as a hostess is balanced by her delicacy as a guest, for she declines to dine oftener at the Park than the Middletons dine with her at the Cottage.

For Elinor and Marianne, their mother sets a standard in hospitality which they are not to experience again until they come to create their own homes. Their passage between the two is fraught with unpleasantness of various kinds. Marianne learns *en route* how to balance the integrity of the self with the legitimate claims of other people; while even Elinor, whose judgement is immaculate, suffers and struggles in steering a proper course. The reward of both is the anchorage of Delaford, with its promise of every rational and physical comfort, where, no sooner have Edward and Elinor settled, than they are visited by 'almost all their relations and friends'. (*S & S, 375*)

It is not suggested that Delaford has ever been an abbey, though it has many of the appurtenances of one; but the failure in hospitality of Northanger Abbey is all the more reprehensible because of the traditions of its former character which it fails to maintain. General Tilney is a poor host both in Bath and in the country, but it is in the latter that he is most to be censured. The socialising that goes on in the Bath of *Northanger Abbey* is mainly in public places and is enjoyed by Catherine, provided she is with her friends. Only the two meals she takes under General Tilney's roof in Milsom Street, one dinner and the breakfast before they set off for Northanger, are unaccountably uncomfortable to her. This is a taste of what is to be, for at the Abbey Catherine's daily, hourly comfort is at the mercy of the General. His deficiencies as a host are very much connected with his greed and tyranny and with his failure to take into account the feelings of his young guest. The attentions he forces on her are destructive of all her comfort, but nothing can prepare her for the downright 'breach of hospitality' of turning her out of his house without ceremony or common courtesy. It is the worst violation of hostly duty in Jane Austen's novels.

If the most serious offender as host is General Tilney, the most serious offender as *guest* is Henry Crawford. At the end of *Mansfield Park* he is left feeling 'vexation that must rise sometimes to self-reproach, and regret to wretchedness – in having so requited hospitality'. (*MP, 469*) It is rather odd to find his adultery expressed in these terms – as if what matters most is the abuse of the trust placed in him when he was admitted to terms of intimacy with the family at the Park. Sir Thomas, not Maria or Mr Rushworth, becomes the one insulted, the one justified in feeling Henry's action as an affront.

Mansfield Park was the first of Jane Austen's novels to have its genesis wholly in the nineteenth century. The remark about requiting hospitality is one of several hints it contains of the bourgeois withdrawal into domesticity which society was beginning to make even in the Regency, though it reached its apogee under Victoria. This phenomenon was the result of a rising population – rising in sheer numbers as well as in aspirations to gentility. Instead of everybody above a certain level mixing at random in public places, or feeling obliged to visit and be visited by all within travelling distance, as had been the case all through the eighteenth century, families were beginning to be more choosy about their company, and to enjoy the power of *shutting out* most of the rest of the world. The family hearth became an almost holy place, the locus of female modesty and as such jealously guarded by the paterfamilias. With this kind of ideology gaining ground, hospitality was more cautiously extended than heretofore.

It is in accordance with this new domestic ideology that the introduction of Mr Yates as a resident of Mansfield Park is deplored at several points in the text, both before and after Sir Thomas's return home, as 'offensive' and 'vexatious' and 'irksome'. Young men, even of good breeding, are seen as potential contaminators of female purity. Edmund himself is brought to take part in the theatricals in order to prevent the admittance of another young man, more harmless than Yates. Edmund describes what would be the end of 'privacy and propriety' in no mild terms to Fanny:

> 'I know no harm of Charles Maddox; but the excessive intimacy which must spring from his being admitted among us in this manner, is highly objectionable, the *more* than intimacy – the familiarity. I cannot think of it with any patience – and it does appear to me an evil of such magnitude as must, *if possible*, be prevented.' (*MP, 153*)

He goes on to talk of the 'mischief that *may*, . . . the unpleasantness that *must*, arise from a young man's being received in this manner – domesticated among us – authorised to come at all hours – and placed suddenly on a footing which must do away all restraints'. (*MP, 154*) Not much hospitality here, and Sir Thomas on his return to Mansfield is just the same, 'wanting to be alone with his family'. Sir Thomas's views of the obligations attaching to a man of his position in society are markedly different from those of Sir John Middleton, Sir William Lucas *et al.* The difference is not just one of temperament, but of changing social perceptions.

Hospitality at both Park and Parsonage, whenever it *is* given, is 'elegant and plentiful . . . according to the usual habits of all'. (*MP, 239*) Meetings are generally deemed pleasant and worthwhile, even by the most intelligent characters. Nothing is wanting once the decision to invite guests has been made; the question in *Mansfield Park* is not, as in the Steventon novels, what makes a good host, but rather how a host can guard the sanctity of his hearth and home from pollution by the wrong guests.

The picture of London given in this novel – while seen only at one remove – suggests that high society there is too heartless and immoral to share these concerns. Mary's letters to Fanny from London are full of parties, including a dinner to which sixteen people sit down and another very grand party to open Mrs Rushworth's house in Wimpole Street. Edmund's looks, rather than his personality and conversation, are what are admired when he mixes with company in London. Fanny thinks 'the influence of London very much at war with all respectable attachments' and her author does not mock her for the idea. (*MP, 433*) Unlike Elinor and Marianne, Fanny does not have to find a balance between the claims of self and society. Fanny's task is to cling to the integrity of the self at all costs and to shut out the attractions of dangerous strangers. Edmund and Sir Thomas have to learn this lesson too. Both come to recognise that at their own hearthside has long been hovering the true angel of their house.

Emma, the next novel, set wholly in one country village, shows enough of the same retreat into domesticity to establish a trend. There are no four-and-twenty families on an equal footing with Hartfield, no dining in company four times in a fortnight for Emma. Of course much of the tone of the social intercourse in this novel is set by either Emma's snobbery, or Mr Woodhouse's dual fear of food and late hours. These are the traits of individuals, not of the community at large – or are they? Emma is given enough rational thoughts on the subject to suggest authorial approval. Emma finds Mr Weston a shade too convivial; and reflecting on the character of John Knightley, by no means a favourite with her, she concedes: 'There was something honourable and valuable in the strong domestic habits, the all-sufficiency of home to himself, whence resulted her brother's disposition to look down on the common rate of social intercourse, and those to whom it was important. – It had a high claim to forbearance.' (*E, 97*) Her original plans for a drive to Box Hill with Mr Weston are likewise approved: 'Two or three more of the chosen only were to be admitted to join them, and it was to be done in a quiet, unpretending, elegant way, infinitely superior to the bustle and preparation, the regular eating and drinking, and pic-nic parade of the Eltons and the Sucklings'. (*E, 352*)

Nevertheless, Emma is a faulty hostess through most of the novel, and has to learn to correct her faults. 'I hope I am not often deficient in what is due to guests at Hartfield', she says on one occasion, smiling complacently, and her father immediately replies, 'There is nobody half so attentive and civil as you are. If anything, you are too attentive. The muffin last night – if it had been handed round once, I think it would have been enough.' (*E, 170*) But Mr Knightley, who is also listening, makes her a more ambivalent reply. As the narrator has taken care to tell us near the beginning of the novel, when Emma is presiding over a supper for guests at Hartfield, this heroine is 'never indifferent to the credit of doing everything well and attentively'. (*E, 24*) The word 'credit' links her with Mrs Bennet. Both are thinking mainly of themselves as they serve their guests. Emma indeed feels little more than contempt for the three old ladies to whom on this occasion she proceeds to 'do all the honours of the meal, and help and recommend the minced chicken and scalloped oysters'.

In the Highbury world in general, dinner-parties are less a regular part of life, more a special occasion, than at Longbourn or Barton. When the Coles give their dinner they are long in the planning. Social aspirants themselves, they segregate their guests into those deemed worthy of a dinner, and those who are invited only for tea and music afterwards. The only dinner-party at Hartfield is given in honour of the new arrival, Mrs Elton, and is a matter of politeness rather than inclination. Although lower down the social scale both dinner-parties and evening-parties are arranged by all Mr Elton's acquaintance to meet his bride, so that she can boast of being 'absolutely dissipated', she plans to 'return their civilities' in the course of the Spring only by:

> one very superior party – in which her card tables should be set out with their separate candles and unbroken packs in the true style – and more waiters engaged for the evening than their own establishment could furnish, to carry round the refreshments at exactly the proper hour, and in the proper order. (*E, 290*)

Mrs Elton is condemned both as a recipient and a giver of hospitality by being wholly motivated by a desire to impress a small country community with her own superior knowledge of the world. She is mean and she is patronising. Her opposite is not Emma, but Miss Bates, who no sooner becomes the recipient of some foodstuff – apples, pork – than she longs to share it with her neighbours, and whose hospitality, though it can run to little more than 'sweet-cake from the beaufet' is offered from the heart, with true generosity and humility.

Of Mrs Elton it is said, 'Her Bath habits made evening-parties perfectly natural to her, and Maple Grove had given her a taste for dinners'. (*E, 290*) This is the distinction also drawn by Elizabeth Elliot in the quotation at the beginning of this chapter. Dinner-parties were associated with country houses; evening-parties, which meant cards, tea and elegant light refreshments such as Mrs Elton's rout-cakes, were all that people troubled to give in Bath.

The association of cards with Bath goes back to the previous novel: in *Mansfield Park*, Mrs Rushworth vacates Sotherton for her new daughter-in-law, removing 'herself, her maid, her footman, and her chariot, with true dowager propriety, to Bath – there to parade over the wonders of Sotherton in her evening-parties – enjoying them as thoroughly perhaps in the animation of card-table as she had ever done on the spot'. (*MP, 203*) This is just half a sentence occurring within the more momentous statement of Maria Bertram's marriage, but with what economy and accuracy it conjures up the tedium and snobbery of Bath evenings. The association with cards is made even more explicit in *Persuasion*, when the following exchange takes place between Captain Wentworth and Anne:

> 'You have not been long enough in Bath,' said he, 'to enjoy the evening parties of the place.'
> 'Oh! No. The usual character of them has nothing for me. I am no card player.' (*P, 225*)

Whereas the Bath of *Northanger Abbey* had been stimulating, the Bath of *Persuasion* is stultifying. The city is an education to Catherine, a prison term to Anne. Something is due to the different plots, the different ages of the heroines and the trials they are required to undergo. But much is due to the changing character of Bath society itself, as observed by Jane Austen and reflected in *Persuasion*. No longer the height of fashion, Bath was actually at the height of its popularity – with many visitors and residents coming from the middling classes. The consequence of this slippage down the social scale was, paradoxically, an *increase* in snobbery and exclusivity – the result, of course, of insecurity. No longer did everybody mix in public places; they confined themselves to their own small circle of acquaintance, and met in their own homes. Guests were not often asked to dinner, because this admitted them too much on terms of intimacy with the family, whose domestic secrets would be revealed. Not all families had moved down in the world like the Elliots, but almost all had a social position they were anxious to retain or improve:

> Elizabeth was, for a short time, suffering a good deal. She felt that Mrs Musgrove and all her party ought to be asked to dine with them, but she could not bear to have the difference of style, the reduction of servants, which a dinner must betray, witnessed by those who had been always so inferior to the Elliots of Kellynch. It was a struggle between propriety and vanity; but vanity got the better, and then Elizabeth was happy again. These were her internal persuasions. – 'Old fashioned notions – country hospitality – we do not profess to give dinners – few people in Bath do – Lady Alicia never does; did not even ask her own sister's family, though they were here a month: and I dare say it would be very inconvenient to Mrs Musgrove – put her quite out of her way. I am sure she would rather not come – she cannot be easy with us. I will ask them all for an evening; that will be much better – that will be a novelty and a treat. They have not seen two such drawing rooms before. They will be delighted to come tomorrow evening. It shall be a regular party – small, but most elegant.' (*P, 220*)

Though Anne is not privy to her sister's musings, she can guess well enough their tenor. Throughout the novel she repeatedly compares the cold formality of her father and sister with the unceremonious warmth of heart of two other sets of people. One set represents the old country hospitality and the other a new kind of hospitality altogether, based on professional brotherhood. Between the old ways, sadly dying out, and the new, poised to invigorate society, the Elliots languish, useless and idle, thinking only of their own importance, with neither the wish nor the capacity of giving happiness to others.

Mr and Mrs Musgrove are portrayed as the last generation to whom simple, friendly country hospitality is a way of life:

> The Musgroves, like their houses, were in a state of alteration, perhaps of improvement. The father and mother were in the old English style, and the young people in the new. Mr and Mrs Musgrove were a very good sort of people; friendly and hospitable, not much educated, and not at all elegant. Their children had more modern minds and manners. (*P, 40*)

A little later, Captain Wentworth is visiting Uppercross almost every day, attracted equally by the young people's agreeable, lively manners and by the fact that 'the old were so hospitable'. (*P, 73*) Their hospitality is further demonstrated by their taking in the Harville children for the Christmas holidays. The Musgroves provide a real old-fashioned Christmas for their own and other people's children: 'tressels and trays, bending under the weight of brawn and cold pies, where riotous boys were holding high revel . . . a roaring Christmas fire, which seemed determined to be heard . . . . It was a fine family piece'. (*P, 134*) The brawn and cold pies at Uppercross are the only specific foodstuffs mentioned in the whole of *Persuasion*; they are also the only Christmas foods mentioned in any of the novels, which never dwell on the season. As Robert Southey wrote in 1807:

> It is part of an Englishman's religion . . . to have pies at Christmas made of meat and plums. This is the only way in which these festivals are celebrated; and if the children had not an interest in keeping it up, even this would soon be disused. All persons say how differently this season was observed in their fathers' days, and speak of old ceremonies and old festivals as things which are obsolete.[4]

Although the food, the fire and the children seem to anticipate Dickens, Christmas at Uppercross, which the elegant Lady Russell finds unbearably noisy, is a remnant of a former age, not a pointer towards a new one. With Christmas as with weddings, Regency manners of the middling classes represented a period of restraint between the unself-conscious bawdy of preceding times and the sentimental excesses of the Victorians, but the elder Musgroves cling to the customs of their youth.

There is nothing expensive, fashionable or showy about their style of hospitality generally. It contrasts favourably with that of the Elliots and is valued and honoured by Anne; but she is accustomed to it, and it is the hospitality of the Harvilles which truly impresses her. The passage containing her reactions is worth quoting at length, because it incorporates some of Jane Austen's most openly avowed feelings on the subject of hospitality:

> Captain Harville, though not equalling Captain Wentworth in manners, was a perfect gentleman, unaffected, warm, and obliging. Mrs Harville, a degree less polished than her husband, seemed however to have the same good feelings; and nothing could be more pleasant than their desire of considering the whole party as friends of their own, because friends of Captain Wentworth, or more kindly hospitable than their entreaties for their all promising to dine with them. The dinner, already ordered at the inn, was at last, though unwillingly, accepted as an excuse; but they seemed almost hurt that Captain Wentworth should have brought any such party to Lyme, without considering it as a thing of course that they should dine with them.
>
> There was so much attachment to Captain Wentworth in all this, and such a bewitching charm in a degree of hospitality so uncommon, so unlike the usual style of give-and-take invitations, and dinners of formality and display, that Anne felt her spirits not likely to be benefited by an increasing acquaintance among his brother-officers. 'These would have been all my friends,' was her thought; and she had to struggle against a great tendency to lowness.

On quitting the Cobb, they all went indoors with their new friends, and found rooms so small as none but those who invite from the heart could think capable of accommodating so many. Anne had a moment's astonishment on the subject herself; but it was soon lost in the pleasanter feelings which sprang from the sight of all the ingenious contrivances and nice arrangements of Captain Harville. (*P, 98*)

Although at this point Anne is hopeless of ever belonging to the naval group, the passage indicates the escape that both she and, to some extent, the nation, will make from the parasitic society of Bath. The Musgroves provide a nostalgic glimpse of what has been lost, but the Harvilles promise a new direction and a new energy.

Their hospitality, like that of the Palmers in *Sense and Sensibility*, extends to making their small house a hospital for the care of Louisa after her fall and is all the more meritorious in that their patient is scarcely known to them before. Moreover, they nurse Louisa themselves. An even more remarkable instance of this kind of hospitality occurs at the very beginning of Jane Austen's next (unfinished) novel, *Sanditon*, in which the injured Mr Parker and his wife are taken in and looked after for a fortnight by the Heywoods, to whom they are total strangers, deposited by accident at their door. 'Every possible attention was paid in the kindest and most unpretending manner, to both Husband & wife. *He* was waited on & nursed, & *she* cheered and comforted with unremitting kindness' and 'every office of Hospitality & friendliness was received as it ought'. (*MW, 371*)

From this supreme example of old-fashioned, selfless, country hospitality, the plot develops into a disquisition on hospitality as commerce – for this surely is the founding principle of a sea-side resort. In the fragment there is unresolved tension between regret that hospitality has moved out of the realm of friendship and Christian concern for fellow creatures into the exchange of money; and acceptance that the country must prosper and thrive by such enterprise as the Sanditon scheme.

Mr Parker, the prime mover behind the enterprise, is viewed with a certain amount of indulgence, for his heart is sound; he desires all Sanditon's visitors to be made more happy and healthy by their stay, and for all the tradesmen of the place to benefit from their spending. But he is blinded by his enthusiasm. One of his rasher actions has been to leave 'the house of my Forefathers', as he calls it, a 'snug-looking place' according to Charlotte, for the windswept new Trafalgar House. The old house is situated in a sheltered dip, 'well fenced & planted, & rich in the Garden, Orchard and Meadows which are the best embellishments of such a Dwelling'. (*MW, 379*) Had he remained quietly there he could have offered true hospitality in the style of the Heywoods; Charlotte draws the connection to her parents' home by remarking, 'It seems to have as many comforts about it as Willingden'. The significance is compounded by Sidney Parker's joke that his brother should make a hospital of the old house. That is exactly what the Heywoods have done of theirs, when occasion required, but without its being a commercial proposition.

If Mr Parker's house is linked to the idea of a hospital, the house of his partner in speculation, Lady Denham, is likened by her to a hotel. Both are ways of offering hospitality to people on a more businesslike footing than a private home. Lady Denham is much more mean-spirited than Mr Parker. Expressing the fear that the price of commodities will rise, she says to Charlotte Heywood, 'Depend upon it, you will be thinking of the price of Butcher's meat in time – tho' you may not happen to have quite such a Servants Hall full to feed, as I have.' (*MW, 393*) A little later she disgusts Charlotte even more by giving her reasons why she won't invite her various poor relations to stay with her. 'I have no fancy for having my House as full as an Hotel. I should not choose to have my 2 Housemaids Time taken up all the morning, in dusting out Bed rooms. – They have Miss Clara's room as well as my own to put to rights every day. – If they had hard Places, they would want Higher Wages.' She adds, 'If people want to be by the Sea, why don't they take lodgings?' (*MW, 401*)

With *Sanditon* Jane Austen brings her discussion of hospitality into a new commercial age. During the course of her career she has considered hospitality under the guises of sensibility, social imperative, domestic retreat and financial enterprise; while welcoming some changes and deploring others, she has held to an ideal of hospitality which is motivated by warmth of heart and true concern for other people's feelings. There is a sense in which with *Sanditon* she comes full circle. In welcoming total strangers to their house the Heywoods are strangely reminiscent of the Webbs, with their exaggerated notions of hospitality. True, this is counteracted by the total absence of romance in the Heywoods' plain, common-sensical characters: theirs is genuine hospitality, fulfilling a real need. Nevertheless it is appropriate to the tone of this fragment, closer to burlesque than the six preceding novels, that it should open with an episode which in any of the completed fiction would seem bizarre. In many ways, not the least of which is its treatment of hospitality, *Sanditon* for Jane Austen is both a departure and a return.

Chapter Seven

Food as Symbol

We have looked at various functions which food fulfils in the fiction of Jane Austen: at how it is used to define character, forward the plot and enhance the theme. We have seen that she never gives a detail without a definite effect in view; often her economy is such that she achieves several different purposes simultaneously. But in certain passages she goes even beyond this, using a specific food as a symbol to suggest some quality about a person or situation that is all the more profound for not being spelled out. With some writers this is a common practice but with Jane Austen so rare that when it does occur it can be quite astonishing in its power. At the same time, because we are not used to looking for this kind of almost poetic complexity in her work, it is easy to pass over, to read her only for her truth to nature and to miss some of the meaning that the text contains.

I want now to turn to some of those details, which seem to occur naturalistically in the narrative, but in fact have a deeper resonance. It is not only with food that this magic is occasionally wrought. A good non-food example would be the 'sleek, well-tied parcels of "Men's Beavers and York Tans"' which are laid out for Frank Churchill's inspection on the counter at Ford's, and which give him time to regain his own sleekness and tie up his emotions before deceptively (yet not downright dishonestly) replying to Emma's awkward question about the degree of his acquaintance with Jane Fairfax at Weymouth. But food often *is* the medium for this kind of allusiveness. On the one hand an everyday, mundane commodity, on the other freighted with biblical and universal symbolism, food is richly capable of bearing multiple meaning.

In a previous Chapter I mentioned briefly the passage in which Mrs Jennings describes Delaford, citing it as an example of how her mind and memory pick out housekeeping detail from any experience as an illustration of her character. Here I want to give the passage fuller consideration, because in it we can observe Jane Austen unobtrusively working on several levels at once. These are Mrs Jenning's words:

'Delaford is a nice place, I can tell you; exactly what I call a nice old-fashioned place, full of comforts and conveniences; quite shut in with great garden walls that are covered with the best fruit-trees in the country: and such a mulberry tree in one corner! Lord! how Charlotte and I did stuff the only time we were there! Then, there is a dove-cote, some delightful stewponds, and a very pretty canal; and everything, in short, that one could wish for: and, moreover, it is close to the church, and only a quarter of a mile from the turnpike-road, so 'tis never dull, for if you only go and sit up in an old yew arbour behind the house, you may see all the carriages that pass along. Oh! 'tis a nice place! A butcher hard by in the village, and the parsonage-house within a stone's throw. To my fancy, a thousand times prettier than Barton Park, where they are forced to send three miles for their meat, and have not a neighbour nearer than your mother.' (S & S, 197)

How characteristic of Mrs Jennings is this speech. Firstly in terms of language, with the homely idioms of 'stuff' and 'stone's throw', the obsolescent ''tis' and her favourite ejaculation 'Lord!'. She uses the word 'prettier' to mean more correct or more pleasing, rather than with any visual connotation, linking it as she does with butchers and neighbours; this is a usage common to other old people in Jane Austen, including Mr Woodhouse, who speaks of people being prettily-spoken or prettily-behaved. It is for practical rather than aesthetic reasons that Mrs Jennings picks out all the features she remembers about Delaford. The majority relate to the provision of food – fruit, fish, meat – and the remainder to that interest in her fellow-creatures which becomes more and more endearing, to Elinor and the reader, the better we get to know this vulgar but very warm-hearted and sensible woman. To talk of meat and butchers – especially at this moment in the action, when Willoughby's faithlessness has just become known to the suffering Marianne and the scarcely less suffering Elinor – is undoubtedly crass, yet it is motivated by the kindliest concern for the happiness of both Marianne and Colonel Brandon, and spoken to give comfort to Elinor.

So the speech gives an excellent insight into the good and bad qualities of Mrs Jennings. It also provides a remarkably vivid and detailed picture of the place where both Marianne and Elinor are to make their homes. Elinor has no inkling that her destiny may lie at Delaford, and only a vestigial hope that Marianne's might do so; she seems to pay no attention to the speech and asks no follow-up questions. The reader's attention, like Elinor's own, is too much absorbed in Marianne's grief to think of the speech as anything but an inept response on Mrs Jenning's part. Yet the picture has been planted in the reader's imagination, all the more retentively because it is not just a vague commendation, but full of precise detail, with the result that, as the plot works itself out, drawing both sisters ineluctably towards Delaford, we can feel comfortable on their behalf. Not just emotional, but physical satisfactions, await them at Delaford. There is nourishment of every kind here; they will thrive as the fruit threes thrive.

It is important that this picture *is* given, because *Sense and Sensibility* is the only novel apart from *Persuasion* in which the heroine has no prior knowledge of her married home. It is appropriate in *Persuasion* that this should be so because Captain Wentworth *has* no home before his marriage; Anne's readiness to set off with him into an unknown future is an important part of that trusting to Providence which she has come much to prefer above caution. But for the other heroines their future homes, their style of life and their duties, both domestic and public, are inextricably linked with their husbands' role and status. Accepting a proposal of marriage also involves settling for a certain home and, virtually, a career. Thus it is artistically important, and not only for the purposes of varying the narrative, that Elizabeth visits Pemberley and Catherine visits Woodston. Fanny and Emma have longstanding knowledge of their future homes, but even Emma must look again at Donwell with grown-up eyes and a maturing heart.

What Jane Austen manages to do with Mrs Jennings's passage of speech is still not exhausted, for it also provides the alert reader with useful information about Colonel Brandon. He is all too apt to be a shadowy figure, with whose portrayal, as it is, many readers are dissatisfied. Designing him to be the sort of modest and well-judging man who abstains from that spontaneous, self-revealing speech in which more foolish characters indulge, Jane Austen has to seek other stratagems to make him known to us. One is this picture of Delaford, for a man's home is a reflection of his values (which is another reason why the heroines must get to know the homes as well as the heroes). From Mrs Jennings's description of Delaford, we learn above all that Colonel Brandon is a good steward. In this he is a precursor, more lightly sketched in, of the admirable Mr Knightley. Colonel Brandon is a good steward of his land and food supplies, just as he has done his best to be a good steward of his charge, the younger Eliza.

If Mrs Jennings remembers chiefly what interests her – the provision of food – those features would not be there for her to remember if the owner of the garden were not a man to cherish such things. Colonel

Brandon's character is thereby linked with a caring, nurturing tradition. Dove-cotes and stewponds were both time-honoured sources of food, which every English monastery and medieval great house possessed. The dove-cote was invaluable for providing a supply of fresh meat through the winter, and the stewpond for the ready availability of freshwater fish. By Jane Austen's day these were being made redundant by improvements in agriculture and transport. Livestock could now be overwintered, and seawater fish brought to inland markets while still in good condition.

At Donwell, too, 'the old Abbey fishponds' are still in existence, though they are perhaps no longer kept stocked: they are viewed as a curiosity by visitors. Twenty years separates the writing of *Sense and Sensibility* and *Emma*. The slightly muddier taste of fish from ponds lost favour, though not with older people who had grown up with it. Jane Austen's mother belonged to this generation, contributing, as we have seen, a recipe for 'a very good white sauce for boil'd carp' to Martha Lloyd's collection. Incidentally, is there not something of Mrs Jennings in Mrs Austen (or vice-versa) in their keen interest in the details of housekeeping? Here is Mrs Austen's report on Stoneleigh Abbey in 1806, another old-fashioned, self-supporting place:

> I do not fail to spend some time every day in the Kitchen Garden where the quantities of small fruits exceed anything you can form an idea of. This large family with the assistance of a great many Blackbirds and Thrushes cannot prevent its rotting on the Trees. The Garden contains 5 acres and a half. The ponds supply excellent Fish the Park excellent Venison; there is also great plenty of Pigeons, Rabbits, and all sort of Poultry, a delightful Dairy where is made Butter good Warwickshire Cheese and Cream ditto. One Man servant is called the Baker, He does nothing but Brew and Bake.[1]

The large family she mentions means the number of servants, as Stoneleigh had been inhabited until a few weeks before by an elderly single lady and had just been inherited by an elderly single man, Mrs Austen's cousin. The quantity of servants is suggested not only by the multiplicity of functions to which they were assigned, but by the fact that this enormous house, which had '26 Bed Chambers in the new part of the house and a great many (some very good ones) in the old' was kept so clean in every corner that 'were you to cut your finger I do not think you could find a Cobweb to wrap it up in' – a homely remark that might have come as well from Mrs Jennings as from Mrs Austen.[2] 'Family' in the sense of household establishment is another link with Delaford, for Marianne Dashwood is described at nineteen as finding herself 'the mistress of a family, and the patroness of a village'. (*S & S, 379*)

There is a sense in which Delaford, with its high walls and proximity to common humanity, is going to confine, domesticate and socialise the free spirit which has formerly delighted in wandering at will on high downs and the wilder parts of the Norland and Cleveland estates. At the same time Colonel Brandon's attachment to the past and disinclination to remodel his old home for the sake of being fashionable is well suited to Marianne's own nostalgia; Elinor is quite afraid to tell her of the improvements which their brother is making to their beloved Norland. As Mrs Jennings says herself, Delaford is a very old-fashioned place. The straight lines of canals, as of avenues, had been largely swept away by 'the hand of the improver' and high walls had come down when views became more highly valued than shelter.

(Yet while John and Fanny are silently censured by Elinor for rooting up the old walnut trees to make room for a green-house, and some old thorns to make room for flowers, she and Edward are not too conservative to 'project shrubberies and invent a sweep' for Delaford Personage. Jane Austen is ambivalent about 'improvements' – but Delaford House takes its place with Donwell Abbey, Uppercross Hall and the Parkers' old house at Sanditon in being approved for its preference of comfort above fashion.)

That Jane Austen can suggest so much in one passage of direct speech – not only the character of the speaker and of the person whose property is being described, but the destiny, spiritual and physical, of a heroine; and that she can do it in a passage which seems but a digression, an irrelevance, at the time – is an example of the wonderful economy of her art. But for economy and resonance, supreme even within this passage is the symbol of the mulberry tree.

A mulberry takes a very long time to come to fruition. So does Colonel Brandon, who is thirty-eight when he marries Marianne, and, if they are to have a family, as they surely are, will be in his forties when his children are born. Though we are to presume a monkish celibacy about his early life, he is not as dried up as Marianne first presumes him to be. Is there even a promise of sexual pleasure for her in that 'Lord! how Charlotte and I did stuff?' Readers who have felt uneasy about the docility with which Marianne allows herself to be married off to Colonel Brandon in the last few pages of *Sense and Sensibility*, should think back and take comfort from the mulberry tree.

Fruit as conjugal happiness and increase? It may be no coincidence that *all* the homes to which the heroines will be taken are fruitful places. Delaford has its mulberry, Mansfield Parsonage its apricot, Woodston its apple trees: 'apple trees too!' as Catherine Morland joyfully observes (as well she might). Donwell Abbey is famous for its orchards and straw-berry-beds, and when Harriet Martin enters Abbey Mill Farm as a bride she will pass between espaliered apple trees laden with the rosy, ripening fruit of late September.

Pemberley also has its fruits, though of a more rare and delicate sort, befitting Darcy's status. These are hot-house fruits, and they have the distinction of belonging to the only mealtime set-piece in any of Jane Austen's novels which is described straightforwardly by the narrator as impinging on the heroine's consciousness. More than ordinary signific-ance must therefore attach to the scene.

When Elizabeth pays her first social visit to Pemberley, there is, for different reasons, a great deal of awkwardness, shyness and silence between the five ladies present. Then:

> The next variation which their visit afforded was produced by the entrance of servants with cold meat, cake, and a variety of all the finest fruits in season; but this did not take place till after many a significant look and smile from Mrs Annesley to Miss Darcy had been given, to remind her of her post. There was now employment for the whole party; for though they could not all talk, they could all eat; and the beautiful pyramids of grapes, nectarines, and peaches, soon collected them round the table. (*P & P*, 268)

Why does Jane Austen deviate in this one instance from her usual practice to show us the heroine registering what she is about to eat? She is suggesting several things here, beyond the mere exemplification of the elegance of arrangements at Pemberley. The pyramids of fruit are symbolic of the rigid social pyramid which the love between Elizabeth and Darcy must find the will to topple. Elizabeth, confronting an arrangement that might intimidate anybody with less social grace, proves, by her own better manners than Miss Bingley, that she is worthy of her elevation. At the same time she is presented with the motivation necessary to surmount social obstacles. Just as she is beginning to acknowledge Darcy's real humanity, she is given this sign of the ripeness of his affection, which is no longer the arid and emotionally immature infatuation against his better judgement which had got the better of him at Rosings.

Moreover, as a prefiguring of the coming together of Darcy and Elizabeth, the instinctive movement to gather round the table breaks down awkwardness as healthy appetites are given free play. Jane Austen is showing that our natural appetites can lead us right and do more than all our social refinements to connect us joyfully to other people. Words have sometimes been the enemy of Elizabeth and Darcy's feelings for one another. They must learn to be guided by their needs and emotions as well as by their cleverness and wit. We can appreciate now why the narrator must take it into her own hands to describe the scene. It is a moment with a significance beyond words for Elizabeth.

In the pyramid of fruits at Pemberley nature and artifice are held in perfect balance: the produce of nature shaped by man. The shape itself is suggestive of the shape of the novel, placed as the scene is exactly at the point where Elizabeth's antagonism tips over into self-acknowledged love. The apex of the pyramid is the fulcrum of the plot. When next we enter Elizabeth's thoughts, the following day, it is to learn that 'Never had she so honestly thought that she could have loved him, as now . . .' (*P & P, 278*) It is the first time she has used the word love of her feeling for Darcy. She has tasted the fruit of Pemberley; as at Delaford, Donwell and Abbey Mill, fruit is a potent symbol of sexual attraction and love.

The apricot tree which grows against the stable wall of Mansfield Parsonage bears a slightly different interpretation. It is a symbol not so much of the fruitfulness of Fanny's eventual union with Edmund (though perhaps of that too) as of Fanny herself – her growth and maturity during the course of the novel.[3] Transplanted from one part of the country to another, rather tender, with aspersions cast upon its pedigree, the Moor Park apricot is like the sapling Fanny. Mrs Norris is the prime mover in the acquisition of both, but the bill for the fruit tree – seven shillings, for like Fanny, it has a Price – is paid by Sir Thomas, as the whole of Fanny's maintenance is to be. To Dr Grant's coarse and over-indulged taste, the fruit is insipid and not worth gathering. Just so is Fanny considered by almost everybody through the greater part of the book. In fact, Fanny has been transplanted to a spot that suits her: she thrives; with the 'stable wall' of Mansfield tradition and Edmund's love to support her, the novel sees her grow into a 'noble' woman.

In a novel so much concerned with fostering and nurturing, it is apt that symbols from the worlds of horticulture and husbandry should be applied to Fanny's career. When Mrs Norris – whose name is ironically given, for she is no nurse – accepts Mrs Whitaker's gift of the four pheasant's eggs at Sotherton, she immediately plans to get the Park dairy maid to set them under 'the first spare hen', and then, if they hatch, to borrow a coop – in other words, to have no trouble or expense in the business herself, beyond making a great fuss. (Perhaps that is why she is in the poultry yard on the occasion of her 'triumph' over Dick Jackson.) Fanny is like those pheasant's eggs – taken away from her mother, largely at the instigation of Mrs Norris, but nurtured up not at the White house, but at the Park, and there given her own borrowed coop – the East Room, her 'nest of comforts'. Whether the pheasant's eggs 'come to good' is unknown, but Fanny, no thanks to her aunt Norris, certainly does.

Mansfield Park is perhaps the most symbolic, patterned and poetic of all Jane Austen's novels. These qualities are what make innumerable rereadings of *Mansfield Park* deeply satisfying, in the way that other patterned works of art, poetry and music are satisfying. There is no equivalent, elsewhere in the oeuvre, to the day at Sotherton foreshadowing the adultery of Maria Rushworth with Henry Crawford; or to *Lovers' Vows* mimicking the 'play' that is going on in 'real life'; or to the significance of Henry's necklace not going through William's amber cross. The brilliance of these contrivances has been pointed out admiringly by many commentators. I have also drawn attention to another level of patterning, less spectacular but still meaningful, in the pairs of housekeepers who circle Fanny.

These are all major devices, requiring the full span of the narrative to work themselves out. There is another, more localised way in which *Mansfield Park*, more than the other novels, tends toward poetic practice: the use of metaphor.

Fanny, whose appetite for real food is easily frightened away by emotional disturbance, is often described as living off metaphorical food. Sometimes it is her imagination, sometimes her despair, that is fed. In Mrs Grant's garden, she observes to the uninterested Mary Crawford, 'One cannot fix one's eyes on the commonest natural production without finding food for a rambling fancy'. (*MP, 209*) Less happily, when Edmund joins them and begins to converse in coded terms with Mary about the kind of life they might live together, this is 'sorrowful food for Fanny's observation'. Significantly, this episode in the Grants' garden is to close with that invitation to eat a real, specified food – turkey – which introduces Fanny to Henry Crawford's attention and appetite, and thence to the trial of her life.

Still in the Parsonage garden, Mary Crawford avows that a large income is 'the best recipe for happiness' she knows. If a woman in a garden is temptress, and if love of money is the root of all evil, Edmund is surely being perversely blind to the biblical overtones here. This scene is extraordinarily rich in every kind of significance, and the heightened language used is highly appropriate. Even the myrtle, which Mrs Grant is in danger of losing, has its symbolic significance, for myrtle is the traditional bridal wreath.

At Portsmouth the metaphor continues: in the first letter Fanny receives there from Mary she finds 'great food for meditation . . . and chiefly for unpleasant meditation'. (*MP, 394*) Edmund shares her propensity to nourish his more desponding thoughts this way. Returning to Mansfield after his ordination, and expecting Mary already to have left for London, he rides into the village 'with spirits ready to feed on melancholy remembrances, and tender associations, when her own fair self was before him, leaning on her brother's arm'. (*MP, 334*) Fanny is described as being able to 'live on' expressions of affection from Edmund while his confidences can turn her 'too sick for speech'. (*MP, 262, 268*)

In *Mansfield Park* the characters even occasionally employ food metaphors themselves. 'I am inclined to envy Mr Rushworth for having so much happiness yet before him. I have been a devourer of my own', says Henry Crawford of landscape improvements. It is the fleeting happiness of Maria's sexual favours that he envies, and he will end with devouring the peace of mind of many beside himself. When he concocts his plan to make 'a small hole in Fanny Price's heart', he again uses metaphors of consumption. 'I do not like to eat the bread of idleness', he tells Mary. (*MP, 229*)

Mrs Norris uses the same word, this time as a metonym, in her hypocritical enquiry, when the subject of adopting Fanny is under discussion: 'Is she not a sister's child? and could I bear to see her want, while I had a bit of bread to give her?' (*MP, 7*) Fanny will get never so much as a piece of bread, let alone a square meal, still less the love which food both embodies and symbolises, from Mrs Norris.

If the presence of fruit trees signifies conjugal happiness and increase, the proximity of that most mundane of establishments, the butcher's shop, seems to guarantee emotional as well as physical nourishment. There is a butcher in the villages of Delaford, Mansfield and Highbury, all places associated with solid comfort, whereas Barton and the Prices' area of Portsmouth have no such shop within easy reach. Although Barton Park is very different from Portsmouth in its elegance and hospitality, both equally fail to nourish the soul. The city of Bath too is found wanting, metaphorically, when Mrs Thorpe laments that there is hardly any veal to be got at market.

'One shoulder of mutton, you know, drives another down', says Mrs Jennings in her forthright way, referring to the hoped-for succession of Colonel Brandon to Willoughby in Marianne's heart. (*S & S, 197*) It is fitting that this undereducated old woman should find in an old proverb with its mundane imagery the language to clothe her ideas about love and lovers. Colonel Brandon *does* turn out to be that source of emotional nourishment which Marianne requires to return her to a full and fulfilled life. The proverb, crude as it is, exactly expresses what happens to Marianne, the heroine who once tried to starve herself to death, but whose appetite for food and life is restored.

Meat has another moment of significance in *Sense and Sensibility*. Despite the dozens of elaborate dinners the characters evidently must take together, the only meal Jane Austen thinks it fit to give the details of is Willoughby's snatched lunch at a coaching inn in Marlborough. We know that this consisted of cold beef and a pint of porter because he tells Elinor so, in order to refute her imputation that he has had too much to drink. But the menu does more than that; it has a moral dimension. Willoughby's choice of good, plain, honest, manly, English fare is, on however subliminal a level, a mark in his favour. He is behaving honourably and with feeling, at last; he is not so foolish as to starve himself in his haste to reach Marianne before she dies; but neither will he waste time ordering a more elaborate dish or caring what he eats. Jane Austen does not spell this out, and Elinor does not consciously reflect upon it, but the detail does contribute to the reassessment of Willoughby's worth in her estimation and ours. Some of the sterling character associated with the roast beef of old England attaches to Willoughby in this, his final appearance in the book.

That the association was well established in the public consciousness by the time Jane Austen wrote her early novels is proved by the regularity with which it was evoked throughout the eighteenth century. Richard Steele, in the *Tatler* of 21 March 1710, called for a return to the beef and mutton diet on which the battles of Crecy and Agincourt had been won. Robert Campbell, writing in *The London Tradesman* of 1747, brought the golden age a little nearer. 'In the Days of good Queen Elizabeth, when mighty Roast Beef was the Englishman's Food, our Cookery was plain and simple as our Manners', he declared. A mid eighteenth-century print of St George carried a verse extolling 'Gorgeous English Fare / Noble Sirloin, Rich Pudding and Strong Beer'. [4] As late as 1807, Robert Southey was entering the fray. 'Roast beef has been heard of wherever the English are known', he stated in his guise as a foreigner. 'I have more than once been asked at table my opinion of the roast beef of Old England, with a sort of smile, and in a tone as if the national honour were concerned in my reply'. [5]

This emotional defence of roast beef and the English character was occasioned by the growing popularity of French cookery throughout the eighteenth century. F. Massialot, in *The Court and Country Cook* of 1702 described 'vast quantities of exquisite Ragoo's and Sauces that are continually coveted'. Lady Mary Wortley Montagu, in Constantinople in 1717, reported that the Turks enjoyed as many ragouts as nowadays one could find in England.[6] But there were many people ready with forebodings that English taste was being debased, and that what was seen as the trickiness and flabbiness of the French character would be imbibed with the greater subtlety of their cooking. Robert Campbell railed against 'Meats and Drinks dressed after the French fashion' disguising its 'Native properties'. Parson Woodforde complained of a meal eaten out in 1783 that most of the things were 'spoiled by being so frenchified in dressing'.[7]

It was this minor and trivial, yet hotly contested controversy which Jane Austen drew upon more overtly in her next novel, *Pride and Prejudice*, to portray the worthlessness of Mr Hurst in half a sentence: 'and as for Mr Hurst, by whom Elizabeth sat, he was an indolent man, who lived only to eat, drink and play at cards, who when he found her prefer to plain dish to a ragout, had nothing to say to her'. (*P & P, 35*) Not only does this suffice to convey, unobtrusively and in a seamless narrative, that her heroine has simple English tastes and no interest in talking about food, but Mr Hurst is utterly demolished – most of all by that one word, so potent in eighteenth-century argument, 'ragout'. The very first appearance of the word in print in an English context had occurred in the anonymous 'Satyr against the French' of 1691 which included the lines:

> With dishes which few Mankind knew beside
> With Soups and Fricasies, Ragou's, Pottage[8]

When Mr Hurst makes his enquiry of Elizabeth, therefore, he is not to be assumed to be referring to a dish actually in front of them at Netherfield, but asking her where she stands in the debate between fashion and patriotism, sophistication and insularity. In associating Willoughby with roast beef and Mr Hurst with ragout, Jane Austen would have expected her readers to pick up on this debate; to enjoy the joke at Mr Hurst's expense, and to accept her underlying endorsement of Willoughby. Her own patriotism was fierce; she called Southey's book 'horribly anti-English' (which it isn't) and expressed the view that letters from a friend travelling in France 'would not be satisfactory to *me*, I confess, unless they breathed a strong spirit of regret for not being in England'. (*L, 212, 477*) In *Emma*, Mr Knightley and his home are several times associated with Englishness; in the terms of this novel it is English to abhor 'trick or littleness' of any kind, while the charming but less than straightforward Frank Churchill is allowed to be '*aimable*' only in the French sense.

If Jane Austen's exaggerated hatred of France had become something of a byword in her family – three of her brothers travelled for pleasure on the Continent, so this was not a general Austen characteristic – perhaps the ragout was introduced into *Pride and Prejudice* partly as a joke against herself that her family would enjoy.[9] There are many such in-jokes in the Juvenilia and a few, in all probability, which have been left to stand in the novels composed at Steventon.

Mr Hurst, of course, thinks he is the height of fashion and sophistication; yet, as this was a very old controversy, it might rather show his being *behind* the times. Certainly, by the time *Emma* was written some twenty years later, although Jane Austen's own chauvinism remained, as we have just seen, as strong as ever, the debate was so far forgotten that there is no want of patriotism in the fricassees served at Hartfield. They have been absorbed into the English cuisine. Mrs Elton, as concerned as Mr Hurst to trumpet her sophistication through talking about food, cites ice and rout-cakes, not ragouts, as proof of her knowing the ways of the fashionable world.

But *Emma* is so replete with food that it requires a whole chapter to itself. In this novel, rather than individual foods having individual meanings, food itself is a symbol for the social commonwealth in which all people must have their being.

Chapter Eight

The Significance of Food in *Emma*

Among Jane Austen's novels, *Emma* is uniquely laden with references to food. Food anchors the fictive to the real world, contributing to that powerful sense of fidelity to life which so many readers have testified to feeling most especially with this book. This effect of Dutch-school realism, however, is by no means the sole or even the primary function of food in *Emma*. More profoundly, the giving and sharing of food becomes a symbol or extended metaphor for human interdependence, resonating through the entire text.

There are sound artistic reasons why Jane Austen's method should differ in this novel. Unlike the plots that go before, *Emma* focuses on the heroine as a member of a community. Other novels show the heroine in her own family, or interacting with other families of much the same rank, and their narratives follow the heroine away from home. *Emma* is quite different. It is static, but to compensate for this in interest, as it were, it embraces far more levels of society. There are the shopkeepers, Mrs Ford, Mrs Wallis and Mrs Stokes; the schoolteachers, Mrs Goddard, Miss Nash, Miss Richardson and Miss Prince; the professional semi-gentlemen, Mr Cole, Mr Perry and Mr Cox; the ostler, John Abdy; the farm manager, William Larkins; and of course the tenant farmer Martins themselves. Though most of these characters are never heard in direct speech, we are aware of them conversing both among themselves and with other, more prominent, members of the *dramatis personae*. Information often comes to Emma, hence to ourselves, by a very circuitous route; for example she learns of what Mr Elton said about his errand to London via Mr Perry, Miss Nash and Harriet, who all pass on his words, one to another.

Then there are the servants, Serle, Wright and Mrs Hodges, Patty, Hannah and James. Not only are there more named servants in this book than in any other, but they belong to various households, not just to the heroine's. They are also allowed lives and family relationships of their own: James and Hannah are father and daughter and like to visit each other; John Abdy's father is held an affectionate remembrance by the Bateses.

The village has its rising generation too, from the young Coles and Perrys to the children round the gingerbread shop, from the baker's boy to the daughter of the sick cottager. All these people, as well as most of the major characters, are to a greater or lesser extent subject to the patronage and goodwill of Emma. She has been placed by her creator in a more comfortable and privileged position than any other of the heroines, and the lesson she must learn in the course of the novel is how to fulfil the duties which go with it. In one sense the community exists to test Emma; this is a novel about village life because Emma's particular character demands this particular trial. In another sense, of course, the community has a life and reality of its own, and Emma over-estimates her importance to it.

Thus, for the purposes of teaching Emma how to live, Jane Austen creates the only organic community of her fiction, and the device she uses to show its interdependency is food. The cultivation, distribution, cookery and above all the sharing of food play an important part in both the physical and the moral life of Highbury. Food is a symbol of goodwill, and Emma must learn to be as generous with her heart as she is with gifts of pork and arrowroot.

One thing we can be sure of is that nobody will ever starve in Highbury. Food is always passing hands there. Indeed we hardly ever hear of anybody eating anything that has not been given by somebody else. Sometimes it seems that people only exist to feed their neighbours: a moral or religious truth which the plot of *Emma*, albeit at an often comic level, enacts.

The very first food to be mentioned in the novel is wedding-cake. This is a supreme example of Jane Austen's economy of method; consider the work which this simple, homely item is made to perform. First, it announces one of the motifs of the novel: weddings, the match-making that leads up to them, and the changes that come in their wake. As has often been noticed, this novel opens with one wedding, encompasses two others – the Dixons' and the Eltons' – and closes with three more, as the characters choose their partners and their destinies, and the way is prepared for the next generation to be given life. Wedding-cake is surely the ultimate in a foodstuff designed to be handed round among friends and eaten not for its own sake only but in celebration of a joyful development in the life of a community. This is, after all, an almost wholly happy book, an almost wholly happy *world* that we are entering. Wedding-cake thus sets, or at least signals, the tone of *Emma*.

It is fortunate that Mr Woodhouse cannot foresee just how much wedding-cake is going to be in circulation at Highbury within the course of the year. For the Westons' wedding-cake, we are told, is 'a great distress to him':

> His own stomach could bear nothing rich, and he could never believe other people to be different from himself. What was unwholesome to him, he regarded as unfit for anybody; and he had, therefore, earnestly tried to dissuade them from having any wedding-cake at all, and when that proved vain, as earnestly tried to prevent anybody's eating it. (*E, 19*)

Here is presented Mr Woodhouse's maddening but lovable character, with its combination of self-centredness, for he cannot see any point of view but his own, and tender solicitude for the welfare of others. These characteristics will be displayed repeatedly over questions of food. But this is not all Jane Austen does with the wedding-cake, for in Mr Perry's reaction she shows a little truth about human nature generally – that we usually do as we wish, if not actually constrained to do otherwise – and offers a telling illustration of the apothecary's relation with his most important patient. Mr Perry is prepared to defer to Mr Woodhouse and to agree with him, yet he will exercise a sturdy independence in his own home, as any free-born Englishman would and should: this is a hierarchical, but not a feudal, society. The second chapter ends on a comic note: 'There was a strange rumour in Highbury of all the little Perrys being seen with a slice of Mrs Weston's wedding-cake in their hands; but Mr Woodhouse would never believe it.' (*E, 19*)

But it is a comic note not without a serious point to make. Despite his pre-eminent position in the community, despite the fact that everybody defers to him, Mr Woodhouse cannot prevent people doing what they like and eating what they like; he cannot prevent their marrying and, happily, he cannot prevent other people sharing in their joy.

Nor are his efforts to foist his own favourite foodstuff, gruel, upon everybody, any more effectual. 'A basin of nice smooth gruel, thin but not too thin' is not the stuff from which a healthy, enterprising, self-reliant population can be built – let alone a mighty empire founded and maintained – and it is right and proper that Mr Woodhouse's recommendations should find but little favour in the microcosm of early nineteenth-century England which is the Highbury world.

When friends come to supper at Hartfield, his monologue is comic. With exquisite civility, each lady is addressed in turn:

> 'Mrs Bates, let me propose your venturing on one of these eggs. An egg boiled very soft is not unwholesome. Serle understands boiling an egg better than anybody. I would not recommend an egg boiled any anybody else – but you need not be afraid – they are very small, you see – one of our small eggs will not hurt you. Miss Bates, let Emma help you to a *little* bit of tart – a *very* little bit. Ours are all apple tarts. You need not be afraid of unwholesome preserves here. I do not advise the custard. Mrs Goddard, what say you to *half* a glass of wine? A *small* half glass – put into a tumbler of water? I do not think it could disagree with you.' (*E, 25*)

'Emma allowed her father to talk' – as Mr Perry had done – 'but supplied her visitors in a much more satisfactory style.' What she helps them to, we learn, is minced chicken and scalloped oysters. On this particular evening, alive with schemes for taking Harriet in hand, she is motivated by 'the real good-will of a mind delighted with its own ideas'. But it is not always so, as Jane Austen informs us within the same complex sentence. Often Emma acts from no more than 'the common impulse of a spirit which was never indifferent to the credit of doing everything well and attentively'. In other words, appearances, rather than genuine care for other people's comfort, too often motivate Emma. She can never be indifferent to appearing the gracious hostess; but she is often all too indifferent, occasionally even hostile, to the feelings of the recipients of her attentions. This is a fault of which her father, for all his deficiencies of understanding, his inability to sympathise with feelings different from his own, is never guilty. Neither father nor daughter has the balance between intellect and feeling quite right. Beneath the rival claims of soft-boiled eggs and scalloped oysters, which is funny, lies a subtext of moral attitudes towards other people, which is not. This is the point which will be picked up as a recurring thread in the novel, as Emma manipulates her father with various degrees of success on various occasions over muffin, and gruel, and pork, over asparagus and fricassee of sweetbreads, the comedy always gentle and affectionate, until the shocking moment when Emma will be made to confront her own heart.

Meanwhile among the other characters food is used to show kindness, even love. While Harriet is staying at Abbey Mill Farm, Robert Martin performs two kind actions to please her, one of which is connected with food. Harriet tells Emma: 'He had gone three miles round one day, in order to bring her some walnuts, because she had said how fond she was of them.' (*E, 28*) Robert's willingness to go out of his way, and Harriet's

EMMA:

A NOVEL.

IN THREE VOLUMES.

———◆———

BY THE
AUTHOR OF "PRIDE AND PREJUDICE,"
&c. &c.

———◆———

VOL. I.

═══════

LONDON:
PRINTED FOR JOHN MURRAY.
——
1816.

Title page to the first edition of *Emma*

readiness to be pleased by simple things, are both admirable qualities, and moreover are in harmony with one another. Of course Emma does not see it that way. She thinks scathingly that 'the girl who could be gratified by Robert Martin's riding about the country to get walnuts for her', can easily be manipulated into loving someone else. (*E, 35*)

Jane Austen does not *assert* that Harriet and Robert are really well suited. Rather she uses the incident of the walnuts, brief and simple though it is, to show that they are, so that their eventual union, entered into as the next crop of walnuts ripens on the tree, promises to be fitting and fruitful. Indeed, every symbol about Abbey Mill Farm points that way. To reach the front door it is necessary to pass between neat rows of espalier apple trees. When Harriet is carried over that threshold, all the portents will be in her favour. The tree of knowledge from which she will taste has been domesticated and trained to be decorative, serviceable and bountiful all at once.

As modes of courtship, Robert Martin's offering of walnuts is to be compared with Mr Elton's conversation with Harriet when Emma's contrivances throw them alone in the lane. He talks to her about the courses which he has eaten – but which she can have no share of – the previous night, and Emma herself is forced to catch them up in time to hear about 'the Stilton cheese, the north Wiltshire, the butter, the celery, the beetroot and all the dessert'. (*E, 89*) Such an unusually detailed menu – even for this food-laden novel – should alert us that the speaker has got things out of proportion. Exulting, pedantic Mr Elton to mention even the butter! Self-centred, small-minded Mr Elton not to be able to think of a topic of conversation more edifying, even with the aim of being no more than ordinarily polite and considerate to Harriet! But Mr Elton, we hear, has more invitations than there are days in the week, so ready are the citizenry of Highbury to feed an eligible bachelor – consequently his head has been turned. Nobody but a Harriet deluded by an Emma could find equal charm in these two would-be lovers, one unselfish and kind, the other wholly self-centred and self-satisfied, as can be deduced by their dealings with food.

Harriet of course is a goose; and it is perhaps a little joke at her expense that Harriet should have something to relate about a goose – a goose which features in a double act of generosity. First Mrs Martin makes a gift of it to Mrs Goddard, and then Mrs Goddard shares the eating of it with her employees. Harriet tells Emma, 'Mrs Martin was so very kind as to send Mrs Goddard a beautiful goose: the finest goose Mrs Goddard had ever seen. Mrs Goddard had dressed it on a Sunday and asked all the three teachers, Miss Nash, Miss Prince and Miss Richardson, to sup with her.' (*E, 28*)

One of the virtues of Mrs Goddard's school is that she 'gave the children plenty of wholesome food'. (*E, 22*) We are left in no doubt that this is of far more importance to them than her academic provision. Indeed, business generally is conducted with remarkable generosity of spirit in Highbury. Another woman with her living to make, the baker, Mrs Wallis, is similarly ungrasping towards her customers. We hear that she is attentive to the Bateses, baking their apples for them in her hot oven and sending them back by her boy, even though they eat so little bread that their custom is not very valuable to her. This is very neighbourly of her; and neighbourliness is a quality much praised and discussed in *Emma*, for it is one of the novel's contentions that life proceeds more pleasantly when neighbours help one another out. Miss Bates's own happy nature elicits the best from Mrs Wallis, who is capable, we understand, of giving a sharp answer to other people on occasion; neighbourliness is thus self-perpetuating in the ideal social commonwealth, and this ideal is attainable when every member is well-disposed. Self-interest and consideration for others are not mutually exclusive.

However humble their circumstances, people try to contribute to the welfare and enjoyment of their neighbours. The Bateses more often receive gifts of food than make them, but even they are anxious to dispense hospitality in their own small way. Miss Bates offers Emma sweet-cake from the beaufet, telling her, in a passage of free indirect speech: 'Mrs Cole had just been there, just called in for ten minutes, and had been so good as to sit an hour with them, and *she* had taken a piece of cake and been so kind as to say she liked it very much; and therefore she hoped Miss Woodhouse and Miss Smith would do them the honour to eat a piece too.' (*E, 156*)

These are all acts of genuine, unpretentious kindness. Others have more mixed motives in giving food: the Coles, for example, do it partly to stake their claim to a place in Highbury society. We have no reason in the world to think ill of the Coles – they are, in Highbury parlance, very worthy people – but we can see that, socially insecure, they are anxious to do everything correctly and with a show of abundance. Their dinner consists of two courses, with a rather long interval between them, when perhaps the servants, new to this formality and aware of important guests in the room, are getting flustered. The atmosphere certainly becomes a little strained. It is not until 'the table was again safely covered, when every corner dish was placed exactly right', that the diners can relax once more. (*E, 218*) We feel that at Hartfield, Donwell or Randalls the dishes would be placed exactly right without the guests being made aware.

Notable as people who are never shown giving dinners are the Eltons. Mrs Elton boasts that 'I should be extremely displeased if Wright were to send us up such a dinner, as could make me regret having asked *more* than Jane Fairfax to partake of it . . . . My greatest danger, perhaps, in housekeeping, may be quite the other way, in doing too much, and being too careless of expense.' (*E, 283*) These boasts are not followed through by any example of hospitality. It is unclear whether the 'pigeon-pies and cold lamb' settled between Mrs Elton and Mr Weston to be taken on the ill-fated picnic to Box Hill are actually provided by Randalls or the Vicarage. One rather suspects that the directions emanate from Mrs Elton, but that Mr Weston, or at least his wife, actually supply the provisions.

The only other notice which Mrs Elton takes of Highbury hospitality is to denigrate it as being unfashionable: a grave failure in true neighbour-liness on her part, though doubtless she imagines that she is speaking out for their own good. 'She was a little shocked at the want of two drawing rooms, at the poor attempt at rout-cakes, and there being no ice in the Highbury card parties.' (*E, 290*) In all the giving and thanking, sharing and appreciating of food that goes on in this community, the only negative remark falls typically to Mrs Elton. Anyway, does not she supply ice of the soul enough?

Mrs Elton is associated with, is indeed the prime mover behind, the two occasions when food is consumed out of doors, both of which end in ruffled tempers and hurt feelings. Eating out of doors is evidently a dangerous innovation, imported by ill-bred town-dwellers into the country where there is a better sense of what is fitting. It is dangerous because of its tendency to break down those careful rules of behaviour which have been built up over generations to protect men and women from their baser selves. The whole veneer of civilisation begins to slip. Emma would prefer to conduct the outing to Box Hill in 'a quiet, unpretending, elegant way, infinitely superior to the bustle and prepar-ation, the regular eating and drinking, and picnic parade' beloved of Mrs Elton. (*E, 352*) This is not just an example of Emma's being snobbish, for not only is it true that more impoliteness and lack of self-control arise from the picnic than from any other social gathering in the novel, but Mr Knightley, whose judgement is much more trustworthy than Emma's, is always adamantly opposed to the idea of eating out of doors.

It is not often that Mr Knightley has much say in Highbury's social arrangements, but when it comes to the strawberry party in his own grounds, he simply will not countenance Mrs Elton's suggestion of a table spread in the shade. 'Everything as natural and simple as possible', she trills, in her best vivacious manner. 'Is not that your idea?' 'My idea of the simple and the natural will be to have the table spread in the dining-room', he responds gravely, even ponderously. 'The nature and simplicity of gentlemen and ladies, with their servants and furniture, I think is best observed by meals within doors.' (*E*, *355*) This rebuff is surely tantamount to telling Mrs Elton that she does not know how ladies and gentlemen should comport themselves; but as usual she is too thick-skinned to notice.

Mr Knightley's own character is further revealed to us in this simple conversation, apparently on such a trivial matter. He has sufficient obligingness to go along with Mrs Elton's strawberry-gathering scheme, but not even to be polite to a neighbour will he transgress his own code of decorum. Mr Knightley has achieved an exemplary balance between submission to the wishes of other people and adherence to principle, a balance which all characters in all Jane Austen's books are required to attain. The antithesis is expressed by Mr Knightley himself as he says, 'When you are tired of eating strawberries in the garden, there shall be cold meat in the house.' (*E*, *355*) Strawberries here represent the more superficial things of life, which can be safely compromised on in the interest of social harmony, while cold meat stands in for the fundamentals of human conduct. The cold meat part of life cannot be tampered with, as Mr Knightley knows, without dangerous consequences – as is proved the very next day when the cold lamb, against his and Emma's better judgement, is carried up Box Hill.

Nothing could be farther from the heat, the artificiality, the idleness and the ill-assorted company of that day on Box Hill than the other occasion in the novel when lamb is consumed (except that, in keeping with the homely, unpretentious nature of the meal, this time it's called mutton). The date is 24 December, the weather is cold enough for snow, the characters are out of doors for a purpose, and the meal has been well-earned. I refer to the time when Emma and Mr Elton, having enquired after the sick Harriet, are overtaken by 'Mr John Knightley returning from a daily visit to Donwell, with his two eldest boys, whose healthy, glowing faces showed all the benefit of a country run, and seemed to ensure a quick despatch of the roast mutton and rice pudding they were hurrying home for'. (*E*, *109*)

That is what the country is for: air and exercise and the creation of a healthy appetite. *That* is what food should be: simple, wholesome meals to be eaten with honest relish. *That* is what the best company is: a happy, harmonious family party. The instinctive, natural hurrying-homewards Christmas Eve scene also stands in counterpoint to the ill-timed and unnatural dinner-party that same evening at Randalls, which begins in the ill humour of John Knightley, proceeds through the fears and alarms of Mr Woodhouse, and ends in the débâcle between Emma and Mr Elton, the latter encouraged to overstep his rightful bounds by the too free consumption of Mr Weston's good wine.

The big set-pieces which punctuate the novel are the dinner at the Westons; the dinner at the Coles; the ball at the Crown; the day at Donwell; and the picnic on Box Hill – all occasions when the cast of principal characters come together to eat. Of these, only the ball at the Crown remains to be noticed. At one time, in the face of difficulties about the rooms, Mrs Weston had 'proposed having no regular supper; merely sandwiches etc set out in the little room; but this was scouted as a wretched suggestion. A private dance, without sitting down to supper, was pronounced an infamous fraud upon the rights of men and women.' (*E, 254*)

So Mrs Weston and Mrs Stokes contrive a fully-fledged supper, but we are given no details of the menu – because, in accordance with Jane Austen's practice, it has no intrinsic importance – except for what we glean from Miss Bates's monologue. 'Supper was announced. The move began; and Miss Bates might be heard from that moment, without interruption, till her being seated at table and taking up her spoon.' There follows a page and a half of miscellaneous unconnected remarks, until, with characteristic wonder and gratitude, and still thinking first of other people, she registers the spread before her eyes and exclaims, 'Dear Jane, how shall we ever recollect half the dishes for grandmama? Soup too! Bless me! I should not be helped so soon, but it smells most excellent, and I cannot help beginning.' (*E, 330*)

Emma is the only one of Jane Austen's novels in which a farming family plays a significant part. This has been noticed as Jane Austen extending her social range, admitting a class of people who were to thrive in the coming decades as the middle classes expanded and exerted their claims to be taken into account. Certainly, inclusion of such a family as the Martins shows her understanding of the social changes happening in her lifetime; but it also happens to fit very well into the themes and symbolic structure of the novel.

Even the hero, uniquely in the Jane Austen canon, is a gentleman farmer who *works*. The production of food is the real, serious business of Mr Knightley's life. He eagerly discusses with his brother the disposition of various fields for wheat, turnips or spring corn; even when entertaining guests at Donwell, he keeps an eye on the clover to see if it is ready for cutting. Emma ranks his sheep equal to his library as sources of satisfaction to him; she thinks – or affects to think – that he mistakes good news about a prize ox for news of Robert Martin's success with Harriet; and Mr Knightley's contentment in William Larkins' company is a standing joke in the novel. Moreover, even the pleasure part of the grounds of Donwell are famous not for any elegant improvements such as were all the rage in *Mansfield Park* but for 'the old Abbey-fishponds', like those at Delaford, the orchards and the highly-productive strawberry beds.

Emma's eulogy of Donwell, and of the view from it of Abbey Mill Farm, 'with all its appendages of prosperity and beauty, its rich pastures, spreading flocks, orchard in blossom' (*E, 360*) is expressed in quite different terms from, say, Elizabeth Bennet's praise of Pemberley, Fanny's of Sotherton, or Marianne's of Norland. Scenic beauty in this novel is seen in terms of thriving agriculture rather than of fashionable landscape gardening or picturesque, romantic views.

The seasons, too, are more forcibly present in this novel than in any other. *Emma* completes the cycle of the year from one October to the next: from harvest to harvest. Harriet Smith's visit to the Martins, before the action of the novel gets under way, takes place in September and early October; it is a Michaelmas goose which Mrs Martin sends back with her to Mrs Goddard. Harriet's infatuation with Mr Elton is a wintry, barren, artificial affair; her sap rises again when the warm weather returns and she fancies she is in love with Mr Knightley; she is reunited with her true mate, Robert Martin, as the year reaches its peak of mellow fruitfulness.

Curiously, no fewer than four of Jane Austen's novels start in the autumn – *Sense and Sensibility*, *Pride and Prejudice* and *Persuasion* are the others – and the two former also complete the year; but though in all of them the changing weather is given most realistically, as it is in *Mansfield Park* as well, a novel whose main action runs from midsummer to midsummer, there is, with the exception of the famous country walk in *Persuasion*, and the hay harvest in *Mansfield Park*, not nearly so much sense of the farming year outside *Emma*. That Emma herself, in her musings at Donwell, equates the beauty and prosperity of the farming scene with *Englishness* – 'English verdure, English culture, English comfort' (*E, 360*) – seems to imply that the self-sufficiency and interdependence which this novel celebrates in terms of food are moral no less than economic qualities, making the nation impregnable to attack from her formidable enemies. We must remember that *Emma* was written after two decades of war against the French, a feature of that war being the Continental System, by which Napoleon attempted to exploit England's dependence upon imported food as a means to bring about her submission.[1]

It is no coincidence that while the over-friendly Mr Weston serves wine which is presumably French, or at any rate continental, Mr Knightley, that supreme English gentleman, that perfect blend of uprightness, benevolence and reserve, brews his own spruce beer. The recipe for spruce beer is, of course, the memorandum which Mr Elton wishes to jot down on that occasion when – as she later confesses – Harriet snatches up the discarded end of his pencil. For the purposes of the plot, in so far as exemplifying Harriet's nonsense is concerned, Mr Elton might have been making any kind of note: it is evidence of the wholeness of Jane Austen's vision in the world of *Emma* that this merest trifle should be a recipe. Moreover, there are not many recipes that a clergyman might realistically be made to write down, so to hit on one for beer, with its associations with Englishness, and to have it emanate from Mr Knightley, is surely a minor stroke of genius.

So pervasive is the food imagery in this novel that like air it fills any available vacuum. The famous scene when Emma, waiting for Harriet to complete some purchases at Ford's, goes to the door and looks idly down the main street of Highbury, is a case in point. What Emma *expects* to see is a variety of people going about their business, quite unconnected with food: 'Mr Perry walking hastily by, Mr William Cox letting himself in at the office door, Mr Cole's carriage horses returning from exercise, or a stray letter-boy on an obstinate mule'. But what does she see in fact?

> The butcher with his tray, a tidy old woman travelling homewards from shop with her full basket, two curs quarrelling over a dirty bone, and a string of dawdling children round the baker's little bow-window eyeing the gingerbread . . . (*E, 233*)

Four vignettes whose common factor is food. It is evidently not Emma's mind, but her creator's, which is running on this topic. And to the purpose – for we know that Jane Austen is never guilty of digression. There is something she wants us to know about Highbury, something that relates to the contentment of its population. The scene that meets Emma's eyes is on the whole a cosy and a socially cohesive one. The dogs may be quarrelling and the children presumably are without money for the gingerbread, but this hardly means they are starving; the woman has a full basket and decent clothes to wear, while there are evidently enough families in the village who can afford butcher's meat to warrant that tradesman setting off with his tray. The view down the main street of Highbury is as comforting as that more rural one from Donwell Abbey.

Indeed the only characters excluded from the well-fed, well-ordered world of Highbury are the gypsies and the chicken thieves – but this is because they try to take for themselves what to the deserving and grateful poor is freely given. To prevent lawlessness and disaffection spreading beyond these easily contained margins of society it is necessary, the novel posits, that the leaders of local communities keep the mechanism of giving and sharing in good working order, alive to the real wants of the population and informed by genuine warmth of heart. Multiplied throughout England, such local efforts will secure the social stability which is so desirable, in the novelist's view, both for individuals and for the nation.

This is the true moral of *Emma*. 'I hope I am not often deficient in what is due to guests at Hartfield', Emma says, smiling because she has not yet learnt to doubt herself, and her father replies instantly, 'If anything, you are too attentive. The muffin last night – if it had been handed round once, I think it would have been enough.' (*E, 170*) Only Mr Knightley can see that Emma has deficiencies – not, he admits, in her manner or comprehension, but in her heart. Early in the novel, we see Emma visiting a poor family and sending them a pitcher of broth; she is genuinely compassionate, but such charity accords with her role as great lady and comes effortlessly. Even when she sends the hind-quarter of pork to the Bateses, it is done very graciously and without stinting, but it costs her nothing, either in pride or in material terms. Her conversation on the subject with her father is very comfortable and she has the added advantage of having Mr Knightley know and approve her action.

Meanwhile Mr Knightley is giving Emma – and us – an example of how to do good by stealth. His gift of apples to the Bateses is made in the true spirit of being kind to a neighbour who is worse off than himself. He tells nobody; it is only from Miss Bates we learn that he sends a sack every year; and in her own words, 'he will not wait to be thanked'. Moreover, his gift does cost him something: by giving away his last bushel – as we know from William Larkins – he deprives himself of apple tarts for the rest of the Spring.

This extra gift is made because he finds out that the Bateses have got through their supply more quickly than usual, for not only are Miss Bates and her mother very partial to Patty's apple dumplings, but a baked apple is one of the few foods which can tempt Jane's meagre appetite. When, under emotional stress, this fails still further, other neighbours rally round with offers of delicacies. 'Never had anybody such good neighbours', as Miss Bates cries in gratitude.

Miss Bates stands at the centre both of the Highbury community and of Emma's moral universe, in this theme of giving and sharing which I see as so happily embedded in the metaphor of food in *Emma*. It is in relation to Miss Bates's niece Jane, equally deserving but more discerning, that Emma is to have the disagreeable experience of being found wanting in true philanthropy. Jane knows that the heart which prompts the gift of arrowroot – 'some arrowroot of very superior quality, speedily despatched with a most friendly note' – has not always been kindly disposed towards her, and she rejects it. Emma has never had her charity rejected before. She is rightly mortified and shocked. Miss Bates and the sick cottager are too easy and grateful as recipients: Emma must learn how to give to more proud and sensitive people, and to give her time and her love as well as her largesse, before she is fit to be the wife of Mr Knightley, and thereby doubly patroness of the village. From broth to arrowroot, Emma travels a long and testing moral road.

The reading I have been giving of *Emma* is one which concentrates on character, on personal morality, and on the integration of self into the community. It is a reading which the text overtly supports. It is unproblematic, some would say too cosy. I am aware that a different interpretation, also focusing on the role of eating and giving food in the narrative, is possible, and ought to be aired.

In such a reading, delving beneath the surface of the text exposes the ideological substructure on which it appears to be erected. Whether Jane Austen is aware or unaware of this substructure, whether she is deliberately concealing or desperately signalling or simply herself oblivious to the constraints it imposes on her, is not to the purpose in such an enquiry, which can only be conducted by interrogating the text.

Such an enquiry reveals the exploitative as well as the protective nature of the social hierarchy embedded in Jane Austen's fictive rural world. We see not so much Emma's charity as the abject poverty of the hovel she visits, where the family cannot even afford the simple dish of broth. We might notice too the brevity of Emma's visit, and worse, the actual *omission* of the parish clergyman's visit when something more attractive occurs to divert him – and the way that neither of them appear to think on the subject again. We see that an honest old man like John Abdy, who was clerk to the parish twenty-seven years and is now bed-ridden, has no pension, no livelihood, no means of ending his days in dignity but must beg for parish relief or be a drain on his son. Now what we notice in the High Street scene are the pauper children hungrily eyeing but unable to buy the gingerbread – while Harriet dithers over muslin and ribbon. The gypsies and the chicken-thieves compound the picture of grinding rural poverty co-existent with privileged, sheltered lives. *Emma* presents to us, apparently without criticism, a well-fed ruling class who can choose whom to chase off and whom to reward, for their subservience, with parish relief or broth.

We might question what Mr Woodhouse does to deserve to live in pampered comfort while others around him starve or are driven to pilfering. We might question why the Martins, who produce the food on which the whole community depend, are not only 'precisely the kind of people' with whom Emma feels she can have nothing to do, but are not invited even by the hospitable and friendly Westons to join in the ball at the Crown.

If the social inequalities do not seem to be noticed by the author of *Emma*, the gender inequalities do. They were closer to home. She knew what it was for the widow and daughters of a clergyman to have no or little income of their own. The question is whether there is suppressed anger in the presentation of the Bates household, dependent on good neighbours for little treats of food, always having to say thank you; and in the situations of Harriet Smith and Jane Fairfax, the one full of health and the other full of intelligence, both young and at the start of their adult lives, who can yet do nothing to help themselves. At one point in the novel, Emma actually muses about the different destinies of women; but though full of sympathy for Jane, the thought of challenging the system does not cross her mind. The ostensible message of *Emma*, that it is the duty of us all to help others less fortunate, and be made happy and comfortable ourselves thereby, is not apparently undercut by any funda-mental questioning of the social and sexual order.

Only in Jane Fairfax's refusal of food does the dearth of options open to a woman, either to express her anger at or make her escape from an intolerable situation, pierce the surface of the narrative distressingly. But the moment is brief, and is dissolved in a fairy-tale ending to Jane's romance. She is relieved not by any mode of life than can bring her financial independence and self-respect, but because she takes the fancy of a rich man who when he looks at her head sees it not as a person but as a modelling-block for jewellery. What do Jane and Harriet actually do, at the end of the novel, but sell their (attractive) flesh that they may have food to eat for the remainder of their lives?

Emma herself, for all her wealth and status, health and intelligence, wastes most of her waking hours either on the kind of schemes for which she *is* condemned by her author, or on humouring a silly old man for which she is not. If Mr Woodhouse were a woman, would Emma's sacrifice be presented as equally noble? Mr Woodhouse himself – is he the lovable, benevolent character I described in relation to the wedding-cake, or is his irrational attitude to food the symptom of a seriously disturbed personality which is in retreat from sex, love and life?

To ask such questions is to be aware, at least, that it is possible to come away from *Emma* with a different impression from the one that Jane Austen puts forward for our consumption. This is not necessarily either wrong or presumptuous in us. A great text cannot be silenced. Neither one impression nor the other need prevail, certainly need not exclude the other entirely. The imaginative world of *Emma* is capacious enough and realistic enough and symbolic enough that both cosy and subversive readings can profitably be held in play at the same time.

Food in the world of *Emma* is the voluntary currency of love and caring; or it is instrument by which one class, or one sex, keeps another in a desirable state of servility and quiescence. It is a network of support, or a web of entrapment – or perhaps something of each. Jane Austen uses food for many purposes in her art, as this book has attempted to show. It is fitting that in the most food-laden novel of all, it should have so much to say to us.

Index of Food and Drink
in Jane Austen's Fiction

Notes

Page references to Jane Austen's novels and letters are given in the text. The editions and abbreviations used are:

The Novels of Jane Austen ed. R.W. Chapman (3rd edn, 5 vols, Oxford, 1923):

E	*Emma*	P	*Persuasion*
MP	*Mansfield Park*	*P & P*	*Pride and Prejudice*
NA	*Northanger Abbey*	*S & S*	*Sense and Sensibility*

MW   *The Works of Jane Austen*, vi, *Minor Works*, ed. R.W. Chapman (Oxford 1954)

L   *Jane Austen's Letters to her Sister Cassandra and Others*, ed. R.W. Chapman (2nd edition, reprinted with corrections, Oxford, 1979)

Chapter 1: Domestic Economy in Jane Austen's Life

1. Irene Collins, *Jane Austen and the Clergy* (London, 1994), p. 54.
2. R.A. Austen-Leigh, *Austen Papers* (London, 1942), pp. 31–32.
3. Ibid. pp. 25, 29.
4. Caroline Austen, *Reminiscences of Caroline Austen* (Jane Austen Society, 1986), p. 56.
5. Robin Vick, 'The Sale at Steventon Parsonage', *Annual Report of the Jane Austen Society, 1993*, p. 14.
6. Ibid., p. 15.
7. Test of advertisement in *Reading Mercury* kindly supplied in a letter to me by Robin Vick.
8. J.E. Austen-Leigh, *A Memoir of Jane Austen by her Nephew* (London, 1870; Oxford, 1926), p. 11. Many surviving charades and light verses attest to Mrs Austen's pleasure

in word-play. She herself referred to her own 'Sprack wit'; her wit was of both kinds – verbal and common-sensical.

9. Tom Fowle died before the marriage, delayed by shortage of money, could take place.
10. *Memoir*, p. 39.
11. George H. Tucker, *A Goodly Heritage: A History of Jane Austen's Family* (Manchester, 1983), p. 78.
12. *Austen Papers*, p. 23.
13. Ibid., p. 249.
14. Trevor Fawcett, 'Eighteenth-Century Shops and the Luxury Trade', *Bath History*, 3 (1990), p. 50.
15. Robert Southey, *Letters from England by Don Manuel Alvarez Espriella* (London, 1807; reprinted 1951), p. 472.
16. *Bath Guide for 1800*, in Bath Reference Library.
17. John Britton, *The Autobiography* (London, 1850), p. 58.
18. Lefroy family MS quoted in Constance Hill, *Jane Austen, her Homes and her Friends* (London, 1905), p. 177.
19. Caroline Austen, *My Aunt Jane Austen: A Memoir* (new edn, Jane Austen Society, 1991), pp. 3–4.
20. Information kindly supplied to me by Jean Bowden, Curator of Jane Austen's House at Chawton.
21. *Austen Papers*, p. 249.
22. Appendix to *My Aunt Jane Austen*, p. 20.
23. Ibid., p. 21.
24. *Austen Papers*, p. 249.
25. Ibid., p. 264.
26. 'Aunt Jane', *Cornhill*, 973 (London, 1947) pp. 72–73.

Chapter 2: Mealtimes, Menus, Manners

1. *Memoir*, p. 39.
2. *Austen Papers*, p. 245.
3. Quoted in Jean Latham, *The Pleasure of Your Company: A History of Manners and Meals* (London, 1972), p. 31.
4. André Parraux, *Daily Life in England in the Reign of George III* (London, 1969), p. 37; *Carl Philipp Moritz in England in 1782* (London, 1924), p. 33.
5. Dorothy Marshall, 'Manners, Meals and Domestic Pastimes', *Johnson's England*, ed. A.S. Turverville (Oxford, 1933), p. 348.
6. *Austen Papers*, p. 245.
7. Elizabeth Raffald, *The Experienced English Housekeeper* (8th edn, London 1782).
8. *Caroline Austen's Reminiscences*, p. 40.
9. There is an excellent discussion of these terms in Myra Stokes, *The Language of Jane Austen* (London, 1991), pp. 1– 9.
10. Sara Paston-Williams, *The Art of Dining: A History of Cooking and Eating* (London, 1993), p. 244.
11. James Boswell, *The Ominous Years, 1774–1776*, p. 79.
12. Walpole, *Letters*, xiv, February 25 1789.
13. Byron, *Don Juan* xv, stanza 61.
14. *Memoir*, p. 30.
15. James Woodforde, *The Diary of a Country Parson, 1759–1802*, ed. John Beresford (Oxford, 1949).

16. Jane Austen mentions that the visitors were welcomed in the hallway by all Henry's servants except for the cook, Madame Bigeon, who was 'below' 'dressing' this dinner. Two mornings later, writing to Cassandra before breakfast, Jane informed her, 'At eight I have an appointment with Madame B., who wants to show me something downstairs' – further proof, surely, of the sisters' familiarity with and interest in kitchen affairs. (*L, 322*)
17. Iris Brooke, *Pleasures of the Past* (London, 1955), p. 32.
18. *Austen Papers*, p. 243.
19. *Memoir*, p. 30.
20. Appendix to *Emma*, p. 500.
21. Emily Climenson (editor), *Passages from the Diaries of Mrs Lybbe Powys* (London, 1899), p. 320.

Chapter 3: From White Soup to Whipt Syllabub

1. Jane Grigson, *English Food* (2nd edn, London, 1993), p. 5.
2. *Margaretta Acworth's Georgian Cookery Book*, ed. Alice and Frank Prochaska.
3. Fernand Braudel, *The Structures of Everyday Life*, trans. Miriam Kochan and Sian Reynolds (London, 1981), p. 136. This book explores the way in which staple foodstuffs have influenced the culture and commerce of the various peoples of the world.
4. *Memoir*, p. 32.
5. Information kindly supplied by Robin Vick.
6. *Austen Papers*, p. 30.
7. *English Food*, p. 44.
8. William Cobbett, *Cottage Economy* (London, 1822; reprinted Oxford, 1979), p. 51.
9. 'Ah, what an excellent thing is an English pudding!' the quote continues. 'To come in pudding-time, is as much as to say, to come in the most lucky moment in the world.' François Misson, *Memoirs and Observations on his Travels over England in 1696*, trans. J. Ozell (London, 1719).
10. Woodforde's *Diary*, 7 January 1783.
11. *Annual Report of the Jane Austen Society*, 1993, p. 14.
12. J.C. Drummond and Anne Wilbraham, *The Englishman's Food: Five Centuries of English Diet* (2nd edn, London, 1991), p. 53.
13. See note 11 above.
14. Dorothy Hartley, *Food in England* (London, 1954), p. 100.
15. Information supplied by Irene Collins.
16. *Letters from England*, p. 472.
17. *The Art of Dining*, p. 212.
18. *English Food*, p. 352.
19. Ibid., p. 61.
20. *The Art of Dining*, p. 124.
21. It is an interesting sidelight on forty years ago that the 1954 editor and tester of the collection should add, 'The labour would have been so arm-aching that we promptly obtained a small electric gadget that would do the beating for us. It is an American invention; nothing of the kind is yet made in England.'
22. Walpole, *Letters*, iii, 6 June 1752.
23. Peggy Hickman, *A Jane Austen Household Book* (Newton Abbot, 1977), p. 96.
24. *Food in England*, p. 546.
25. *Letters from England*, p. 90.

26. *Food in England*, p. 545.
27. *Austen Papers*, p. 131.
28. *The School of Salernum*, trans. Sir John Harington (London, 1608).

Chapter 4: Greed and Gender

1. John Trusler, *The Honours of the Table for the Use of Young People* (London, 1787); Elizabeth Burton, *The Georgians at Home* (London, 1967), p. 196.
2. For a sustained discussion of this, see Brean S. Hammond, 'The Political Unconscious in *Mansfield Park*', *Mansfield Park* ed. Nigel Wood (Buckingham, 1993), pp. 56-90.

Chapter 5: The Sweets of Housekeeping

1. *Austen Papers*, p. 291.
2. When Jane Austen creates a servant with ideas above her station, she gives her a name ending in 'a'. Thus Rebecca, in Portsmouth, wears a flower in her hat (*MP, 408*) and Jemima, the nursery-maid at Uppercross Cottage, is 'always upon the gad . . . such a fine-dressing lady that she is enough to ruin any servants she comes near'. (*P, 45*) Sally, Patty, Nanny and Betty, names belonging to servants who have no such pretensions, are diminutives respectively for Sarah, Martha, Anne and Elizabeth, and are used to distinguish them from gentlewomen of those names.
3. 'Dilapidations' referred to the sum an outgoing clergyman, or his widow, was legally obliged to pay towards the repair of the parsonage; as can be imagined, it was a frequent source of friction and dispute. In this case, almost certainly Mrs Norris would have manipulated Sir Thomas into footing the bill.
4. This network is exhaustively investigated by Deborah Kaplan, *Jane Austen among Women* (Baltimore, 1992).

Chapter 6: Town and Country Hospitality

1. A facsimile of the note by Cassandra Austen of the date of composition of her sister's novels is printed in *Minor Works*, facing p. 242. Broadly speaking, *Sense and Sensibility*, *Pride and Prejudice* and *Northanger Abbey* are Steventon novels (though revised and published after the move to Chawton), while *Mansfield Park*, *Emma* and *Persuasion* were wholly written during the Chawton years.
2. *Caroline Austen's Reminiscences*, pp. 44–45.
3. In *The Honours of the Table* (1787), for example, the Reverend John Trusler found it necessary to advise against scratching, spitting, nose-blowing, teeth-picking, leaving the table in an obtrusive fashion 'from any necessity of nature' or advertising what one had been doing by adjusting the dress on returning to the room. (Quoted extensively in *The Georgians at Home*, p. 196; *The Art of Dining*, p. 258.) Trusler also offered advice to servants on how to be attentive yet unobtrusive when waiting at table.
4. *Letters from England*, p. 362.

Chapter 7: Food as Symbol

1. *Austen Papers*, pp. 245–46.
2. Ibid., p. 247.
3. Jean Nursten first suggested this idea and I am grateful to her for allowing me to develop it.
4. *The Englishman's Food*, p. 215.
5. *Letters from England*, p. 89.
6. Letter dated 18 April 1717; quoted in *The Georgians at Home*, p. 197.
7. Woodforde's *Diary*, 18 August 1783.
8. *Oxford English Dictionary*, s.v.
9. James spent some time in France during 1786 or 1787; Edward did the Grand Tour in 1787–88; Henry took advantage of the Peace of Amiens in 1802 to visit France to try to recoup some of his wife Eliza's property (her first husband, the Comte de Feuillide, had been guillotined and his property confiscated in the Terror). Jane's two youngest brothers, Frank and Charles, had a different relationship with what Captain Wentworth calls 'the Great Nation' (*P, 66*), since both were naval officers during the Napoleonic Wars.

Chapter 8: The Significance of Food in Emma

1. Though there was never any real danger of famine in Britain – or the riots that might go with it – the propertied class, mindful of the Revolution across Channel, had been anxious that 'the kingdom may experience no anxiety' at least since March 1795, with *Hints Respecting the Culture and Use of Potatoes* (see above, Chapter 3, note 5). In 1808, for example, John Loudon, who was to go on to be one of the great garden design innovators of the first half of the nineteenth century (developing the ideas of his predecessor Humphry Repton with the style he termed 'Gardenesque'), published a pamphlet entitled *An Immediate and Effectual Mode of Raising the Rental of the Landed Property of England, and Rendering Great Britain Independent of other Nations for the Supply of Bread Corn*. Could this be one of the 'stupid' pamphlets which engage General Tilney after Catherine has gone to bed, 'poring over the affairs of the nation for hours after you have gone to sleep', his eyes 'blinding', as he claims, 'for the good of others', and conveniently learning to increase his own income at the same time? (*NA, 187*)

Bibliography

JANE AUSTEN AND HER FAMILY

To list all the works of Austen biography and literary criticism to which I am indebted for general knowledge and understanding of the subject would be unwieldy and superfluous, since comprehensive Jane Austen bibliographies can be found elsewhere. This selection therefore is confined to those works which I have consulted in writing the present book.

Austen, Caroline, *My Aunt Jane Austen: A Memoir* (new edn, Jane Austen Society, 1991)

—, *Reminiscences of Caroline Austen* (Jane Austen Society, 1986)

Austen-Leigh, J.E., *A Memoir of Jane Austen by her Nephew* (London, 1870; Oxford, 1926)

Austen-Leigh, R.A., *Austen Papers, 1704–1856* (London, 1942)

Bloom, Harold (editor), *Jane Austen's Mansfield Park* (New York, 1977)

Collins, Irene, *Jane Austen and the Clergy* (London, 1994)

Hickman, Peggy, *A Jane Austen Household Book* (Newton Abbot, 1977)

Hill, Constance, *Jane Austen, her Homes and her Friends* (London, 1905)

Johnson, Claudia, *Jane Austen: Women, Politics and the Novel* (Chicago, 1988)

Kaplan, Deborah, *Jane Austen among Women* (Baltimore, 1992)

Kirkham, Margaret, *Jane Austen, Feminism and Fiction* (Brighton, 1983)

Lane, Maggie, *A Charming Place: Bath in the Life and Novels of Jane Austen* (Bath, 1989)

—, *Jane Austen's England* (London, 1986)

—, *Jane Austen's Family through Five Generations* (London, 1984)

Nicolson, Nigel, *The World of Jane Austen* (London, 1991)

Stokes, Myra, *The Language of Jane Austen* (London, 1991)

Tucker, George Holbert, *A Goodly Heritage: A History of Jane Austen's Family* (Manchester, 1983)

Wiltshire, John, *Jane Austen and the Body* (Cambridge, 1992)

Wood, Nigel (editor), *Mansfield Park* (Buckingham, 1993)

FOOD AND SOCIAL HISTORY

Ashley, Maurice, *The People of England: A Social and Economic History* (London, 1982)

Black, Maggie, *Georgian Meals and Menus* (Bath, 1977)

Braudel, Fernand, *The Structures of Everyday Life*, trans. Miriam Kochan and Sian Reynolds (London, 1981)

Brooke, Iris, *Pleasures of the Past* (London, 1955)

Burton, Elizabeth, *The Georgians at Home* (London, 1967)

Cobbett, William, *Cottage Economy* (London, 1822; reprinted Oxford, 1979)

Davidson, Caroline, *A Woman's Work is Never Done: A History of Housework in the British Isle, 1650–1950* (London, 1982)

Drummond, J.C. and Wilbraham, Anne, *The Englishman's Food: Five Centuries of English Diet* (2nd edn, London, 1991)

Fawcett, Trevor, 'Eighteenth-Century Shops and the Luxury Trade', *Bath History Volume III* (Gloucester, 1990), pp. 49–75

Filbee, Marjorie, *A Woman's Place* (London, 1980)

Girouard, Mark, *Life in the English Country House* (New Haven, 1978)

Grigson, Jane, *English Food* (2nd edn, London, 1993)

Hart, Roger, *English Life in the Eighteenth Century* (London, 1970)

Hartley, Dorothy, *Food in England* (London, 1954)

Jarrett, Derek, *England in the Age of Hogarth* (London, 1974)

Latham, Jean, *The Pleasure of Your Company: A History of Manners and Meals* (London, 1972)

Paston-Williams, Sara, *The Art of Dining: A History of Cooking and Eating* (London, 1993)

Stead, Jennifer, *Food and Cooking in Eighteenth-Century Britain* (London, 1985)

Southey, Robert, *Letters from England by Don Manuel Alvarez Espriella* (London, 1807; reprinted 1951)

Tannahill, Reay, *Food in History* (London, 1973)

Taylor, Duncan and Dobson, Dennis, *Fielding's England* (London, 1966)

Trevelyan, G.M., *English Social History* (London, 1942)

Turberville, A.S. (editor), *Johnson's England*, 2 vols (Oxford, 1933)

White, R.J., *Life in Regency England* (London, 1963)

Williams, E.N., *Life in Georgian England* (London, 1962)

Wilson, C. Anne, *Food and Drink in Britain* (London, 1973)

Woodforde, James, *The Diary of a Country Parson, 1759–1802*, ed. John Beresford (Oxford, 1949)

Index